ASTROLO[barcode]

Rising of KUNDALINI

"Barbara Hand Clow presents a way to make midlife crisis both meaningful and more manageable. Her descriptions of kundalini rising are lovely and compelling. She offers a strong argument for this spiritual emergence as a universal experience, not an achievement of the very few."

PEGGY PAYNE, AUTHOR OF THE KUNDALINI NOVEL *COBALT BLUE*

"Finally! A book that makes spiritual sense out of life's passages and does so not only on a personal level but a cosmic level as well."

ROSEMARY ELLEN GUILEY, AUTHOR OF *HARPER'S ENCYCLOPEDIA OF MYSTICAL AND PARANORMAL EXPERIENCE*

"This exciting new book contains the vision of a new human state whose 'primary goal will be the complete evolution of consciousness.' The erotic and cosmic qualities of shamanic, astro-mythic, and Goddess cultures is brought into the now of Western left-brain (technological societies) to heal, magnify, and balance us if we, as men and women, can unify our goals."

ROWENA PATTEE KRYDER, PH.D., AUTHOR OF THE *GAIA MATRIX ORACLE* AND FOUNDER OF THE CREATIVE HARMONICS INSTITUTE

"A lot of interesting astrological information is presented in a direct and accessible manner. The information is clearly written and moves from the very personal through the collective."

TANTRA MAGAZINE

"Barbara Hand Clow helpfully provides Cliffs Notes for the midlife crisis and much, much more. This is must reading for anyone feeling midlife dissatisfaction. Her ideas can help avoid costly and unnecessary mistakes often caused by misinterpretation of a natural process of evolution. She heals by explaining deeper reasons."

SPIRIT OF CHANGE

"Barbara Hand Clow's years of experience as an astrological counselor and her understanding of subtle cosmic energies have led her to draw some striking conclusions regarding the midlife phenomenon. The message in *Astrology and the Rising of Kundalini* is that we can move through these critical points with grace rather than confusion."

CONNECTING LINK

ASTROLOGY
and the Rising of
KUNDALINI

The Transformative Power of
Saturn, Chiron, and Uranus

BARBARA HAND CLOW

Bear & Company
Rochester, Vermont • Toronto, Canada

Bear & Company
One Park Street
Rochester, Vermont 05767
www.BearandCompanyBooks.com

SUSTAINABLE FORESTRY INITIATIVE Certified Sourcing
www.sfiprogram.org
SFI-00854

Text stock is SFI certified

Bear & Company is a division of Inner Traditions International

First edition originally published in 1991 by Bear & Company under the title *Liquid Light of Sex: Kundalini, Astrology, and the Key Life Transitions*
Second edition published in 1996
Third edition published in 2001
Fourth edition published in 2013 by Bear & Company under the title *Astrology and the Rising of Kundalini*

Library of Congress Cataloging-in-Publication Data
Clow, Barbara Hand, 1943–
 [Liquid light of sex]
 Astrology and the rising of kundalini : the transformative power of Saturn, Chiron, and Uranus / Barbara Hand Clow.
      pages cm
 Rev. ed. of: Liquid light of sex : kundalini, astrology, and the key life transitions. c2001.
 Includes bibliographical references and index.
 Summary: "Revised and updated edition of the classic astrology text on predicting and navigating life crises"— Provided by publisher.
 ISBN 978-1-59143-168-8 (pbk.) — ISBN 978-1-59143-849-6 (e-book)
 1. Astrology and sex. 2. Astrology. 3. Sex—Miscellanea. 4. Chakras—Miscellanea. 5. Kundalini—Miscellanea. 6. Midlife crisis—Miscellanea. I. Title.
 BF1729.S4C57 2013
 133.5—dc23
                                                        2013010324

Printed and bound in the United States by Lake Book Manufacturing, Inc.
The text stock is SFI certified. The Sustainable Forestry Initiative® program promotes sustainable forest management.

10 9 8 7 6 5 4 3 2 1

Text design and layout by Virginia Scott Bowman
This book was typeset in Garamond Premier Pro with Novarese used as the display typeface

To send correspondence to the author of this book, mail a first-class letter to the author c/o Inner Traditions • Bear & Company, One Park Street, Rochester, VT 05767, and we will forward the communication, or follow the author at **www.HandClow2012.com**.

Contents

List of Illustrations

Acknowledgments

I WOULD LIKE TO THANK all my clients who have shared their deepest secrets with me and who have given me permission to share their stories about their own progress, so that this knowledge about the key life passages could be presented to as many readers as possible.

I would like to thank the members of my own family and close friends, who have been my greatest teachers about the mysteries of human physical and spiritual maturation.

I am deeply grateful for Dr. Richard Gerber's introduction, which helps support this theoretical linking of energetics medicine and astrological cycles. I would like to thank Dr. Percy Seymour of England for his groundbreaking research on solar magnetism and astrology, and for his scientific presentation of the causal principle of astrology.

I would like to thank fellow astrologer Gail Vivino, for her assistance on the tables at the end of the book; designer and illustrator Marilyn Hager Biethan, for her work on this book; editor Barbara Doern Drew, for her careful copyediting and intelligent suggestions for the final text; and editor Meghan MacLean for her superb content suggestions and editing for this new edition.

Thanks especially to Jerry Simon Chasen, who helped me write this book in a form that is accessible to many people. And I would like to deeply thank editor Gerry Clow, who lent great clarity to this text and who supported me with honesty and power throughout the ten years of doing research. I honor Diana LaDue Hand and Darlene Yusuf of Wiseawakening.com for their devotion and excellence in promoting my work.

Lastly, I would like to acknowledge Inner Traditions • Bear & Company for promotion and sales and all the details behind bringing this book to the people.

Preface to
the Fourth Edition

WHEN IT WAS FIRST published in 1991 under the title *Liquid Light of Sex, Astrology and the Rising of Kundalini* offered a new hypothesis: predictable planetary cycles or transits can be used to determine the onset, progress, and completion of human growth cycles, the most critical one being midlife crisis. Now, after more than twenty years of feedback in workshops and countless letters from readers, the time has arrived to assess the accuracy of this idea. This idea has really worked for people who know little about astrology, the tool we use to predict our personal growth cycles. In particular, *Astrology and the Rising of Kundalini* examines the nature and timing of *kundalini rising*—healthy fire that rises in our chakras, or energy centers in our bodies—a key body dynamic that is activated as we mature physically and emotionally. The most intense kundalini activation occurs during midlife crisis in our early forties, and this process is virtually synonymous with *spiritual emergency*—extreme anxiety that often occurs when people process difficult emotional issues.

My hypothesis in this book is the result of observing astrological clients going through midlife crisis, most of whom exhibited mild to very strong symptoms of kundalini rising. They were having what is also called "spiritual emergencies." Once I became sure this was what was going on with my clients, I noticed that I could use specific planetary transits to predict the onset and completion of this very stressful energy activation. I found ways to help them make the best of this important growth opportunity, just as you can by using the tables at the end of this book. In addition to this new preface and updated chapters 8–10, this edition updates these tables to include those born between 1992 and 2000, because this group is growing up and needs this information.

In my original preface I discussed the text with cultural historian William Irwin Thompson and theologian Timothy Sedgwick. I sought their opinion because I wanted a nonastrological perspective on the possibility that we can time human growth. Their thoughts have withstood the test of time and are very provocative now, since my hypothesis has been strongly verified over the past twenty years. Initially Thompson and Sedgwick were both deeply skeptical of my idea; however, they were willing to consider it, even though it essentially challenged the basis of their own ways of thinking. I did *not* seek out astrologers, because I knew that if I were right, most astrologers would just agree with me. They would not tend to challenge the *implications* of my hypothesis because they would instantly see the value of my idea, since they already have experience with observing how planetary patterns influence human behavior. Astrologers all know that planetary transits influence human growth passages, so I sought instead good arguments from nonastrologers to challenge my premise.

Thompson and Sedgwick both have remarkable capacities to consider all possibilities, so they were able to think about whether *there may be astrological and astronomical influences on human behavior.* They were both intrigued that the astronomer Dr. Percy Seymour had published an astronomical causal theory for astrological influences and that Dr. Richard Gerber suggested that the energetic systems of our bodies actually are stimulated by planetary patterns (see Dr. Gerber's introduction).

Thompson and Sedgwick are and were both deeply skeptical of deterministic approaches to human behavior, as am I. Such theories often result in what Thompson calls "misplaced concreteness," a tendency to attribute fixed reasons for things that are inherently speculative, such as people who say the Fallen Angels in the Hebrew Bible are spacemen. Both thinkers are highly skeptical of ideas that trample on or reduce the potential for subtlety in human nature, qualities they value so deeply. Both feel that narrowing the range of human comprehension about what is possible often ultimately results in tyranny and delusion. I agree!

Beginning with William Irwin Thompson, the disturbing issue raised by *Astrology and the Rising of Kundalini* is that if my central theory is correct—kundalini energy rises according to the cycles of the planet Uranus, which triggers a spiritual crisis in all people during their early forties—then this suggests that all people could attain enlightenment, because kundalini rising is what triggers enlightenment by means of intense meditation practices. He notes that kundalini rising may *enable* some humans to attain mystical attunement, yet he points out that kundalini rising does not necessarily *accomplish* enlightenment. To him, such a state of being cannot exist without compassion and the opening of the heart, and I totally agree with him.

My finding that everybody experiences kundalini rising during midlife crisis presents similar difficulties for any person who has used Eastern meditation practices, such as kundalini yoga, to attain enlightenment. Until this book was published in 1991, Eastern spiritual teachers taught that kundalini rising can only be attained by practicing intense yogic asanas and breathing techniques; only a few practitioners might attain enlightenment, which is the full opening of the heart. I was worried that people schooled in Eastern meditation might accuse me of blasphemy. So I've emphasized the point that kundalini rising in the masses is a stressful experience that requires guidance; it is not an easy path to enlightenment. I describe in detail the widely reported stress symptoms of kundalini rising during midlife crisis and show they are the same as the spiritual emergency symptoms. Both midlife crisis and spiritual emergency trigger a cascading series of problems for people as they struggle to save their marriages, and even their homes and jobs.

What about enlightenment for the masses? Well, if you are actively seeking to open your heart and achieve bliss, you are more likely to accomplish this if you successfully navigate through your midlife crisis.

To be truthful, kundalini rising during midlife crisis usually does *not* result in enlightenment for most people; it just causes intense stress. The physiological and emotional symptoms of midlife crisis are *exactly* the same as the symptoms of kundalini rising described by people using Eastern practices to intentionally activate kundalini rising. Therefore therapists helping clients with midlife crisis can draw on the extensive sources on spiritual emergency for advice—including, of course, those offered in this book. One of the great joys for me since this book came out is that I've heard from many therapists who use this book and have given it or loaned it to their clients.

The spiritual emergency literature is extensive, because many people in the West activated their kundalini by meditating with Eastern gurus starting in the 1960s. Many experienced spiritual emergency and even psychosis, which also can happen during midlife crisis. This is why my therapeutic recommendations for help with too-much-fire-energy abound in this book. Dubious energy experimentations with gurus were going on all around me during the 1980s. I discovered in my practice that most people benefit by processing midlife crisis as a spiritual emergency, rather than reducing it to just an aging, health, or relationship crisis. Now, after twenty years of feedback from people who have used the advice in this book, I am so happy I wrote it. People have thanked me for giving them tools to save their marriages and their basic health, which has helped open my heart!

Back to our question about mass enlightenment, maybe the agenda of our times *is* the enlightenment of many people so they can guide us during our critical evolutionary leap, an idea I discuss extensively in many of my other books. If we need enlightened guides to help us eliminate ecocidal behavior, then perhaps this book will be a good resource for some people. We know that compassion seems to flower in people who integrate the spiritual fire and then consciously direct the divine elixir—kundalini—to open their hearts. Chapter 7 offers advice on enlightenment processes that utilize the potent healing powers of Chiron, a small body orbiting between Saturn and Uranus. My Chiron book—*Chiron: Rainbow Bridge between the Inner and Outer Planets*

(1987)—posits that Chiron's discovery in 1977 heralded the mass awakening of our species. Hopefully *Astrology and the Rising of Kundalini* can help people personally handle the intensity of this mass awakening.

Now on to Timothy Sedgwick, who wondered whether I even understood the implications of what I was saying, which made me chuckle. I assured him that I was well aware that if we can "time" human growth processes and identify their energetic causal basis, this could open humanity to a new form of behavioral analysis that could be dangerous. Then we went on to intelligently discuss the *positive implications* of this theory. For example, maturation could be consciously directed if personal and family disruptions were reduced as much as possible while an individual changes and expands his or her consciousness. If many people could grow and expand more easily and safely, society as a whole would improve.

These critical questions arose in my discussion with Sedgwick: (1) Will this idea foster a herd mentality and make humans into sheep who predictably get stuck or grow at specified times? (2) If it is possible to understand the human as this theory posits, then once the knowledge in this book is integrated, will we go beyond the conflicts and problems existing now that must be due to previously misunderstood causes? (3) Does not the possibility of such knowing about the timing processes at birth somehow devalue the brave struggles and pain that define us as humans in the first place? I answered each question as best I could years ago, and now I can add what I've learned from twenty years of feedback.

Regarding a "herd mentality," yes, there is a herd mentality inherent in the key life passages because they are universal growth processes that occur again and again due to the ceaseless orbiting of Earth and all the other planets around the Sun. But this collective solar influence simply *is,* and I've been literally astonished to see clients using these processes intentionally instead of being used *by* them. This approach may be the best way for ordinary human beings to *grow out of* the herd level caused by the repetitive solar cycles. The key life passages are when people can ignite their unique potential, individuate, and really become themselves. Regarding being able to transcend current levels of conflict and problems, I now see many people moving beyond excessive stress during the key life passages by having this knowledge; we *are* attaining new stages of growth that will benefit our planet! Judging by some people's experiences with this book, they are using the key life passages as intentional "initiations," carefully crafted psychological turning points. My great joy now is that this really improves their lives.

The ideas in this book have been used so successfully by many people that I find most other writers who discuss spiritual emergency and initiation don't even realize some of their ideas came from this book! This is fine, because people are just doing the work that is radically transforming society at this time. That is what matters to me, not being credited for an idea whose time has simply come.

Regarding Sedgwick's concern that knowing *when* we are most likely to struggle could lessen or devalue human pain, I say, "Yes!" We have been on the cross for too long, and it is time to come down. More and more people are tired of this strife, especially when they see that the destructive aspects of the striving are either destroying Earth or are causing Gaia—the living Earth!—to eliminate humanity from her surface. I predicted that many people would become wiser by intentionally using the potential of the key life passages. They *have* and they *are*. And as a result they are changing the planet. Countless people have told me that they believe the *planet is in a midlife crisis* because enough people are prepared to face the music and learn to co-create with nature.

When this book first came out, many people expressed an aversion to its analytic view of personal growth cycles. Now, as time has passed and so many have benefitted from its advice, people seem to realize that we are influenced by the solar orbits; the only question is whether we use them or get used *by* them. The Sun is the source of energy for all existence and life—this helps people feel more organic because they realize we are actually just a plant that seeds, grows, and then dies. We grow in the Sun like an iris, a corn plant, or a tree, and when you find yourself reflecting on yourself as an organic being, life is exciting and creative. This organic view of the human enables us to escape from cages and sheep pens that limit us. It is by consciously abetting the solar growth cycles that we live the fullest life possible and then can die very consciously.

So welcome to *Astrology and the Rising of Kundalini,* which offers a way to grow into your light body by letting go and just allowing the natural cycles and energies trigger growth. Let yourself realize that you are a plant or a tree in the Sun!

Introduction

....

Richard Gerber, M.D.

ALTHOUGH "MIDLIFE CRISIS" has become a popular term these days for individuals going through major life turbulence, it has probably not been looked at in quite the same way as Barbara Hand Clow has done in this impressive synthesis of clinical casework and astrological insight. We all tend to associate midlife crisis with some type of redefinition of our sexual identity and vitality. However, as you will find in the following pages, the rising of kundalini has less to do with discovering new techniques of sexual fulfillment than it does with understanding the energetic nature of human beings and their relationship to the subtle currents of life force that animate and vitalize the living form.

There is reason and purpose behind the timing of key events in our lives, not the least of which is the midlife crisis. Most of the time the nature and meaning of these cycles is hidden to us or dealt with only at the most superficial psychological levels. Astrology, if utilized correctly, holds tremendous insights for understanding the hidden meaning behind these important struggles of everyday life. Barbara Hand Clow's interpretations of astrological cycles and their implications for midlife crises are quite remarkable in that they lead us to a whole new way of understanding the process of growth and transformation as a part of everyday life.

The transformational process is becoming an increasingly viable option in our lives as we are beginning to understand human beings from an entirely new and different perspective. Such a new perspective may even hold the key to understanding how planetary positions in the solar system could have the slightest influence on human behavior. This newly emerging vision of humanity has to do with viewing human beings not merely as biological machines but as unique energy systems. The medical world has tended to conceptualize humans from a Newtonian mechanistic perspective for nearly the last two hundred years. Recent discoveries in medicine, the development of new technologies, and the integration of New Physics into biology have begun to create a vastly different picture of people as more than just the sum of their physical components.

What we are beginning to discover is that the physical/cellular body that medicine has begun to understand all the way down to the molecular level is nourished, structured, and almost invisibly guided by a variety of spiritual and life-force energy systems. This new perspective of human physiology is based on an understanding that the atomic structure of the body, at the quantum level, is actually made up of particles of frozen light. The idea that all matter is really another form of energy is the essence of the Einsteinian worldview. Thus, rethinking the body in terms of interactive energy structures as opposed to moving cogs in a machine holds the beginnings of Einsteinian medicine.

In addition to viewing the molecular and cellular structure of the body as complex patterns of frozen light or compressed miniature energy fields, we are now understanding that the cells are also guided and nurtured by a variety of structured energy systems. These systems, such as the acupuncture meridian system, the chakra system, the etheric body, and the emotional, astral, and mental bodies, form a complex energetic network that feeds life energy to the cells of the body in highly specialized ways. The acupuncture meridians are a type of biocircuitry network that supplies life energy to the different organs of the body. The meridians have surface points, known as acupuncture points, that are like energetic pores. These acupoint pores take in a type of vital environmental energy (known as *ch'i*) and distribute it internally throughout the body in an orderly fashion. The acupoints are also a connecting link or interface between the human organism and its surrounding energetic environment, which includes man-made electromagnetic fields as well as the geomagnetic and cosmic energy environment.

The meridians are also linked to a specialized, holographic energy template known as the etheric body, which provides structural pattern information to the cells of the body during growth and development from the embryonic state all the way through adulthood. The meridian system and the etheric body, as well as the other life-energy systems, work in concert with the well-known biomolecular and cellular systems that medical science has already begun to understand in great detail, though the larger part of the medical establishment has not yet accepted these higher-energy control systems. But there are increasingly greater numbers of enlightened health-care practitioners who have begun to acknowledge the existence of these systems. These practitioners have already begun to utilize therapeutic modalities such as acupuncture, homeopathy, and flower essences because of their powerful effects upon these so-called subtle-energy regulatory systems of the body. The evolving subspecialty of medicine that utilizes various forms of energy (or vibration) for diagnosis and treatment of illness is known as "energy medicine," or "vibrational medicine."

The subtle life energies that flow through the meridians are of a subtle magnetic character. In addition, these energies are negatively entropic in nature (they create order from disorder). Remarkably, subtle energy or life energy appears to have been predicted by Einstein's relativistic equations. Although many physicists will have a hard time believing it, subtle energy is tachyonic, or supraluminal, in character, meaning that it travels faster than light. Preliminary experiments with healers' energy fields have already begun to confirm various theoretical aspects of this evolving (Einsteinian) model of life energy.

The body possesses other life-energy distribution networks in addition to the acupuncture meridian system. Another major subtle energy network of the body is known as the chakra system. The chakras are specialized subtle-energy transducers. They transduce, or step down, subtle-energy signals into chemical and hormonal bioinformational signals that instruct and direct various physiological processes in the body. In addition, the chakras are also emotional and spiritual energy processors. The chakras are not actually part of the physical body but are vortexual energy centers that exist in the higher subtle bodies known as the etheric, astral, and mental bodies. Each of these higher bodies (that has its own specialized functions) is formed from etheric, astral, or mental matter, a variety of "subtle" matter that vibrates at speeds beyond that of physical matter, allowing the subtle bodies to interpenetrate the physical body. These subtle bodies and their associated chakras actually exist at higher dimensional levels.

Thus, the term "multidimensional reality" implies interactions not only in the physical body but also in the higher dimensional bodies (such as the etheric and astral) as well.

Each of the chakra centers corresponds to and feeds subtle magnetic energy to the major nerve and glandular centers of the body. In addition to providing a nutritive function, each chakra is related to a different emotional or spiritual issue of personal spiritual evolution. An understanding of the chakras and of human multidimensional anatomy is critical to making sense of how humanity's relationship to planetary positions at birth can influence psychological, behavioral, and spiritual patterns throughout an individual's life. In other words, astrology as a predictive science will make sense only if we view human beings from a higher energetic perspective that takes into account the meridians, chakras, and subtle bodies as energy systems that help to coordinate and regulate the physical body.

The chakra system is linked by special channels that travel the length of the spinal cord. In the yogic and tantric traditions, there is an energy force, referred to as the *kundalini,* that usually lies dormant in the root chakra at the base of the spine. The kundalini is sometimes referred to as the serpent energy because it is sleeping like a coiled serpent at the base of the spine, waiting to strike forth. In reality, the kundalini is an evolutionary and creative subtle life energy that ascends the spinal pathway, progressively activating each major chakra along its path. Traditional wisdom has taught that the kundalini begins to rise naturally during the life cycle of the individual as a consequence of following any major form of spiritual practice.

As the kundalini energy rises, it may encounter resistance from so-called blockages in the major chakras. These obstructions to energy flow are usually related to an unconscious difficulty the individual has in dealing with particular emotional and spiritual issues that are associated with the blocked chakras. For instance, the issue of the heart chakra is dealing with love—that is, love in the sense of being able to express love to others as well as to oneself (to truly love oneself), along with the ability to express unconditional love. When the kundalini energy encounters resistance to ascent due to a blocked chakra, the energy will continue to hammer away at the area of resistance until the individual either resolves the "blocked emotional issue" or begins to manifest physical symptoms in the particular chakra-associated body region. In the case of the kundalini ascent encountering a blocked heart chakra (which might be due to difficulties in acting toward the self in a truly loving manner), the individual might actually begin to experience chest pains similar to angina. The physical symptom is often a symbolic message from the higher self to examine the way the individual is dealing with the "lessons of the heart."

The kundalini energy process may actually be a kind of natural stress-release mechanism that discharges stresses traumatically locked into the body over the course of a lifetime. It chips away at the character armor we protectively surround ourselves with and forces the individual to deal with major issues of personal integration that are critical to human spiritual evolution. If we could know in advance the timing of such a cataclysmic inner process, it would obviously be of great interest. Therefore, Barbara Hand Clow's theory on the astrological timing of the kundalini ascent is of major importance (even though the kundalini, a universal human phenomenon, is not yet recognized by Western medicine).

In her discussion of possible mechanisms behind the astrological timing of the kundalini ascent, Barbara examines the theories of Dr. Percy Seymour. Seymour postulates that astrology is based on magnetic influences upon the body. Specifically, he suggests that astrological influences are related to solar magnetic activity in relation to the planets of the solar system. According to astrological theory, major events take place when planets are in unique geometric relationships to the Sun, especially with respect to their original positions during the time of birth. Seymour's research suggests that there are major magnetic fluctuations in the solar magnetic field during particular geometric configurations of planets (such as during planetary oppositions, conjunctions, and squares). It is suggested that the fetus is influenced by the Earth's magnetic field at the time of birth. According to Seymour, activation of the fetus's sensory system during the birth process causes the fetal nervous system to integrate a type of geomagnetic coding at the cellular level. The Earth's magnetic field, in turn, is indirectly influenced by the solar magnetic field. In examining Seymour's theory of solar magnetism as a mechanism to explain astrological influences on human behavior and emotions, I felt that it might indeed be plausible. However, I have a slightly different theory that may also explain the astrology phenomenon.

Returning to our discussion of the life energies and subtle matter that guide the physical body, it was noted that these specialized life-energy systems are actually magnetic in character. Quantitatively, the energy of this subtle magnetism (or animal magnetism) is different from ferromagnetism (the magnet- and iron-filings variety of magnetism). Subtle magnetic energy is exceedingly difficult to measure with conventional magnetic detectors (with the possible exception of exquisitely sensitive SQUID [Superconducting Quantum Interference Device] detectors). Thus, it may only be possible (at this point in our technological development) to indirectly measure subtle magnetic fields and currents by observing their powerful effects upon living systems. Qualitatively, subtle magnetic energy has biological effects similar to high-intensity conventional magnetic fields. Subtle magnetism is negatively entropic, meaning that it seems to push biological systems to create order out of chaos, driving living systems toward states of increasing order and organization. This negentropic behavior of subtle magnetism is a primary characteristic of the life force as well.

One other peculiar characteristic of this subtle magnetic energy is that it can have effects on living systems at exceedingly great distances. For instance, certain healers could have the same growth-enhancing effect on plants whether they were in the same room or some six hundred miles away. This faster-than-light subtle magnetic energy (involved in healing and life-energy systems) does not follow the inverse square law of electromagnetism, whereas electromagnetic and gravitational field intensities decrease (inversely) according to the square of the distance.

The chakras are actually spinning magnetic vortices made up of this same subtle magnetic energy. It is suggested here that, at the time of birth, each of the chakras becomes encoded with a particular subtle magnetic orientation. Using a crude analogy, one could view each of the major chakras as pieces of iron. When a bar of iron is exposed to a magnetic field, the iron becomes a magnet itself, oriented with particular north and south poles that become permanently fixed. In the same way, the human multidimensional body (specifically, the astral, or emotional, body) has a series of malleable protomagnets (analogous to the pieces of iron) that attain their (permanent) magnetic orientation at the exact moment of birth. (The astral body is actually more fluid than fixed, but it is made up of subtle magnetic matter.)

The magnetic chakra vortices may become locked into a specific magnetic orientation at the moment of birth. The magnetic influence that creates this orientation comes from the subtle magnetic fields of the planets of our solar system. Each spinning planetary body is like a subtle magnetic vortex in space. (It should be noted here that just as human beings have higher subtle bodies, so do planets have etheric, astral, and higher subtle bodies as well. To quote an age-old aphorism, "As above, so below.") In addition, each of the major chakras may be primarily responsive to a single planet in the solar system, depending upon planetary geometric configurations at the time of birth. This would mean that different planets have their strongest effects upon particular chakras in the astral or emotional body.

According to this theory, the magnetic orientation and responsiveness of the astral/emotional body and its chakras become fixed at the time of birth by the subtle planetary fields. But the sources of magnetic influence to the astral chakras, the planetary vortices, do not remain fixed, as the planets continually move in cyclical orbits around the sun. As the planetary vortices move throughout the solar system, they produce a direct (albeit subtle) effect upon the astral/emotional body of the individual. When the planets reach the particular geometric position (relative to the Earth) that is the same as during the birth time, there is a reactivation of that same magnetic pattern in the resonating chakra, causing a cascading energy transfer from the astral to the etheric and down to the physical body. The so-called Saturn Return would thus be caused by the planet Saturn returning to its original birth position in the sky, thus energetically influencing (via subtle magnetic connections from the planetary vortex to the resonant chakra vortex) the individual's multidimensional energy system. According to Barbara's theory, it is the positioning of the planet Uranus 180 degrees opposite to its position at the time of birth (the Uranus Opposition) that appears to trigger the buildup and accelerated ascent of the kundalini energies from the root chakra. (Metaphorically speaking, this astrological influence of Uranus causes the movement of subtle energy up the spine and away from or opposite to "your anus!"—no pun intended.)

Therefore, there may indeed be a kind of energetic coding that takes place during the time of birth. This encoding may actually occur at the level of the chakras in the subtle bodies. The coding energies may be geomagnetic, solar magnetic, or subtle magnetic influences from the planets themselves. Only future vibrational medicine research will be able to confirm any of these theories of astrological influence upon human emotional energy patterns. Such theories do suggest possible multidimensional mechanisms that would explain how planetary positions in the solar system might affect the energetic character of individual human energy systems, and that these energetic influences are maximized at times of key geometric planetary arrangements.

It is important to recognize that the patterns of life manifestation are not merely the result of planetary motions, although their subtle energetic influences can affect the timing and character of certain events in our lives. We must remember that we are multidimensional beings whose lives are affected by many different factors, from our inherited genes to our diet, our learned patterns of behavior, and even our environment. The environmental factors can range from local chemical and electromagnetic influences to even solar and planetary subtle magnetic influences. Astrological energies are energetic patterns that can best be thought of as potentials for manifestation and expression. These energies affect our subtle energetic makeup, especially our chakra systems, which, in turn, strongly affect our physical bodies, especially our nervous systems.

The importance of this rather lengthy discussion is that the human energetic system is much more complex than Western science had previously suspected. Also, it appears that there are cyclic transformational phenomena such as the kundalini process that are triggered at critical periods in an individual's life. According to Barbara's clinical research and theory, it may be possible to use the astrological model to predict exactly when these key transformational times occur in a person's life. It is a matter of being aware that your own subtle inner clocks may have preset alarms for potential spiritual awakening that are, so to speak, already built into the human energetic system.

Barbara's theory hinges on the idea that as evolving spiritual beings we have hidden agendas of soul growth that our conscious personality does not always recognize. However, our higher self is always aware of this hidden spiritual agenda. This hidden agenda has to do with becoming highly conscious, spiritually aware beings who are able to physically manifest our inner potentials. We come into the physical plane with this preprogrammed agenda that is structured in terms of "timed" learning experiences at key energy intensity points in our lives. Astrology helps us to identify individual energy intensity points in the life cycle by interpreting the coded, symbolic meaning of these intensity points. In identifying their coded meanings, we can be given assistance in terms of direction and approaches that will help us to best assimilate these intense life experiences, utilizing them to transform ourselves through the powerful energies of change that are a part of the soul's learning experience on the physical plane.

The conscious personality is usually unaware of specific

learning experiences that may be contained in the soul's hidden spiritual agenda. What is even more unfortunate is that the majority of Western culture does not recognize or prepare its members for the types of potentially transformational experiences that are contained within this hidden agenda of soul growth. Western medicine and psychology only see symptoms of bodily discomfort and stress in terms of superficial models of cause and effect that do not take into account the multidimensional nature of human beings. In other words, we as a culture are often more interested in figuring out how to make a symptom or illness go away than in figuring out why it happened at a particular point in a person's life. There is a deeper symbolism and synchronicity to such life events. While Western cultures have tended to ignore the symbolic nature of life changes in terms of soul lessons, there have been many earlier cultures that were more in tune with this viewpoint.

Many ancient cultures, including Native Americans, had a very different focus than is found today in Western society. These cultures lived in harmony with nature. In fact, they worshiped the Goddess energy that we sometimes refer to as Mother Nature. Today they are often referred to as Earth Mother societies. In ancient times, such cultures were commonly matriarchal in orientation. Many of their symbolic rituals were expressions of their desire for attunement with the guiding forces of the planetary and cosmic environment in which they lived. They had a deep abiding respect for all life. Today we would consider them to be highly right-brain oriented because they lived their lives with a greater recognition of the symbolic and synchronistic nature of life. They paid tremendous attention to symbolic information that came from their dreams and often used such information as an aid in making important decisions. These societies were frequently guided by the tribal elders, who were often shamans or medicine men—keepers of the sacred wisdom. The shamans would attain mystical states of awareness to obtain symbolic guidance from waking visions and from the dream state that would assist them in seeing deeper levels of truth, especially when they were confronted with difficult dilemmas. Many of their communications and archives were through symbolic pictographs. Such ancient cultures nurtured creativity and growth of the individual.

In contrast, Western societies are extremely left-brain oriented, analytical, and precise in language and communication. These societies tend to be materialistic by nature. Lives frequently become focused upon the search for power, control, and material acquisition. Happiness is often defined by the amount of goods and properties owned. This materialistic philosophy has been summed up rather appropriately by the popular saying "He who dies with the most toys wins." Western societies have gradually weeded out mysticism from the experience of everyday life. Individuals have begun to pursue science as a type of new religion where technology is the fruit that the scientific priesthood has harvested. Western society is now guided by a sterile scientific philosophy that has become obsessed with an overly mechanistic, reductionistic viewpoint of life. Yet there are many who struggle to find deeper meaning in their lives.

The older mystical, shamanistic societies were highly aware of the importance of key life events and created special ceremonies honoring specific rites of passage. Such initiatic rites were a common part of a shaman's training. Each different rite was a form of personal transformation and ascension along the pathway toward attaining higher wisdom. As the higher wisdom was attained and shared with the rest of the tribal culture, all life could be seen as part of an integral webwork of cosmic life energy, infused by the god/goddess into many different forms of earthly expression that included rocks, trees, fish, and animals, as well as people. Through the awakening of their third eye chakras, the shamans grew increasingly aware of the multidimensional nature of the universe. All parts of nature were viewed as a part of the unfoldment of cosmic life patterns. The shamanic elders were the evolved individuals within these cultures who helped to explain the mysteries of life to the rest of the members of their society. These knowledge keepers frequently looked to the Sun, Moon, and stars as important cosmic forces in their lives. Astrological timekeeping helped to synchronize the timing of the planting and harvesting of crops. In addition, astrology provided information that suggested the most favorable timing for important symbolic rituals as well as for ceremonies (such as the solstices) that celebrated the guiding forces of nature.

Today, there is a movement toward rediscovering the uses of astrology and the importance of the shamanistic viewpoint of the world. There is, by some, a turning away from the scientist-priests as the purveyors of all knowledge and wisdom. What we are beginning to realize is that left-brain knowledge alone is sterile and incomplete. We cannot comprehend the bigger picture unless right-brain knowledge is also incorporated into the greater worldview. As a result, we have seen an explosion of right-brain paths of consciousness exploration over the past three decades. A deeply buried need to experience mystical ways of knowing and perceiving the world is reawakening. In this search for greater self-knowledge, many have sought to learn the shaman's path to inner knowing. These trailblazers seek to revive the ancient right-brain technologies of learning through following sacred paths of initiation, exploration, and ascension via symbolically meaningful rituals. They search for ways of adapting shamanistic knowledge gathering and the creative, harmonious use of power to rediscover, through the magic of ritual and dreamtime exploration, the reenchantment of the world. They quest for deeper meaning in their lives.

A new form of whole-brain learning and perceiving the world around us is developing. We have begun to integrate our left-brain analytical skills with our recently rediscovered intuitive, symbolic right-brain skills of knowledge gathering. As we combine the best of both worlds to understand the meaningful symbolism of events in our own lives, we accelerate our spiritual learning and integration of life experiences. We have, as a culture, just begun to uncover the hidden spiritual agenda of soul growth and attainment of higher wisdom. The shamanistic path of exploration holds great power for us to begin to integrate our right and left brains to achieve personal transformation and spiritual awakening. It is a tradition that works with the forces of nature to create harmony on both the personal, microcosmic level and the planetary, macrocosmic scale. There is a tremendous potential for mass transformation of the entire human race if people could begin to utilize shamanistic and scientific knowledge as well as left- and right-brain skills to integrate the wisdom of ancient Eastern and modern Western cultures and to harmonize and balance their masculine and feminine sides.

This trend has already begun with a small but growing group of evolutionary spiritual explorers. They have set out on a course of rediscovery of ancient mystical knowledge that is based, in part, on a rediscovery of the multidimensional self and all of its higher potentials. *Astrology and the Rising of Kundalini* is a guidebook for those of us who wish to begin to integrate our outer and inner worlds by uncovering the hidden meaning and synchronicity in our lives. This book, if properly utilized, can help us to make sense of the sometimes puzzling life journey we have embarked upon, and it can give us guidance about avoiding the pitfalls and obstacles along the way. And, if we are lucky, we can use the tremendous potential energy of midlife crisis to become more conscious, spiritually awakened beings who can begin to make a difference in the world.

RICHARD GERBER, M.D.
LIVONIA, MICHIGAN
JUNE 1991

Dr. Richard Gerber (1954–2007) received his medical degree from Wayne State University School of Medicine in Detroit. He was highly respected for his thirty-one years of progressive research into alternative methods of diagnosis and healing. He is the author of *Vibrational Medicine: The #1 Handbook of Subtle-Energy Therapies.*

ONE

I'm in Midlife Crisis Now!

IT IS 11 A.M. NEAR Stinson Beach, California. Bob walks on the beach with his wife and two children. The sun is hot, yet the air is cool from the remnants of the thick fog sucking into the San Francisco Bay opening just to the south. His children—a daughter who is 7 and a son who is 9—wander quickly away from him as they feel the hot sand underfoot and the cool water beckoning about a hundred feet away. His wife, with whom he has lived very happily for twelve years, continues the conversation they were having at brunch.

Her voice drifts off into the crystalline rays of light from the sparkling water and misty sunlight. Bob doesn't hear her; his attention is on the pulsating waves of eroticism in his body as he watches nubile California girls in skimpy bikinis walking and running at the water's edge. He wonders if it is obvious that he is staring at their young bodies. What is it? Their exquisite shining hair? The blue eyes dancing over wet cheeks? He worries about having an erection as he rubs his thumbs back and forth across his index and middle fingers, just like an infant searching for the pleasures of fluff on a beloved baby blanket.

His wife asks, "Are you there?"

He has shared a close and monogamous relationship with her that allows for honesty when safe, and so he replies, "I just realized I will never go to bed with a young woman again."

The rest of the day passes with conversation about what it's like to be actually getting older. She attempts to penetrate into his very bones to figure out what he is thinking about as insecurity creeps insidiously into her mind. He is interested only in what it could mean that he will never pursue and bed a nubile California girl. He knows his reality is forever different now because he has just noticed that limitation might be a possibility in his life.

Bob is at a turning point in his life, which is commonly referred to in psychology as "midlife crisis." When midlife crisis hit me, I shook for eighteen months. I had been counseling others on midlife crisis, but when I finally experienced it myself, I was appalled by how little I actually knew about the force of it. Through my own experience, I've learned about the astrological implications of this key life passage. This turning point is never easy, but the rewards for passing through it successfully are great.

During midlife crisis, the energy of life—eros—is rising or flowing upward in the physical body through all the subtle energy systems—the chakras and meridians—and opening the chakric centers of feeling so that it flows through the body more intensely. If we are counseled to honor and assist the opening of expanded energy channels at this time, to not resist the powerful flow of erotic energy through the whole body, which I refer to as the "liquid light of sex," the cells in our bodies vibrate as if they are actually making love. An opportunity now exists to move beyond just genital sex as our own bodies evolve into shivering receptors of electromagnetic forces. The liquid light of sex—greatly increased electromagnetic field potential in the body—is the rediscovery, the remembering, and the reexperiencing of sex in an *elemental* way. Full sexual knowing involves all the elements—water, fire, earth, and air—which causes a massive opening of *physical feeling,* creating subtle communion with all that is, even the spiraling center of our galaxy. God/Goddess, the Divine, laughs with the union of beings. Experiencing elemental energy reawakens memory of the first creation of matter itself.

Midlife crisis is a very different experience for men and women. Men must open the heart, and they are overwhelmed by feelings at this time. Women at midlife crisis must take on their power, and this process is generally manifested less sexually for women than for men. A woman's sexual discovery often emerges after the crisis has passed. Her crisis involves her conflict about finding her inner male and using her power without losing her female role.

For both men and women, the challenge is to balance inner sexual polarities, but their processes for dealing with the polarities are very different. In both cases, however, the discovery of individuality is to be found by exploring one's inner male or female. The male cannot attain full sexual maturation without accessing the inner female, which allows him to feel, to open the heart. The female cannot attain full sexual intensity without awakening the inner male to help her take on her power. That's what my client Alice found out.

THERE IS MORE TO LIFE

About seven years before her actual midlife crisis began near age 40, Alice found herself feeling *profoundly* depressed. This is an early vibration of midlife crisis that many people confuse with the real thing. Those who do experience this early depression in the mid-thirties usually experience a rough midlife crisis when it actually comes to pass.

A chaotic blackness that made her feel like everything in her life was exhausting and meaningless settled in on Alice. She went into extreme denial first by doubting herself, asking, "Am I getting serious and deep about my life? I hate people who are like that—I've been avoiding them all for years."

She would go out to get the morning paper after her husband got on the train and her two sons left for school. She would emerge from the magazine store and linger for a moment idly watching career women getting on the commuter train. She would feel hot bile rising in her throat; she would glare at them, despising the very ground they walked on. She hated their briefcases, their smooth trench coats, their perfect hair. She would feel fat and dumpy and stupid, and then she would stop herself and wonder if she was losing her mind.

This angry and negative reaction to other women involved in a life-style different from her own was loaded with information for Alice, if she just could have seen it. Therapists term such responses *projection,* and such responses to others often contain the answer to what the person really wants for herself or himself! Alice probably needed a job in order to discover who she really was.

This depression in the early to mid-thirties is the first warning that big changes are coming, and a lot of pain can be avoided by paying attention at this point. This is usually not the time to actually make changes according to the eventual pursuit of our quest, but it is a time to begin to move out of our "cultural suit of clothes"—living our whole lives according to the ideals of the media, our own generation, or the preordained plans our parents created when we were born. It's time to quit being cool! That is not why we come here, and now is the time to separate ourselves from outside definitions and prepare ourselves for a new path in life more closely aligned with inner needs.

Alice was depressed at this point because she had thought it was all going to be easy in life if she just raised her sons and was a charming wife, which was all her parents had expected of her. Now, however, it was time to develop herself as a person and not just as a wife and mother. She began considering the whole meaning of her life and was looking at her eventual death for the first time.

As we approach the midpoint of our lives, thoughts of death occur, and the need for greater life force intensifies. This early warning is about eros—the exquisite sexual/physical nature of all life's energy—which is the only antidote to thanatos—the death urge. The main thesis of this book is that the eros/thanatos balance is held by planetary transits of Saturn/thanatos and Uranus/eros, so as we begin moving into the *causes* of the key life passages, I will introduce the case for planetary influences and their timing in our lives.

At this point, however, it would be good to just consider that we all live in a balance between life and death, and this process can actually be attributed to planetary forces. For example, the growing understanding in popular culture that addictions are slow death processes is actually a new awareness about the "Saturnian influence," or the idea that *too much form* can lead to deathliness. Seven years before we actually enter midlife crisis, we get a glimpse of that mortality, which wakes us up to the only revenge against inevitable aging: living each moment of our lives at the peak of creativity and sexual ecstasy. This counterbalancing life force is the "Uranian influence." The old roles we bought into no longer suffice as we really see that we will eventually die.

Alice was depressed because she became aware that she couldn't fight time, and, ideally, she would realize that her revenge would be to live time better (the concept of the Saturnian influence is also deeply related to time). As the wife and mother who felt rage toward working women, she needed to prepare herself to balance her responsibilities as parent and begin to train for a career of her own.

We, like Alice, must pay attention to the depression that comes about seven years before midlife crisis, because if we deny growth, particularly at this time, and avoid doing the work called for by the transformation patterns triggered by planetary transits (to be explained later in this book), *we begin dying right at that exact moment.* With my clients, I have seen that some people die in spirit at the first key life passage—Saturn Return, which occurs at ages 29 to 30, when Saturn has orbited back to its original position in the birth chart—the transit that always sets the stage for midlife crisis. Others die in spirit but stay in body at the second key passage—midlife crisis, when Uranus opposes its position in the birth chart. People who die in spirit but keep on living physically are like the characters in the prophetic film of the 1960s *Night of the Living Dead.* The depression that occurs around ages 33 to 36 is a big warning signal. It is time to begin opening and changing so as to be able to handle the energy of Uranus Opposition, which always hits like an earthquake.

Fortunately for her, Alice paid attention. From the onset of her depression, she began developing the buried side of herself, which had begun to go underground as she focused on the choices she had made in her twenties to get married and have a family. After developing into a very accomplished wife and mother, these choices had culminated in a completion of this form at about age 29—Saturn Return, or basic formation of self—when she had literally mastered child rearing and wifely skills. When the early midlife-crisis warning set in, she began to expand her focus. She took on part-time work in a field that interested her while supplementing her education.

As she approached age 40, Alice put all of her time and energy into succeeding at a challenging job. She worried about not having enough time for her family, but she was amazed to discover that they could take care of themselves. At first, her husband was threatened by her new-found freedom and power, but that passed when he discovered that he didn't have to worry about losing her. As more time passed, he found he was much more interested in her just as a person, and he appreciated her contributions to the family income. He even began to enjoy himself more because she had taken some financial pressure off of him.

Another example of the midlife-crisis situation is the woman who gives all her time to her career in her twenties and early thirties and then decides to have a child in her thirties or early forties. Either way, the crisis for women involves the demands of family and finding the self in work, even if that work is the family only. After observing hundreds of women face their rites of passage, I have noticed that women who work at some point before the arrival of midlife crisis often do better with the stress of the passage.

Women who have never succeeded "out there" have an extremely hard time taking on their power. If our culture valued homemaking, this might be different, but our culture does not value the wife and mother. Volunteer work can be somewhat helpful, but much of the volunteer work paradigm is based on patriarchal structures: a woman supported by a man. Women find it hard to figure out how to take on their power in the context of patriarchal structures. Lastly, a woman who succeeded in work before marriage will often choose to remain in the home, because she already knows about the pros and cons of the outer world.

SOUL, MIND, AND BODY

At midlife crisis, Alice made the right moves on three levels: her soul, her mind, and her body. For her *soul's agenda,* she began to question the meaning of her life, of all reality around her—even the meaning of existence itself. Why am *I* here? Have I been here before? Where am I going after this place? By taking on work in a field that fascinated her, she was free to discover her own special contribution. The present culture considers metaphysical ideas to be unimportant, although this is changing, but Alice realized she had to create time and space to become familiar with her soul needs. She even felt comfortable seeking some therapy, which her husband was leery about because *she* was paying for it. Soul needs are just as real as stomach needs, and Alice would have been very vulnerable to deep unhappiness without feeding that part of herself.

For her *mind's agenda,* Alice needed to allow herself the fullest exploration of her intelligence by means of study, travel, and expression of her unique gift. Jungian analytic therapy, psychosynthesis, past-life regression therapy, or the various New Age body/mind therapies are also helpful to a person when he or she enters the really intense phases of midlife crisis. I tell my clients to treat themselves to therapy during midlife crisis because every dollar you spend at this time in your life is worth a hundred.

Astrologically, we mainly perfect the physical plane—jobs, houses, marriages, money, and body care—up to age 30. By that time, Saturn, the planet that causes us to *form,* has orbited all the way around the Sun and has completed a full cycle or has "returned" to its position in the birth chart. Then from age 30 until ages 38 to 42, we perfect our emotional reality, seeking relationships we need in order to really find the heights and depths of our feelings. We have *transformed* the original form, and this process is triggered by the planet Uranus moving gradually into opposition to its location in the birth chart. When Uranus reaches its exact opposition point at around ages 38 to 42, we begin to focus on the full development of the mind—left-brain cognitive skills and right-brain intuitive skills—for the next ten years. The last major life transit occurs at about age 50, when the relatively recently discovered planet Chiron has gone all the way around the Sun and returns to its original position in the birth chart. This transit triggers the total integration of the left- and right-brain hemispheres, resulting in a spiritual awakening. We *transmute* the form that was *transformed* at midlife. These are the three major life transitions, and passing through them successfully is the fulfillment of the magical teaching "Knock three times, and the magical gateway to the soul will open after the third knock."

Alice was able to pursue mental expansion successfully because her emotional reality was sufficiently stable and mature to allow her growth. It was good that she had her own income to pursue her needs at this time, for this allowed her to gently release her husband's control over her reality. The divorce rate skyrockets at midlife crisis, and Alice might have needed to abandon her marriage if her husband could not allow her soul and mental needs to emerge. However, she was cautious at this juncture since she had been married for twenty years.

Midlife crisis is incredibly stressful: you shake, you fear for your sanity, you often have really frightening physical-body symptoms, and you deeply question everything you have ever thought about in life. In most cases, this is the worst time to end a stable relationship because often half of your potential learning is right with your own mate, even if that learning is all about parts of yourself you've been avoiding. I usually ask clients not to terminate a long-term or very intense, deep relationship until after the last opposition of Uranus. (Over a period of eighteen months, there are three oppositions of Uranus during midlife crisis, and the actual process will be covered in detail later in this book.) I also tend to advise clients *not* to marry during Uranus Opposition because a potentially superb marriage can go on the rocks due to the level of stress those going through Uranus Opposition feel. For the most part, only mature and highly valued marriages can handle the stress well.

Like others in her place, Alice found staying in a primary relationship incredibly hard, even though her primary partner was the best person in the world for her. To attain the pinnacle of emotional maturity, she needed to question all that she felt. She stopped feeling and responding based on what she thought everybody else needed. She stood apart in the relationship in order to really *see* herself. From a simple perspective, Alice couldn't find her inner male without seeing it reflected in her partner.

Mastering Uranus Opposition involves learning to see how we are mirrored in others, and this teaching is very subtle. What was important for Alice to know and honor was that she had to find a way to stay with her mirror—her other side—and yet create a great deal of time and space for herself. It is impossible for women to tolerate the emotional stresses of midlife crisis without having a great deal of private time. Women might need to take a few trips alone, attend a meditation group, or have a day a week to themselves. They might need to create permission to not have sex occasionally and not feel like they are depriving their mate. As for their children, women must have freedom to discover that children can handle their own lives perfectly well or, if their children are very young, that child care may be needed for a few years.

What exactly were the emotional changes Alice experienced? If all was going well, she was immersed in a culmination of all she had learned about her feeling needs during her thirties. She found that all those years of giving to the family were a basis for her to explore herself. She gained a new love for her husband when she realized he loved her new self. She realized he didn't love her *role,* he loved *her.* She stayed in this primary relationship and discovered a deeper trust, which was actually trust in herself.

IN PHYSICAL REALITY

The *body agenda* is last. To understand what happens with the body requires some astrological information. Astrology has more than its share of skeptics, who argue that little heed should be paid to it because of a perceived lack of "scientific verification." But skepticism doesn't diminish the extraordinary verification of repeated personal experience at key stages of life. And in any event, current research on the scientific front begins to provide the desired corroboration.

The first area to explore is a growing field of research that is not fully accepted by contemporary "science": the field of subtle energetics medicine, which involves the study of body parts not yet *visible* or *verifiable* to classic hard science. This is the landscape of energy fields such as the chakras, meridians, and *nadis* utilized by acupuncturists, homeopaths, and radionic practitioners, and investigated in the research of neuroscientists. "Energetics medicine" teaches that the subtle-energy fields can be worked with for healing purposes and disease prevention. This field is rapidly moving into scientific credibility due to healing successes by practitioners and the groundbreaking research presented in *Vibrational Medicine: The #1 Handbook of Subtle-Energy Therapies* by Dr. Richard Gerber.

Secondly, astrology is now moving into the realm of scientific credibility as a result of the 1989 publication of *Astrology: The Evidence of Science* by Dr. Percy Seymour, who theorizes that astrology is based on magnetism. (Dr. Seymour's theories are discussed more fully in the next chapter.) Based on my own successful results with many clients, I believe that these two theories together explain what is going on in the body during midlife crisis.

In conventional natal astrology, Uranus rules electricity, surprises, lightning levels of change. The research by Robert O. Becker, M.D., and Gary Selden in *The Body Electric* demonstrates the electrical nature of energy in the physical body, and Uranus rules that electricity. My theory is that Uranus also rules "kundalini energy," the life force in the body according to ancient Indian philosophy.

Kundalini energy is said to be contained at the base of the spine, in the root chakra, in the form of a coiled snake. With certain spiritual practices such as yoga, the snake uncoils and rises up the spine through the chakras, eventually shooting out through the crown chakra. According to Eastern mystical wisdom, the snake communes with the divine or stellar realms, offering the seeker a new level of vision, then returns through the crown, goes down the spine through the chakras, and repositions itself at the base of the spine. The rise of kundalini is said to reinvigorate the body with great electrical power since it is the life force—eros—itself. Figure 1.1 is a drawing of a meditator raising kundalini, and as you can see, I envision Uranus—the ♅ symbol—as the kundalini energy in the spine, which culminates in the crown, or top chakra.

It has been traditionally assumed in Eastern practice that kundalini has to be forced to rise by means of meditation practices for any spiritual illumination to occur. Thousands of years of exploration of such meditation techniques have demonstrated that the natural flow of kundalini energy in the body can indeed be tampered with—such techniques can *force* the coiled serpent in the spine to rise. However, in my opinion, there have been many abuses of this practice, especially by Westerners who have adopted Eastern meditation techniques during the last thirty years.

If kundalini is forced to rise before it is time for the normal integration of this power into the physical body, damage to the nervous system can occur, and new healing techniques have been developing to assist with imbalances created by forced kundalini rising. *Spiritual Emergency* by Stanislav Grof, M.D., and Christina Grof is a superb work on spiritual crisis. With properly supervised meditation practice, many imbalances and nervous disorders can be healed and rebalanced; however, by allowing kundalini to rise naturally according to its own cycles, severe imbalances are much less likely in the first place. The Grofs' significant contribution has been to point out that the crisis itself is an opportunity for healing.

If properly understood and treated as difficult stages in a natural developmental process, spiritual emergencies can result in spontaneous healing of various emotional and psychosomatic disorders, favorable personality changes, solutions to important problems in life, and evolution toward what some would call "higher consciousness."[1]

As a result of my own research, I believe that the maximum rise of kundalini occurs at Uranus Opposition, the transit point when the powers of Uranus are the most intense for each one of us. If my theory is correct, then the vast research on spiritual emergency and kundalini crisis can be utilized to counsel and heal individuals in the midst of difficulty during this time. Since Uranus rules the kundalini rise, the

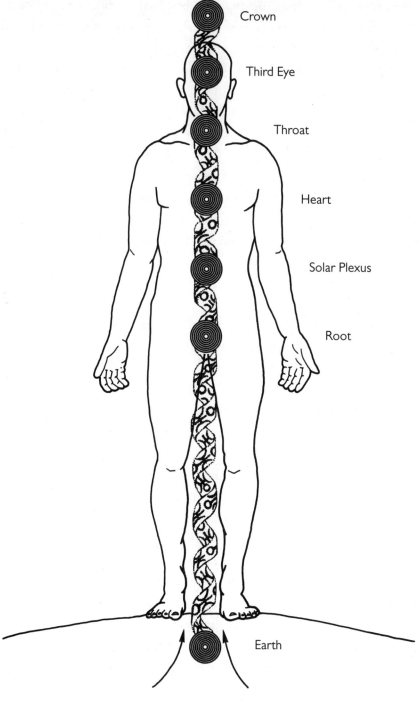

Figure 1.1. Person raising kundalini

actual flow of kundalini energy in the body can be timed according to the natal chart and transits. It is this astrologically prompted surge of energy that triggers the onset of midlife crisis.

What do I mean by Uranus Opposition? When each of us is born, Uranus is in a certain position in the sky, which is indicated by the birth chart when it is cast. But it does not stay there, as the planets continue in orbit around our Sun. It takes Uranus eighty-four years to make one orbit around the Sun. Due to its slightly elliptical orbit, it opposes its natal position at about ages 38 to 44, approximately halfway through its orbit. The energy of Uranus maximizes at the opposition in a way very much like the effects of the full Moon—when the Moon is opposite the Sun. This heightened electrical energy sparks an oscillating magnetic field best imaged as liquid light, since the waves in electromagnetic fields travel at the speed of light. Because Uranus rules electricity, at opposition time the most intense kundalini rise is experienced.

From what I have observed, kundalini rises naturally in all humans during Uranus Opposition. I maintain that it happens to everybody, even though many people believe that it lies dormant through life unless one forces it to rise. After watching hundreds of clients during exact transits (planetary passages over key points in the natal chart) of Uranus opposite their natal Uranus, I have not found a single one who didn't experience energetic shifts. Also, I've noticed that many clients have experienced nonforced kundalini rising at various ages. This is caused by an unusual sensitivity to Uranus, triggered by aspects between Uranus and other planets in their birth or natal charts and then by transits of the planets to those electrically sensitive points. These experiences are extremely traumatic, especially in young children; however, such individuals often turn out to be unusually spiritually and intellectually evolved.

For some people, kundalini rising is very subtle and would not fit the classic description: white-light explosions; possible temporary paralysis; visions; intense heat in the spine; "shakti," or intense shaking; hot sweats at night; or complete blackouts. But most of these classic descriptions of kundalini rising are based on reports by meditators who have forced the energy to rise or on ecstatic responses to great spiritual teachers who are able to cause kundalini to rise in the body just by touching or staring into the eyes of a seeker.

Many of my clients have exhibited the full range of symptoms just described, but many others have totally transmuted their physical-body density very gently. Either way, the purification process is very thorough when it occurs at midlife crisis and is not blocked. I have noticed that individuals who forced kundalini rising before this time still seem to have more transformation and purification to complete because the physical body was not mature enough to carry and balance all the electromagnetic force. By understanding Uranus Opposition and following certain dietary, therapeutic, and meditation advice, kundalini rising can actually be pleasant.

Not only does Uranus affect the kundalini rise, I strongly suspect the kundalini rise really works only at the right time—Uranus Opposition at midlife, when the individual's personal and spiritual life is likely to be mature and prepared for this infusion of spirit. I am convinced that forcing this energy in a body and psyche that is not prepared is the cause of totally unnecessary pain, near insanity, and possible permanent damage to the body. In seeming agreement with my research on midlife crisis, the ancient wisdom of India suggests that a person should raise a family and do business until age 40, and then become a meditator after that time.

When the kundalini rises at the right time—as Uranus comes to opposition—the maximum electrical forces are released in the body. It is similar to the fullness of energy we all feel when the Moon opposes the Sun at the time of the full Moon. Kundalini is electromagnetic, and that is why Uranus is the key to the timing of the rise. Since the whole body is bathed in healing electromagnetic fields at midlife—when the rise occurs in the spine—there is sufficient force to activate the chakras. As the energy rises, each one of the chakras is cleansed.

Looking at the process through the chakra evolution is very useful. For example, those who have sexual confusions will be purifying the solar plexus chakra and the root chakra, or genital area, and more information is available if they observe physical symptoms or sensations in those areas of the body. Most people seem to be helped by learning that different parts of their bodies relate to their experiences. As already mentioned, many men must open or purify their hearts at midlife crisis. They have been blocked from their natural feelings, and now they must allow love to bathe their hearts with healing forces, creating new healing powers of love and compassion. If the throat is blocked—as it is in many women—it is time to energize the throat and take power, to speak the truth so the person can give his or her gift to the planet. If the third eye, the subtle-sight center, has not opened, it will open, and the person will begin to develop extrasensory perception. Then the crown opens. The crown is the opening to the Divine, to God/Goddess, and a person does not know the Divine until the crown opens.

We can be deranged by triggering this process before the right time. First of all, there are many ethical dilemmas created for people when kundalini rises. The energy is erotic, it is power, it is the very core of the life force. It is risky to trigger such power in young people. They have not yet had the life experience to handle it well, and their physical bodies are not yet mature enough for the infusion of subtle energy. Secondly, in spite of the refusal by hard science to seriously investigate kundalini energy and subtle-energetic systems in the body, the results of kundalini rising in the immature body are really traumatic, as demonstrated by the work of Lee Sannella, M.D., on some of these physical-body symptoms.

As for kundalini rise at midlife, the exact opposite paradigm applies. *It is just as dangerous to block kundalini rise at midlife as it is to trigger it sooner in an immature body.* At midlife, the snake will rise naturally in the spine, and blocking it with fear and anxiety is like trying to contain lightning. In an aborted midlife crisis, an individual may ruin his or her family, have a heart attack, become substance addicted, or feel like he or she is going crazy.

The mechanics of the birth process are a great way to see the difference between a natural and a forced kundalini rise. When a woman goes into labor naturally, the cervix and lower pelvic muscles relax and release their normally tight grip. When the hormone in the baby's pituitary gland releases the hormone that triggers labor, the body is ready to pass the baby through. Kundalini rising is the rising of your inner spirit—a coiled snake seeking light—and it feels like a birth of an inner or divine child. It creates a second lease on life that offers you a whole new opportunity to be an open, holistic being. It is as if your reptilian self rises and transforms into a phoenix rising from the ashes of your old self. But when you force the snake to rise too soon, it is the same as when labor is triggered early by inducement—the lower body is locked up tight and is not prepared to release the child. Then, as the passage of the baby occurs, the muscles cramp up and fight the emergence of the child. It is painful, hard on the body, and the natural ecstasy of birth is not given by the child to the mother.

Midlife crisis—the triggering of kundalini rising by the transits of Uranus—results in the erotic emergence of the divine self in preparation for the second half of life, when we become holistic beings. We give birth to ourselves for a new life. We are moving into a phase of our evolution in which we will all consciously choose to create a brilliant, healthy, and ecstatic second half of life. At any moment in our lives, we are either activating a tendency toward more life or more death. The necrophilic structures of our world are largely the creation of death-oriented old men. We now are discovering how to cure addictions, which are a sign of a death-oriented human, and the time has come to consciously activate the maximal power of life—the healing force of a heightened electromagnetic field in our bodies.

BACK TO BOB

Let us return to Bob, described at the beginning of this book as the man who loved bikinis. Bob did not want to take the option of having an affair and possibly losing his wife and children. Fortunately, he received excellent counseling as he came into midlife crisis. For one thing, he was asked to notice if he was experiencing any "mystical" experiences, such as vivid dreams, psychic attunements, or newly found interest in spiritual concerns. He realized that he was beginning to experience an interest in psychic events and more subtle realities, and by diverting his attention to these new insights, he avoided "chasing bikinis" and began to discover a new consciousness within himself. His range of new interests greatly widened his ability to see what Woman/Earth/Goddess actually is, a sign that he was integrating his own inner female. He discovered that his wife was *all women*. He found in her his source for his own maleness. She became his communion with the essential feminine, and he became whole.

Bob became more and more fascinated by experiences in other dimensions. First he took a course in DMA, a self-help program created by Robert Fritz, and discovered that he could be in charge of his life, that he could create his own reality. He learned to consciously create what he really wanted, and then his sense of individual possibility began to widen. After some guided-imagery work during sessions of Reiki, a healing technique that integrates thoughts and feelings with energy in the body, he found himself spontaneously remembering events from other lives. Next, he did some past-life sessions, which helped him see that he was playing out certain themes in this life and in past lives. He discovered that he had been a warrior and major abuser of women in past lives, although outwardly he showed no such tendencies in this life. Bob was a "good guy," but now it was time to explore all the fascinating inner themes to enrich his life.

He did an astrological reading with me at a very intense phase of his transit, and he got angina during the reading. I advised a complete physical to make sure there was no heart disease, which, it turned out, there was not. The reading also triggered a conflict between who he is *now* in relation to who he was *before*. Of course, we have all been other things before, but the triggering of this conflict at this time was what he needed to open his heart chakra. Being a good guy was now less important than his opportunity to deeply explore the fascinating inner depths of being. He needed to discover mad passion, so intense was his power and inner being. He saw that it was his heart chakra causing angina.

I have observed that angina triggered by the heart chakra can cause a heart attack if the person panics, and my observations are given theoretical support by Dr. Lee Sannella's findings[2] and in the latest research of Dr. Deepak Chopra in *Quantum Healing: Exploring the Frontiers of Mind/Body Medicine.* Bob realized the pain in his heart was a heart opening, and he could see by means of astrology that it was exactly related to the timing of his transits. He saw that what he thought about the angina influenced whether it needed to manifest as physical heart disease or not! I advised him to get a puppy, which is a fantastic heart opener for those going through midlife crisis. The puppy cured what was going on with him; she lay right on his heart while he napped after work or watched television.

As his heart opened, Bob began to experience a lowered sexual potency; energy was moving up his spine, and the reorganization lowered his sex drive. He didn't like that, but because he understood it, he kept on working at integrating his intense inner being. Next, his throat chakra started to open, and he began to look at power issues. He had tended to lose a lot of energy by not being sure if he had exactly the work he wanted. He began to realize that where he was, was exactly where he needed to be. He took his power and began to expand with it. His third eye opened easily because he had done so much metaphysical work.

Then, as I had promised him, Bob's sexual potency returned as a result of all his transformation and purification work, but now his sexuality was all-body instead of just genital. He was amazed to discover what it was like to have sex with his whole being. As he came to orgasm, his heart was hot and pounded with healthy power, and he was flooded with great feeling for his wife, children, his close friends and relatives, and for all the people, creatures, and life systems on the planet. He found that making love actually heightened his compassion and increased the elemental and personal fields around himself—that is, he became symbiotic with things and people around himself, and others became energized by him. His crown chakra opened, and he reported being mystified by all the light and energy in his body—the liquid light of sex. Not only had sex become a cosmic experience, which would obviously intensify for the rest of his life, but life itself had become erotic. He found happiness in each day as a result of the elemental fusion with eros, which is the only antidote to aging.

TWO

The Fundamentals of Astrology

IMAGINE KNOWING IN ADVANCE the timing and form that a major life crisis might take. That knowledge could help diffuse the "crisis" nature of the circumstances and create the possibility of understanding the experience *while it was happening.* And what if that "crisis" was the major crossroad of midlife passage? Identification of the true source of this crisis—transformational powers rising spontaneously from within—helps us to focus on demanding inner needs instead of concluding that outside events are the cause of the difficulty. And knowing the exact timing of the intensity levels of the crisis creates very accurate observation of its processes plus the awareness that it will eventually end.

Uranus Opposition pushes the flow of kundalini energy to its peak during midlife passage, and the timing of this maximum-pressure cycle can be determined in advance. The key is astrology, the study of individual life in relation to planetary patterns. This chapter presents some fundamental ideas of astrology that, though basic to any useful employment of astrology, have been distorted and misunderstood as a result of Western culture's attachment to a Newtonian concept of the universe. Curiously, now that we as a culture are more aware of the limitations of Newton's model, scientific explanations and acceptance of astrology are beginning to emerge.

During the last four hundred years of Western civilization, roughly equal to the rise of science as the model for how to think, all fields of scientific and metaphysical thought, including astrology, have been very influenced by the Newtonian mind-set, named after Sir Isaac Newton. Newton's work on physics was the basic scientific model during this period. Grossly simplified, the Newtonian universe is a gigantic clock that has specific and identifiable parts that do precise and predictable things according to patterns that can be calculated.

The Newtonian climate created a very predictive and deterministic form of astrology until the twentieth century, asking astrologers to forecast specific events that were to come to pass because of the placement of the planets, a task for which astrology is only moderately equipped. Since the worldview of astrologers is always influenced and shaped by cultural paradigms, many astrologers have fallen into predicting events based on Newton's clocklike concept of the universe and his mechanistic view of the lives of individuals. Furthermore, individuals seeking the advice of astrologers have often conceived of themselves as cogs in a turning wheel, and their personal needs and questions have reflected their own concepts of self.

In recent times, the simple Newtonian mechanistic cause/effect theory has been increasingly subject to challenge. First, science continually realizes that it does not have all of the information or perception necessary to determine the scientific principles that rule cause-and-effect relationships. There is a growing awareness of subtlety, of dimensionality, of the possibility of larger and more complex systems operating.

Secondly, and more importantly, other theories that are generally acknowledged as valid—Einstein's theory of relativity, for example—don't fit simply within Newton's model. Regarding the field of astrology, Percy Seymour of Great Britain, an astronomer whose text *Cosmic Magnetism* was well received in 1986, has put forth *a new theory that grounds astrology in science!* A fellow of the Royal Astronomical Society, a principal lecturer of the Plymouth Polytechnic Institute, and the director of the William Day Planetarium in southern England, Dr. Seymour stunned both astrologers and astronomers with the recent publication of his new book, *Astrology: The Evidence of Science,* which bases astrology on magnetism, a universal force as significant as gravity. Seymour's theory holds that astrology is not mystical or magical, but "magnetic." Dava Sobel, who wrote about Percy Seymour in the December 1990 edition of *Omni* magazine, commented:

> Astrology can be explained, he [Seymour] says, by the tumultuous magnetic activity of the Sun, churned to a lather by the motions of the planets, carried to Earth on the solar wind, and perceived by us via the Earth's magnetic field while we grow inside our mother's wombs.[1]

In fact, Seymour contends that the horoscope can actually identify some of the genetic characteristics of the individual.

According to Seymour, the moment of birth is synchronized by a set of magnetic fluctuations.[2] The fetus is influenced by the geomagnetic field but is sheltered from external sensory stimuli. Activation of the fetus's sensory apparatus at birth causes a fusion of the geomagnetic coding and the sensory apparatus, and that is why the birth chart is so critical. As the fetus begins to respond to its environment during the first three months of life—the time of the first "solar square"—the magnetic field imprint is exceedingly intense. Seymour notes that one of his students demonstrated that *changes in the magnetic field of the Sun correspond to certain aspects or angles between the planets that astrologers deem significant.*[3] To be specific, these aspects include *oppositions* (180-degree angles between planets as viewed from Earth), *squares* (90-degree angles), and *conjunctions* (0-degree or close angles), all of which create momentous shifts in people's lives.

Western astrology starts with the birth chart or natal chart, which maps the basic energy field of an individual. That energy field encompasses environmental influences, genetic tendencies, and past-life history. The natal chart is the description of a seed or a new bud, reborn after a journey into other dimensions. After analysis of the birth chart, the advanced astrologer observes the inner unfoldment of the client's basic energy field through time by studying progressions and the outer unfoldment by means of *planetary transits.*

The use of progressions is a complex diagnostic technique similar to observing plant growth by means of time-lapse photography. The original bud—the birth chart—is time-lapsed through a lifetime by the astrologer, and the mysterious unfoldment of the birth energy field can be observed through time. We can image the progressions as a rose or lotus, which is a compact bud at birth that gradually unfolds and opens into its encoded exquisite flowering.

This subtle inner opening of the individual to the cosmos, as seen by the study of natal progressions, has always been one of the most accurate and mysterious astrological tools, and Dr. Seymour's magnetic theory offers the first scientific idea on why it works. During the first ninety days of life, there is much shifting in the solar magnetic field: there are three lunar cycles; Mercury, Venus, Earth, and Mars move great distances; and the slower-moving planets move slightly. This shifting sky makes a pattern imprint on the individual that continues to mature through time. These concepts are based on the belief that a created form contains seed patterns that will unfold according to patterns, just as an acorn will eventually become a gigantic tree if it is planted, is watered, and receives sunlight.

Transits—when planets return to form significant angles in relation to the birth chart—are the key to prediction of human response patterns to outside events. Beginning with the moment of birth, transits of the planets continuously "set off" life events when they return to conjunctions, squares, oppositions, and less critical angles to birthchart positions. I like to image them as beacons of light that shine into key parts of the birth chart, activating events for predictable periods of time. Like the forces triggering the growth of an oak tree, these transits are seasonal and are large patterns related to the energy of the Sun that creates weather patterns and electromagnetic fields.

The key transition growth points occur at the return of Saturn to its original position in the birth chart at age 30 (conjunction); at the opposition of Uranus to its position in the natal chart at ages 38 to 44; and at the return of Chiron to its natal position (conjunction) at age 50. If one lives to age 84, Uranus returns to its natal position, and this conjunction is the completion of the evolution of consciousness, just as

Saturn Return is the completion of structural evolution. Notice how these aspects creating the key life passages are also the aspects that have the greatest impact on the solar magnetic field.

What about astrology's potential to accurately predict things in our lives? Before we get deeply into the power of astrological influences, let us explore just exactly what astrology *can* reveal. Astrology can offer a very specific energy analysis of trends, the quality of possible outcomes, and the nature of events likely to occur based on transit patterns. An astrologer can be strikingly accurate with a specific prediction by using some general information about energetics, and then can take a potshot at the nature of an event to come and even guess its outcome. For example, if an individual's chart shows that he or she will be experiencing financial loss, a comment about the loss of someone's house or business might turn out to be true. But the overall influence and tendency—the nature of the energy field—is what is really important.

ASTROLOGY AS ENERGY POTENTIAL

When Ellen came to me, she was 38 years old, divorced, and the mother of two small children. All she wanted was a husband. I saw a Venus transit to the 7th house of her natal chart coming up in eighteen months, indicating that "the love of her life" would manifest. Normally, I would have explained to her that she was going to have some significant growth of her receptive potential, which would possibly attract another being who could learn with her while she deepened. But, because she was a single mother and I felt sorry for her, I allowed her to hear that the love of her life was going to appear. I didn't say it would be a man, but I knew she heard it that way.

Eighteen months passed. After having an affair with a person who seemed to be useless as a potential mate, Ellen gave birth, lonely and unmarried, to a baby girl. And it was this little girl—not the man who impregnated Ellen—who became the love of her life! This little girl, who was born prematurely and weighed less than five pounds, opened her mother's heart.

With this example, we can see what astrology is and is not. Not a parlor game for predicting mechanics and events, astrology is a complex, synchronistic science, a science of coalescing energetic fields. Astrology can predict the *quality* of energies presented by general future patterns that appear likely to occur, and by observing a person's reaction to specific planets over time, a good astrologer can tell what the person is, and will be, struggling with.

Astrology predicts upcoming energetic forms, and in order to read natal charts on that basis, the astrologer must develop very good descriptive powers. But to narrow those energetic forms to anything less than the energy form itself—to focus on the form that energy might take, for example—drastically reduces potential growth by limiting possibility. By helping their clients to see the "energy" of what is coming, astrologers offer them the opportunity to (1) prepare themselves, (2) have a very broad view of what is going on as it starts to happen, (3) be able to realize the patterns and synchronicities that make life more subtle, and (4) avoid deep trouble during a tough transit.

If astrologers fix the upcoming phase into specifics, clients are robbed of the very gift that astrology actually can offer them: the information needed to live life consciously. More insidiously, prediction of the form a particular energy might take involves judgments by an astrologer about a client's future possibilities. Such judgments can be dangerous. On the positive side, a reading of a chart for energetics, instead of specifics, may help us get beyond fear. Bob, "the man who loved bikinis," learned how to live life more consciously when his view of what was possible for him got wider and wider, and he learned how to go beyond fear.

Transit phases last from days to years, depending upon the length of a planet's orbit. For example, Venus transits might last only a few days, but Pluto* and Neptune transits last for a few years. The transit has a beginning, middle, and end. During this time, certain issues are likely to arise that will correspond to particular phases of the transit. There

---

*Although astronomers have recently downgraded Pluto's planetary status, in the field of astrology Pluto's history and influence as a planet remain unchanged.

is usually a beginning point, when we realize that a change needs to happen and what that change might be; a middle point, when we do the integration work required for the shift to occur; and an end phase, when we absorb the deeper spiritual meaning of the change. If we can "do" the transit phase—absorb the full meaning and personally integrate the lesson—we are on our way to becoming much more conscious.

Most importantly, the astrologer can advise when it will all end! Fear starts to take us over when we feel lost in the deep forest of the night—the subconscious mind. We panic when we feel like we are falling into an endless pit dug by chaotic events around us. Knowing that there is an end to the crisis can help us not to become unbalanced or even suicidal.

The astrologer can also chart exactly when the energy will be the most intense so that an event that might seem to be irrational actually has an identifiable basis. This also makes it less likely for a person to attribute an inner change only to outside forces, thereby losing the chance to learn the lesson of the transit. For example, someone who is mugged and whose astrologer had warned of the presence of a Mars/Pluto aspect, which indicates a lesson about violence and the underworld, might choose to learn about what violence brings up for him or her rather than move to another community based on a decision that crime had become endemic in the first location.

THE INNER AND OUTER UNIVERSES OF EXPERIENCE

Astrology's basic tool, the natal chart, is divided into twelve sections, called the "houses of the zodiac." In order to begin to absorb the basics of astrology, we need to see how this field operates and how the houses relate one to another. The field is the background map for all the action of the planets, the Sun, and the Moon.

Looking at the "wheel," the zodiac with the twelve houses, let us begin with a view of the lower houses—1st through 6th—as the fields of inner perception, and the upper houses—7th through 12th—as

Figure 2.1. The twelve houses of the zodiac

the fields of outer action, or actual events in life. For example, the 1st
house rules discovery of the self, and the 7th house rules how the self
relates to other people.

Each of the upper six houses of the zodiac—7th through 12th—
are in "polarity relationship" to the lower six houses—1st through 6th.
Polarities are the opposite ends of an issue. During midlife crisis, ideally
the issues represented by the upper astrological houses, as seen by the
status of key outer events such as marriage and career, are deepened by
inner exploration in the lower houses. This polarity growth—greater
ability to expand the inner and outer selves—is a prerequisite for successful resolution of midlife crisis.

Unity lies in the direct midpoint between the polarities. In the
astrological chart, unity is in the center, where the Earth lies: we are
here on Earth to resolve polarities! The birth chart sets up this expe-
riential dilemma exquisitely. The importance of this concept cannot
be overemphasized, because most of our experience is very polarized—
dualistic—and yet peace of mind can be found only in unified resolution. The source of the dualistic confusion that plagues our lives is

perceptual confusion between inner needs and the demands of outer events. To compound the imbalance, in contemporary Western culture the outer reality is considered to be more "real" than the inner world, and the majority of the growth at midlife crisis is actually the acquisition of respect for the importance of the inner world.

As mentioned earlier, the lower six houses rule inner growth, while the upper six houses rule the ways in which we experience the outer world in relation to our inner perceptions. Astrology's version of the New Age teaching that "we create our own reality" manifests as follows: the inner reality seen in the lower six houses is a landscape of energy that will manifest itself as outside events according to the qualities in the opposite and upper houses. Or, to reverse the causal flow, the contents of the upper six houses will trigger "acting out" of events, which can push the individual to identify otherwise invisible inner energies in the lower houses.

Many people cannot see what is within themselves without acting out dramas that teach them about their inner contents. By studying polarized aspects in the natal chart, the astrologer can actually see how a client could resolve the inner and outer worlds and attain unity; the chart is a readable map of inner energy and outside events. Midlife passage always ends up being the resolution or avoidance of the *key unresolved polarity,* which can provide the greatest possible self-knowledge. So let's walk through the houses of the zodiac in order to clearly understand each side of the six polarities.

THE 1ST THROUGH 3RD HOUSES OF THE ZODIAC

The 1st house is identity: "Who am I?" The key word is *me.* At some level, we ask ourselves this question every day, and the answer can come only from life experience. Knowing who we are and why we came is life's big project.

In very early childhood, we sense who we are; ideally, parents take the time to help nurture that intuitive identity, and life feels secure. If awakening identity is not acknowledged because of a dysfunctional

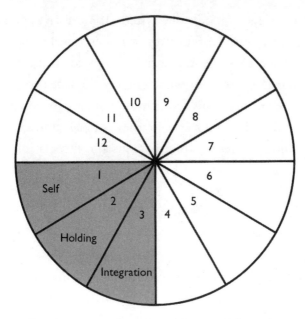

Figure 2.2. 1st through 3rd houses of the zodiac

family or loss of one or both parents, then we tend to search for identity from outside reality to an excessive degree. It may take us years to learn to listen to that subtle knowing that comes from within. As we begin to have experiences with others, this identity is continually challenged and we constantly evaluate ourselves. With each challenge in life, our identity enlarges and shifts, and new parts of ourselves come to the surface. The need to truly know the self builds to its maximum crisis at midlife, when self-knowledge must be attained at all costs.

Once our identity is established, we begin to "ground" ourselves, which is the agenda of the 2nd house. What do I need in order to live? The key words for this house are *I need,* and a mature development of this house indicates a healthy sense of materialism, a true enjoyment of all the things we need for everyday life, such as housing, money, clothing, and health care. If our 1st house of basic identity is well developed, then the values about what we need tend to be sound automatically. If we know who we are, it is easy to figure out what we need.

Along with ruling the gathering of our needs, the 2nd house also rules taking care of things. The ability to care for things is based on a sound identity and a good value system. If a person is careless about material reality, a weak self-identity or undeveloped values are at the core. The 2nd house represents a horizontal development; it is a "spreading out" of ourselves, and our whole life unfoldment depends upon an adequate development of this foundation. We have to gather effectively what we need in order to take the journey through time.

The 3rd house rules communications and integration of the self, and its question is "How do I fit into my reality?" How do I express myself in the world I inhabit in order to get what I need and carry on with a healthy sense of who I am? The key words are *fitting in,* and everybody spends an amazing amount of time trying to do just this.

The 3rd house is a tricky house. Many of us think we have our links to outside reality all figured out, and then we end up in a workshop or party where we feel like we must be from Mars, judging by how other people seem to be reacting to us. The stronger the early identity and sense of values the better, because a really supportive childhood tends to widen the field into which we can "fit." The more we explore different realities as quickly as possible, the more we can easily fit into whatever circumstance in which we may find ourselves.

The 3rd house rules education, which broadens our field of activity. It also rules all the skills of getting along in foreign locations—language skills and the ability to be comfortable with new people. The foundation of our ability to broaden is our basic sense of self, and the opportunity is dependent upon getting what we need, since the chance to obtain the integration skills needed to fit into as many realities as possible is dependent upon material support. Most of all, we need a strong ego or developed sense of self intact within its boundaries in order to explore new realities.

As we move out of the first three houses and go into the second three, notice that we will lack the courage to explore the next three houses unless we have an *ego,* we are *grounded,* and we are *functionally integrated.*

THE 4TH THROUGH 6TH HOUSES
OF THE ZODIAC

Next let us examine the qualities of the 4th through 6th houses. The 4th house is the realm of the unconscious. It is the "nest" from which we emerge, and the key word is *feeling*. The 4th house rules our sense of home throughout life, as well as our ability to feel safe on planet Earth. This is the area of astrological analysis that attempts to determine the solidity of the emotional structure of a person. If 4th house issues—our deepest attachments to loved ones—get disturbed by early childhood trauma, such pain and separations can be healed later in life through therapy and/or life with new people who love us.

The model child we observed in the first three houses would be comfortable with normal human stresses and normal occasional anger and/or boundary difficulties, and he or she would gradually develop emotional complexity and sophistication during grade school. As adults, if we are able to look deeply inside and integrate the unconscious, we will possess a basic trust in our lives. We will not be afraid of the hidden or unexpected events of life.

Once we have been able to explore and integrate the core of our being, we move to the 5th house of creativity and erotic sexuality. The key word is the *inner child;* this is the pool of our desires that come from childhood pleasures and/or deprivations, and as adults we can't get the child to express itself comfortably without having faced the deep-seated desires of the 4th house. Some of the most creative adults I have seen are those who were allowed to really develop their inner child when they were small. That is, the least-controlled childhood environments are the best, provided the environment is structured and not chaotic. The inner child can know how to satisfy its sexual and creative drives in an adult environment, and such adults are less prone to addiction and manipulation of others.

Many artists are masters of the 5th house. They have learned to not resist sinking into the dark, the deepest part of self. When the journey

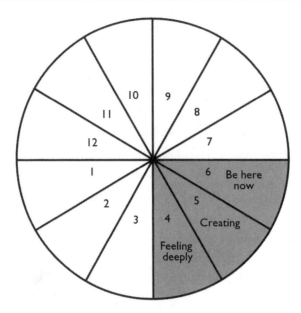

Figure 2.3. 4th through 6th houses of the zodiac

through this shadow is complete, there is emptiness in which to form new creation. Like the 2nd house, the 5th house expands us horizontally, and this development of creativity opens us to new communication and integration skills.

We move into the 6th house once we have really found the child, our inner delight. The 6th house is healing power. Its key words are *"Be here now!"* It represents our ability to be in the present moment instead of having our consciousness in the past or future or in another location. Being able to heal ourselves and others is based upon the ability to be in the present moment.

From a practical standpoint, we must find our correct work in order to be a healing instead of a destructive force. Therefore, the 6th house rules the search for meaningful work, and a hierarchy of power and money makes it hard for people to discover their inherent dignity through expressing themselves in work. We all need to *succeed* in the process of work in order to find ourselves. The 6th house is the starting line for just about everybody; we must find meaningful work in this world so that we can begin to evolve. Also, most people first discover how to be in the moment during engrossing work projects that enable them to filter out all their other conflicts as well as the undeveloped aspects of self.

It is instructive to move through the first six houses in reverse in order to see how the 6th house is the awakening point for most people. This is because Western cultures are extremely dysfunctional at this time, and few people reflect the idealized development of self presented by the first six houses of the zodiac. Nondysfunctional people seem to be an endangered species! So let us move in reverse for a moment in order to better comprehend the qualities of the lower houses before we explore the upper six houses.

We will use John as our example. Although he was 27 years old, he had never found work that interested him. He had no personal partner and felt like he was "nobody," with nothing to offer and no means of self-expression. His crippling self-judgment was based on series of failures caused partly by his own lack of commitment to any job. He had done some carpentry, some cooking, and various other odd jobs. He decided to go back to school for lack of any better plan, and in order to pay his way, he opted to build housing units for a campus environmental group. The group was led by a young professor/architect, assisted by a socially conscious contractor in town.

Within a few months, John became highly valued for his strength, fine carpentry, and quiet good humor. He did an excellent job for the first time in his life because he was instructed to do things right instead of hurrying or cutting corners. He had just integrated the 6th house and moved strongly into the moment. One day while standing on the roof of a new unit, he took a deep breath and fully absorbed the view of a Japanese garden forming below under the careful direction of a young female student. His body suddenly surged with energy, his heart swelled, and he catapulted into intensely feeling the present moment. He came alive.

In the next few weeks, John began working on designs of the units with the architect and the student gardener. He and the student began a romance, kindled by their intense excitement about the way the gardens and units related. He found his inner child, the exquisite pleasure of the 5th house and creativity.

John noticed that he wanted to see his father and mother again after many years of minimal contact, and when he did, he found he actually could talk to them. They admitted that they had rarely been truly present for him when he was a child due to the stress of the normal chores of child-rearing and earning a living. Returning to his new life of Italian dinners and warm embraces in the night with his girlfriend, he felt the numbing neglect of his childhood lift. He began to realize that his parents had done the best they could, and what mattered was that he felt their intense love for him. John began to open the 4th house of the unconscious, his fear of the demanding inner world lessened, and he could identify and respond to emotional processes more easily as he let go of anger about his childhood.

One day John felt a tightness in his throat. The semester was coming to an end, and he was going back out in the real world. He knew all about the alienation out there. The tightness came from fear of losing the work that centered him, the woman with whom he found trust, and his new enjoyment of his parents. But he kept on moving forward. He put on his best clothes and knocked on the office door of the contractor who had assisted the housing project to ask for a recommendation. The contractor offered him a great job, based upon his excellent presentation of what he had to offer after graduation. John had overcome his communication paralysis; he had mastered the 3rd house of communication and integration.

Next, John quickly mastered the 2nd house of physical-plane needs when he built his own house, found that he loved his job, and married his girlfriend. Finally, some years later, he discovered identity, the 1st house, when he gazed into the eyes of his newborn infant and saw himself within those eyes.

THE 7TH THROUGH 9TH HOUSES
OF THE ZODIAC

The 7th house rules partnership, marriage, and the ability to learn from the other side. Not surprisingly, the key word is *relationship*. Recalling the

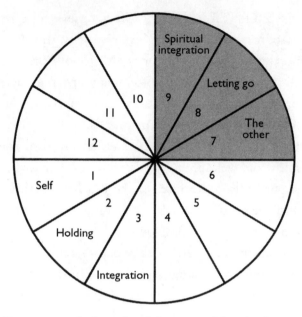

Figure 2.4. 7th through 9th houses and lower polarities

polarity nature of the upper and lower houses, the 7th house is in polarity relationship with the 1st house—self-identity. The 1st house asks, "Who am I?" and the 7th house asks, "How can I deal with the *other?*"

The key word for the polarity is *knowing.* When this polarity is unresolved, we feel like we cannot ourselves grow while being pulled away from our self by the other. And as we relate to the other, we lose the sense of who we are. The unified maturity comes when we have attained enough sense of self so as to relate to the other without losing our own identity, thus finding a mirror of ourselves that offers self-knowledge. Then, the more we develop our individual potential, the more we have to give to the other, and the more we give to the other, the more we find out about ourselves.

The 8th house rules emptying, letting go of everything that is not essential for evolution to our next level. Its key words are *letting go.* Therefore, the 8th house is deeply involved with death and how we feel about it. It is in polarity relationship with the 2nd house—grounding and material values. The 2nd house asks, "What do I need?" and the 8th house asks, "Wouldn't I be more clear if I had less?"

The key word for this polarity is *values,* or an ethical sense of how to use the resources of the planet. Needless to say, this polarity is very poorly comprehended on the planet at this time. When we are stuck in this duality, we may accumulate too many material possessions and have no room for spiritual contact, or we may empty too much, become ungrounded; we may even deny normal needs.

The 9th house represents *God/Goddess* issues, for it rules connection with spirit, and we cannot get to spirit until we have lightened our load by the purification processes of the 8th house. Also, we cannot feel spirit until we are comfortable with emptiness. The 9th house is in polarity relationship with the 3rd house—the house of communication/integration—and the key word of the polarity axis is *connecting.* This polarity offers profound wisdom for us at this time.

In Western civilization, we have been experimenting with Eastern wisdom teachings for many decades, and this yearning for spirit is classic 9th house development, but the 3rd house integration process goes awry when one culture attempts to adopt the spiritual practices of another. Eastern philosophy, as it has been transferred to the West for the last thirty years, has been dangerously unbalanced in the 3rd/9th house polarity, since the spirituality (9th house) of indigenous cultures of the East does not integrate easily (3rd house) into Western environments. The cultural integration of spiritual practices is more easily available to the seeker within his or her own heritage. For example, theologian Matthew Fox has shown in his book *Original Blessing* that spiritual practices from medieval mystical traditions are very deep for people in Western cultures, and I have found the Native American medicine teachings to be very profound for people in the Western Hemisphere.

When the 3rd and 9th houses are balanced, the spiritual seeker carefully integrates the self and communicates with spirit in a balanced way in the body. The balance of the 3rd/9th house polarity occurs when the seeker opens gradually and harmonically. It is critical to take time to integrate spiritual fire in the life while staying in healthy communication with others and living serenely. The seeker is thus in service to humanity while developing oneness with spirit.

Successful resolution of midlife crisis involves activating the vertical axis—Earth to sky—of awareness after the horizontal maturation into form during the first forty years of life. This activation is the work of the 3rd and 9th houses and the 4th and 10th houses, and the qualities of these houses tend to create great rushes of energy, energy that is actually kundalini rising. Notice how the growth in the 1st/7th house and 2nd/8th house polarities is very horizontal and how the growth in the 3rd/9th house and 4th/10th house polarities is very vertical.

THE 10TH THROUGH 12TH HOUSES OF THE ZODIAC

The 10th house rules power—taking on our own power and utilizing our power in the world. Its key words are *I am*. It is in polarity relationship with the 4th house, the subconscious self, and the key word of the polarity axis is *being:* we cannot take on our power without full exploration of subconscious reality. Until we have fully integrated the deepest core of self, we will either abuse others with what power and control we have, or we will remain powerless. The 4th and 10th houses of the zodiac, along with the 3rd and 9th, are where the greatest kundalini energy rise occurs. Therefore, great purification of emotional, spiritual, and power complexes is triggered, and this is where the greatest confusions lie. This clearance of confusion by kundalini purification fire is the *essence of midlife crisis.*

As we work with the intricacies of kundalini rising in this book, we must remember that our kundalini energy is our power, the basic life force, or eros. Triggered by Uranus, this liquid light floods our bodies with electromagnetic pulsation. As we cope with this increased energy at midlife, the psychological and power complexes of the 4th and 10th houses must be exposed and then transmuted by a desire for life rather than death. Otherwise, some individuals become monsters of power abuse driven by a hot, juicy, boiling subconscious volcano within. The 10th house power complexes cannot be resolved when there is avoidance of the dark side of the 4th house. A balanced 4th and 10th house

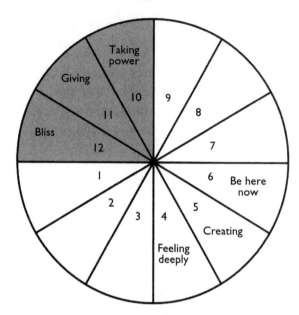

Figure 2.5. 10th through 12th houses and lower polarities

polarity creates a complete clearing of the subconscious, while use of power becomes a love for self and all beings—the open heart.

The 11th house rules the discovery of purpose on this planet in relation to all other beings, and its key word is *gift*. It is through our service that we give back to the planet all that we have created here. The 11th house is in polarity relationship with the 5th house—creativity and the child—and the key word for the polarity is *playing*.

Both houses teach the releasing of energies back into the cosmos with trust, and this process cannot occur without the mastery of these houses. Thus, if power is not mastered, purpose cannot be known, just as without the journey through the dark, new creation cannot emerge. The harmonious state of the 5th and 11th houses is the fountain of creativity that keeps on releasing new creations and delights. The polarity resolution of the 5th and 11th houses occurs automatically when individuals master the conflicts at midlife crisis. Thus, personal midlife crisis resolution will release our creativity back to the planet, and that is why midlife crisis is both a personal and planetary issue.

But why resolve our midlife crisis? The 12th house, with the key word of *bliss,* is the reason. The 12th house is *samadhi/ecstasy/bliss/ divine communion.* We cannot get to ecstasy without knowing our purpose and giving all our powers back, because this emptying creates space for spiritual infusion. The 12th house is in polarity relationship to the 6th house—getting into present time—and its key word is *fusing.* The most curious truth about the six polarities—which create the Star of David—is that you can't get to bliss, to the timeless, unless you enter fully into time! And the real irony is that you lose the bliss if you try to hold it or stop it in time. The way to move into the present moment is to give your gift—that is, give everything away—and then you will discover the key to *samadhi:* every time you totally offer your gift to the cosmos, you go into bliss. We accumulate cosmic poker chips just by giving! This is the same as the Native American teaching of the giveaway. It is our holding on, our need for control, that keeps us from exactly what we desire. Go ahead and take your power, give your gift, and then enjoy fusional ecstasy.

The potential maturity of complex polarities and a broader and more heightened and deep life sounds wonderful, but you are probably asking yourself, "How do *I* do it?" We do it step-by-step as we live through the key passages of life: Saturn Return, Uranus Opposition, and, lastly, Chiron Return. As we move through these passages, our ability to master the polarities gradually matures. We become more subtle, broader, and we learn to reach for the sky and dive into the Earth.

The first thing that all of us must master in order to begin this growth is *structural grounding.* Saturn is the planet that is the basis of all structure in life, the process of *formation.* Next, the job of Uranus is to *transform the structures* once they have served their purpose. Lastly, Chiron *transmutes the transformed form* into the diamond body, a physical body that has been purified by kundalini fire so that all the cells hold the maximum electromagnetic life force. Let us begin with the basic formation process activated by the transits of the planet Saturn up to age 30.

THREE

The Saturn Principle in the Cycles of Life

IMAGINE TRYING TO WALK UP a flight of stairs, but there are no stairs to climb. Or what about trying to paint a picture, but you have no brush in your hands, paints to use, or even a canvas in front of you. Would you set out on a long journey without proper provisions? Doesn't make sense, does it? Neither does approaching one's Uranus Opposition without doing the prep work Saturn provides. On a very real, material level, consciously working with Saturn during the first thirty years of life, or at least examining subsequently the issues that were presented at age 30, helps an individual make the most of Uranus's opportunities. And working with Saturn above all requires balance—a symmetry between the polarities set up by each of the six pairs of houses in the astrological chart. That symmetry then sets up the needed relationship between the structure of Saturn and the creativity of Uranus.

WHY SATURN?

In the Roman pantheon, Saturn was an ancient deity credited with the founding of Roman civilization, and his Greek counterpart, Cronus, was the founder of Greek civilization. Thus, Cronus/Saturn is the Western archetype of structure and form, of order and time, sourced from the emergence of civilization in Greece and the Roman Empire.

Saturn was the youngest of the seven Titans, the Earth-born sons of Uranus. Earth, the mother, persuaded the Titans, under Saturn's leadership, to attack and kill their father, Uranus, and Saturn/Cronus was awarded sovereignty of the Earth after releasing the Cyclopes from the underworld.[1] But Saturn himself ate his children because Mother Earth had prophesied that one of his own children would eventually destroy him.

In such legends, we find graphic and primal sources for the ancient roots of the father/son conflict—the primordial conflict between structure/Saturn and creativity/Uranus. Saturn guides each of us to set up the structures necessary to maximize the transformative opportunities that come when Uranus arrives at a location opposite its place in our birth chart, around ages 38 to 44. Earlier I used the archetype of thanatos/death with Saturn and eros/life with Uranus because the formation process itself will solidify any organism into death without the balancing effect of the quickening force of transformation. So the quickening force adds *life* to the solidity of Saturnian form.

The "theater" in which Saturn rules the movie of life is the houses of the zodiac, the map of psychological growth. You may even want to refer back to the journey through the houses or house diagrams as you contemplate the structural maturation process of Saturn. Saturn's transitions from house to house are major crossroads, times when we all are the most likely to get confused without guidance, and they are also the times when we can accelerate our evolution. At the crossroads, deaths can occur, marriages can be made or broken, creativity can be blocked or released, and major career choices can be made.

It's like driving a car and coming to a fork in the road: with a map, you can always take the direct path. The map that astrology provides offers maximum free will—exactly the opposite of popular opinion about how astrology works. Armed with the knowledge of your life cycles, you can begin to direct each day with keen insight. By knowing when to hunker down and discipline yourself because it is a contraction time, which is ideal for more exacting formation, you'll find that a tremendous amount of basic resistance to living just dissipates.

Later on, there will be an ideal expansion time, and all your structural maturation will be a great foundation for transformation. By observing the beginning, middle, and end phases of changes in your life, you can write, direct, and star in your own movie script. Application of the Saturn principle is a powerful tool for taking control of one's life.

SATURN'S ORBIT THROUGH THE ZODIAC

The orbit of the planet Saturn around the Sun is twenty-nine to thirty years. Therefore, every twenty-nine to thirty years, it returns to the same position in the solar system. When you were born, Saturn was in a certain position in the solar system, which is indicated in your birth chart. When a person is about 29, it *returns* to that exact position, forming what astrologers term a *conjunction* to its location at birth.

As set forth in Percy Seymour's theories on astrological magnetic influences, this return of Saturn to its original location sets off a powerful magnetized memory of the original birth vibration of Saturn. Thus, as Saturn culminates its journey through an individual's twelve houses, one whole phase of his or her psychological maturation is completed. This moment triggers a rebirth of the self based on thirty years of living, a self that already knows much about life.

It takes Saturn two to two and one-half years to move through each house of your natal chart, since the solar orbit of Saturn is twenty-nine to thirty years and there are twelve houses in the chart. At your birth, Saturn is located in a certain house of your chart, and each house represents a phase of life formation. Thus, your structural form—basic processes for actualizing yourself—begins in that house, and then it will traverse certain houses at certain ages depending upon where it first started out at birth.

Since each one of the twelve houses of the zodiac rules a certain area of life experience, and Saturn is the teacher of maturation in all phases of life, integration of the whole structure of personality occurs when the last lesson is presented. As Saturn moves through each one of the houses, it causes the process of that house to form, to develop.

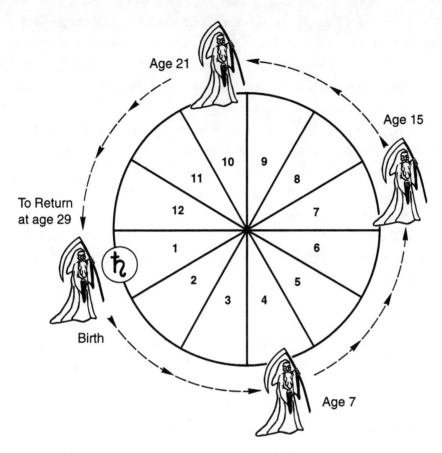

Figure 3.1. Saturn moving through the houses of the zodiac

For example, when Saturn is in the 10th house, you will find yourself experimenting with taking more personal power and taking big risks to garner new opportunities.

At ages 14 or 15, Saturn transits opposite its birth position and sets off your first *polarity paradox,* causing you to see issues as "both/ and" instead of "either/or." As we saw in the previous chapter, the issues of each house are deeply related to those of the house opposite it; they are simply on the other end of the continuum. During adolescence, we have the first double-sided, or polarity, perceptions. Because the polarity initially occurs in the house opposite Saturn's birth house, it causes us to magnify that polarity. For example, Christopher has Saturn in the

7th house. Until age 15, he was totally immersed in relating perfectly to everyone in his environment. However, when Saturn transited into his 1st house and reached opposition to his natal Saturn, he became self-absorbed, much to everyone's surprise. He became totally fascinated with his own inner psychological processes.

This first polarity paradox tends to be the most subtle and well-developed aspect of our personal lives, since it is in that paradoxical experience that we first realize how little we actually know. Christopher was amazed at how little he understood himself! When he attained his second Saturn Opposition at age 42, the next level of this polarity maturation, he realized that it is impossible to relate to others without knowing the self also. The maturation process after the second Saturn Opposition is very profound because we reexperience all of the opposite polarities, just as we did when Saturn transited opposite houses that it journeyed through from birth to age 14. For Christopher, this meant Saturn transited through all the lower houses, deepening his self-knowledge while his observation of the behavior of others became more and more keen. This type of chart is great for a creative writer, a manager of people, or a psychologist.

Obviously, then, adolescence is a key point in the Saturn cycle. Until Saturn has traversed six houses, children have experienced Saturn's structuring only on one side of the personality or polarities. At ages 14 to 15, Saturn will have transited through six houses of the person's birth chart, and as it moves into the 7th house, it activates the house opposite it, which is the birth house of Saturn.

While just one side of ourselves is being developed up to age 14, life is black and white, paradox is not seen, and all is delightfully simple. Then during adolescence, the first awareness of polarity's subtlety and complexity hits hard, often introducing an issue with which we become obsessed until it is resolved at Saturn Return. As we move on to the second, then third polarities, and so on, the tension and knowledge increase, like the tightening and tuning of piano strings. As Saturn Return hits, we reach the development of that last house—the natal house of our Saturn—and it is like a second birth or formation intensified by all the subtle growth first activated during adolescence when Saturn reached its opposition to its birth position.

For parents, this extended maturation may seem bad news, because it means our children may need our assistance much longer than we would like to believe. But the good news is that we cannot be sure a child is dysfunctional until after age 30. I have seen children who seemed to be lost suddenly get it all together when they turned 30, especially kids from extremely dysfunctional families. The first true sight of what a person will become occurs with the birth of the "solar self," or the manifestation of one's Sun-sign personality, at age 30.

Rosemary was a client who was obsessed with questions of who she was in relation to the influences of her parents. She wondered during her adolescence how much of what she did came from their influence on her and their wishes for her future, and how much of what she did, thought, or experienced was genuinely self-generated. These are 4th-house questions. Of course, Rosemary had Saturn in her 10th house—concerned with taking on one's own power and using it in the world—and so the questions Saturn raised during her adolescence would naturally be those of its opposite, the 4th house.

At Saturn Return, Rosemary had a crisis over taking on her personal power. This came after fourteen years of inner-directed exploration of the qualities of her own emotional being triggered by her first experience with polarity when Saturn transited her 4th house of deep feelings during adolescence. She had been in medical school studying to become a psychiatrist, figuring her work would be very analytical and feeling oriented, and suddenly she switched majors and became a surgeon, which she felt offered her immediate power in the medical world.

When Saturn returns at ages 29 to 30, it first reactivates the issue of that primal house—the location place at birth—and that is exactly where critical issues can be seen. But the house opposite to Saturn is the repository of information about a very subtle part of the personality, since in it lies the virginal perception of paradox and duality. It is the part that can become the most sophisticated area of a life, and the more a teenager is encouraged to develop it, the better.

For example, Rosemary became a great surgeon because she possessed unusual abilities to understand how her patients felt about their operations and the subsequent healing process. These abilities were the result of the fourteen years of psychological exploration triggered by her first Saturn Opposition. If this deep and paradoxical part of self is well developed when it is supposed to be—ages 14 to 16—then individuals can easily release themselves to their destinies at Saturn Return. If, for some reason, a person is repressed in adolescence by extremely controlling parents and/or schools, the individual may turn out to be one-sided and robotic, and will be unable to handle paradox, making him or her rigid and judgmental. The house that contains Saturn is the house we *must* master, but the one opposite makes us more complex and subtle; it is the pool of knowledge that fuels our greatest works of destiny.

Since Saturn goes around the Sun every twenty-nine to thirty years, there is a second Saturn Return at ages 58 to 60 and a third return at about 88 to 90. Obviously, our age when experiencing the various Saturn transits through each house tremendously affects the nature of the process itself, and that is what we can become much more conscious of during our second Saturn phase. At each Saturn Return, we experience the maximum pressure to conquer the weakness in ourselves that is blocking growth; we have the opportunity to pierce the resistance that is keeping us from breaking through into our greatest potential evolution.

One of my favorite Saturn stories is of Helen, who drank her way all the way through two Saturn Returns. Helen became a heavy drinker in her late twenties, and she continued to struggle with alcoholism throughout her thirties. Saturn was in her 9th house, meaning that the process she needed to master was integration of spirit, but she had a severe emotional communication block, caused by profound, unexpressed grief over the death of her mother at an early age. This block intensified her separation from spirit; communication, of course, is the subject of the house opposite the 9th—the 3rd house.

Helen managed to avoid integration of her emotional needs at her Saturn Return by drinking whenever she needed to go deeper into herself. She drank more and more to avoid facing the intense emotional pressure that was building inside, as it always does during one's thirties. The most intense phase of her alcoholism peaked during her Uranus Opposition, in her case at age 42. When the family realized she needed to be "fixed," she was "cured" by a hypnotist.

Helen could have progressed to a profound level of consciousness expansion had she undergone depth therapy to help her stop repressing her grief. But in the 1950s in America, you were "insane" if you needed therapy in the first place! If you went to a psychiatrist, you could end up getting electric shock treatments or a prefrontal lobotomy, so Helen sought no deeper therapy. Rather, she just experimented with hypnosis, since it was prescribed by a doctor, which simply programmed her subconscious to avoid drinking.

Helen stayed on the wagon until about age 56, when Saturn was approaching its second return. The pressure again mounted to look at her severe inner pain, and she took another drink, right at a point when she was experiencing intense emotional blockage with one of her children. The disease progressed more rapidly this time, and she attempted suicide.

As soon as the uncomfortable push of Saturn lifted off, she dried up and joined Alcoholics Anonymous (AA), which made it possible for her to stop drinking, just as hypnosis had done almost thirty years previously. However, her ability to communicate has remained almost totally blocked, because she missed a second chance to master the Saturn process. The block with her own child was a potential gateway to her own inner grief, just as the initial loss of her mother could have been a bridge to the spirit world had she been able to deal with it in a healthier way in a more enlightened culture, where therapy is considered to be essential for any emotionally blocked person.

WHAT WAS THAT?

Saturn Return can be smooth, profound, and radically transformative if people experiencing it understand the process as it is occurring. Instead, many of us go through a huge trauma involving outrageous acting out and then ask, "What was *that?*" The intense need to act out new behavioral patterns at Saturn Return can result in some wild scenarios that are as amazing to the actor/actress as they are to the observers. Needless to say, seeing a counselor is always helpful, and it is usually less damaging to our friends and relatives than acting out.

However, Saturn is also the principle of *necessity,* and often Saturn Return *must* result in a lot of acting out. For example, another client, Tony, had Saturn in his 12th house, indicating that he needed to master the process of "living without a why," of just existing in bliss and allowing himself to experience life without self-judgment. Certain aspects of his chart showed that he had come into this life with extensive homosexual past-life experience and that the purpose of this life was to allow himself joyful and very free sexual expression. He had been married to a woman in his twenties and then his Saturn Return initiated his coming out as a homosexual, which allowed him the chance to explore other sexual aspects of himself without judgment. More restrained behavior might have created fewer waves for Tony's parents, his ex-wife, and his friends, but Tony would have died inside. Most importantly, he would have missed a key learning experience.

In each lifetime, Saturn motivates us to learn the lessons we need in order to evolve. Whatever the purpose of our lives, Saturn creates the *process* we need in order to accomplish that purpose. This planet has been called the Grim Reaper, the "taskmaster," and he is the one who forces us to tackle our potential and make it real.

For those who resist growth—like Helen—Saturn can be a real pain. But if we avoid Saturn's push, we'll abort growth, because the only way to avoid the push is to cop out—to drink, do drugs, be a ski addict, chase miniskirts, be a compulsive shopper, or become an ungrounded New Age workshop-junkie. In fact, ages 28 to 31 is the best time to examine all our addictive tendencies and the lazy ways we avoid hard realities, and to make choices about how much of these patterns we'd like to transform.

Since Saturn is the taskmaster, the disciplinarian, for many the natural reflex is to resist. The old conflict over the demands of the father versus the child's desires tempts us all to resist the lessons of Saturn. Activating the principle of structure and form seems to automatically bring up the primordial conflict between control and creativity, but developing structure in life is essential for psychological maturation. Fortunately, at Saturn Return, necessity predominates for most people, and that is what forces us to blast through the resistance. If we consciously employ our best powers of discipline to master the part of ourselves that we have always resisted, we will have a tool for activating our real purpose in life. We will also make life easier for everyone around us, for resistance is what exhausts us all.

SATURN RETURN

Now it is time to consult the tables at the end of the book to see when your Saturn Return already occurred or when it will occur. As you will see, for most people Saturn "hits" occur over a period of time because it conjuncts its natal position three times during the time frame of its return. Some people experience only *one* conjunction, however, and their process happens once instead of in three stages as described here.

At Saturn Return, you are being pushed to actualize the process through which you can constructively approach life. The resistance within yourself that needs to be dealt with manifests at the first "hit," integrates during the second one, and is fully dealt with at the third. If you only get one hit, you will work with all three phases of the transit at once.

If you have an astrological chart cast by any of the available casting services (listed at the end of the book on page 224) or by an astrologer, you will know which house your Saturn is in. Then check the explanation of that house in the previous chapter, and you should be able to ascertain the main issue of your Saturn Return.

If you don't have a chart, it is still possible to figure out the area of your resistance just by noticing which house seems to be your biggest struggle area in this life. Where there is resistance, there is a block.

If you got a divorce at age 30, Saturn is probably in your 4th house (feeling), 7th house (relationships), or 10th house (taking power). If you suddenly found your career at that age, it is probably in your 6th house (being in the moment) or the 10th house (taking power). If you became deeply spiritual, it is probably in your 9th house (spirit) or 12th house (bliss). As Saturn comes to its return, if you have not yet found your true work, such as John of the previous chapter, you may go back to school, change professions, or start a business. Possibly, a marriage is blocking growth, and it must be ended in order to start a new phase of growth. If you have not taken the time to develop a significant relationship, you just might begin that process now.

If you've already had your Saturn Return, review what happened that year. What was your big change? Think about the changes you made around age 30, and try to intuit which house Saturn was in. If you think you know the answer, be sure to see how balanced you are now on that polarity. See whether, as the time of your Saturn Return arrived, you had been obsessively involved for the previous fourteen years with the affairs of the house opposite the one in which Saturn is located in your natal chart. Never forget that it is just that obsession and intense involvement that allowed you to develop an extraordinary wellspring of wisdom in the area opposite your true purpose in life. The goal of Saturn Return is to balance all polarities so that we are able to utilize the powers inherent in all twelve sides of ourselves to achieve emotional maturation during our thirties.

THE POLARITIES

Let's look again at the six polarities, the questions they raise, and some applicable universal resolutions and teachings about these issues. As we do, see if you can figure out where your Saturn lies, and if you have your chart, check to see if your intuition is accurate.

Polarity One: 1st and 7th Houses
The first polarity turns around the issues of self/other. Am I deeply

immersed in myself and not relating to others? Or am I so caught up in a relationship that I have forgotten who I am? *Resolution: merging.* As you discover who you are, give all that you find to your partner. As you are immersed in the other, see clearly and deeply that you are your partner. *Teaching: the Mayan saying "In Lak'etch, I'll Laken"*—*"I am yourself, you are another."*

Polarity Two: 2nd and 8th Houses

The second polarity turns around the issues of grounding and emptying. Am I stuck in a house in the midst of a fifteen-year accumulation of possessions and feeling like I can never leave? Or have I so let go of things I need for living that I am not grounded? *Resolution: higher ethical sensitivity.* Take for yourself what you really need from the Earth and enjoy all your pleasures. Let go of every single thing in your life that is not frequently needed or used. *Teaching: the Native American saying "The Earth is your Mother and she freely offers to you all that you need."*

Polarity Three: 3rd and 9th Houses

The third polarity turns around the issue of integrating in ordinary reality and connecting with spiritual realms. Am I so hooked on my computer, fax machine, telephone, and plane flights that I haven't had a mystical thought or feeling in months? Or am I so spiritually obsessed that I can't stand ordinary reality, which is falling apart because of my lack of attention to details? *Resolution: integration of self as vessel of spirit.* Find the spiritual dimension daily within every act in your life. As you meditate, connect everything you feel and know with everything and everyone in your life. *Teaching: the Zen Buddhist saying "With right words and actions, spirit resides in the heart."*

Polarity Four: 4th and 10th Houses

The fourth polarity turns around the issue of inner knowing and outer power. Am I so deeply involved in my home or inner subconscious exploration that I am disempowered in the world out there? Or am I so involved in power struggles that I have forgotten exploration of my inner world? *Resolution: inner energies create outer reality.* Here you explore your subconscious, come to know your shadows, and find respect for the power of inner urges. As you revel in exercising power in the world, in freely giving of your personal power, you recognize that everything you know comes from the pool of all the desires and visions of Earth and its inhabitants from the beginning of time. *Teaching: the New Age saying "You create your own reality."*

Polarity Five: 5th and 11th Houses

The fifth polarity turns around desires and giving away. Am I so involved in my creativity that I pay no attention to giving to others? Or am I giving everything all day to people who need me and paying no attention to the needs of my inner child? *Resolution: playing creates service.* As your child within plays and creates, you then know how to give from that wellspring of delight. *Teaching: the creation spirituality saying "As the Divine plays, God/Goddess creates through humankind."*

Polarity Six: 6th and 12th Houses

The sixth polarity turns around being in the moment and letting go into divine fusion. Am I so obsessed with my responsibilities that I have lost contact with spirit? Am I so involved in mystical contemplation that I am not existing in the moment, in ordinary reality? If Spirit walked in the back door of my house or filled my car with gas, would I see her/him? *Resolution: be here now.* As you fulfill your duties, notice how absolute focus moves you right into deep cosmic joy. As you contemplate the Divine, notice how it is most easily found in the smallest and most obscure places. *Teaching: from the mythological centaur Chiron, "In the energy of each moment the divine exists."*

You may be able to radically accelerate your growth at Saturn Return by referring back to the concepts of the twelve houses of development and trying to identify the key polarity you are attempting to balance. Maybe you've been deeply absorbed in a time-consuming and challenging relationship, and now you see that you have no idea of who you are anymore. If you do have your chart, reread the section on the house where your Saturn is located as well as that of its opposing house. Saturn Return activates the process you need in order to discover and facilitate the purpose of your life, and the use of the six polarities can be a great technique for maximal conscious growth at any time in your life.

Recall that John's block was finding work. It comes as no surprise, then, that his Saturn was in the 6th house. The opposite house, the 12th, is the house of finding bliss. Since he was a small child, John had always been seeking ways to get blissed out, and then he consciously devoted himself to meditation around age 14. By doing this, he was able to avoid school and facing reality; he was always wanting to tune in to spiritual feelings instead of being in the present time. He continued this pattern once he began to work in the world, and he had trouble tuning in to his job. John would have been best off with Zen Buddhism as a meditation technique, as it focuses on being in the moment, rather than practicing transcendental meditation (TM), which was his first meditation practice and teaches how to still the mind and enter deeply into the inner realms. This technique would be ideal for a person with Saturn in the 12th house, but not for John with Saturn in the 6th house. Neither side of the polarity can mature unless we work on both ends. Thus, once John was able to master work, he was able to find the mystical side he had always been seeking.

Many marriages made in people's early twenties break up around age 30 unless the partners are truly compatible, can continue to grow in the marriage, and are able to tolerate big changes together. We do not know who we are until age 30, and often once we understand who we are, we may see that it no longer serves us to live with the people with whom we've been just existing. Often two people in a relationship are going through Saturn Returns simultaneously and discovering the real needs of their lives. However, if the two people are compatible, they can honor each other's true agenda, and the relationship can continue to benefit both.

Patrick had been unhappily married for six years by age 28, had two children, and had been working in a local bank while taking pre-law courses at night. His wife was very close to her parents, and she did not want to move away from her hometown, where they all lived. She was a shy woman who was totally absorbed in the children, and she hated socializing.

As his Saturn Return approached, Patrick wanted to start law school, which triggered an argument with his wife: she wanted him to promise he would practice law in their hometown if he became a lawyer. However, part of his reason for wanting to become a lawyer was to escape his hometown, where he felt he would psychologically die if he remained. Patrick had Saturn in the 1st house, and he had to master his sense of himself—the question of who am I?—in order to keep on growing. He could no longer put himself aside for a relationship in which his partner did not want to assist his personal growth.

When I first saw Patrick at age 32, his marriage was over and he felt very sad and guilty. His wife was quite angry at him. Through counseling, he was able to see that he and his wife were actually profoundly incompatible—that they could not have grown together. They had to learn to manage separation or both would begin to die.

In contrast, Bob (in the first chapter) had Saturn in the 7th house, and much of his growth up to midlife crisis involved the need to discipline himself within the structure of marriage and family, following an intense focus on himself from age 14 until Saturn Return, similar to that of Christopher (mentioned earlier in this chapter). Bob mastered the process of knowing himself within a relationship, the opposite side of the polarity Patrick needed to master. Notice how Saturn in the 1st or 7th houses always creates major lessons about personal exploration and growth in relationships.

When considering these case histories, it is important to remember that Saturn is only part of the story regarding such major needs in life. For example, Patrick might have been married to a woman who could assist his self-emergence, while Bob might have been married to a woman who could not share in a marriage with him as deeply as he required. Thus, Patrick might have stayed in his marriage and learned a lot from his wife, and Bob would have chased bikinis or found another woman who could share his deep need for a major relationship. After years of being an astrologer, I am still amazed by Saturn's power to trigger key life pursuits based on its placement in the birth chart. For example, I have taught an unusual number of priests, and a very high percentage of them have Saturn in the 9th house—spiritual connection.

Noticing which side of a polarity is not being honored is still my own favorite "tune-up." You may have done this intuitively as you read the description of the polarities, but now we want to take a moment to look at the last polarity, that of the 5th and 11th houses. Let us say you feel like you have no purpose—you serve no meaningful need for others or the planet (which I hear constantly from many of my clients over age 40). That would indicate you are struggling to master the 11th house— "How can I give my gift in this life?" For the answer to this question, look to the opposite house, the 5th—that of creativity and the child within. It is likely that you are underdeveloped there, for Saturn is often in the 5th house when people resist their creativity. So go take a class in a creative endeavor you have always wanted to pursue, and chances are that this will be the first step to finding and developing your gifts for everybody else.

But, you ask, what does all this have to do with Uranus and the liquid light of sex?

THE SEVEN-YEAR ITCH

Saturn transits each house or life issue every two and one-half years, while it takes Uranus seven years to move the same distance. In seven years, therefore, Uranus has moved through one house and Saturn, three. This transit of Saturn through three houses creates a "square," or 90-degree revelation point, of Saturn *to itself*. Remember from the first two chapters that Dr. Percy Seymour has discovered that the astrological aspects that influence the solar magnetic field are *conjunctions, squares, and oppositions:* this is why these Saturn squares each seven years have major influence on your life. This is why ages 7, 14, 21, 28,

35, 42, and so on are known to be key growth stages in all cultures.

As Saturn reaches its complete formation of a stage of growth at these square points, Uranus has fully transited through a house or area of experience and is poised for a new phase of transformation. Like a lightning bolt striking your head—remember being 14?—Uranus explodes our form that could get too rigid and solid, opening it for more and more mature perceptions of life. The age of 21 is such a major turning point because it is the coincidence of the culmination of three seven-year Saturn squares with the *first* Uranus square! People at 21 are thus at a maximum peak of Saturn's structural maturation and Uranus's creative vision, which may explain why we often get serious about goals at this time.

The cycle of Saturn maturation and Uranian creative opening is the *basic foundation and new creation cycle of life* because it is the archetypal formation process that is transformed over and over again into greater expansion. This process is popularly known as the "seven-year itch." It occurs when we have learned enough on a certain level, and it is time to risk a new level of experience. This is a cyclical process that can actually be fun to work with, and it truly is the key to enjoying life. Skiing is a useful image for the mastery of this process because the need for control and balancing is very Saturnian, but a good skier can fly like a Uranian lightning bolt. A bad skier who has not balanced contraction/expansion struggles on the slope is often eventually grounded with a broken bone or torn ligament.

Since contraction/expansion processes can be exactly timed, we can acquire subtle knowing about how structure supports all life. We can understand the old wisdom that "you can't do the right thing at the wrong time" by realizing that we cannot expand during a phase when we need to structure and contract, and we need to allow for transformation when it is needed.

Dave was an artist, a quintessential creative person, who could not see by age 30 the need for a physical/structural basis for his life. As a result, he lost his wife and family because he couldn't discipline himself into providing the basic work and home structure for the growth of relationships. What Dave really needed was to find a way to create and secure physical needs for his family while getting them to help him to be as free of "things" as was reasonable so he could pursue his artistic development. If he had been able to identify these major astrological patterns earlier in life—at age 21 or even 27—he might well have been able to hold on to structures for his life lessons.

If people can master structure, the miraculous life-infusing powers of Uranus become available for utilization of the structural matrix for personal transformation. Saturn and Uranus have a *contraction/ expansion action* that operates all the way through the life of each one of us. Honoring the need for structure, even while knowing how stressful it can be, is made easier by knowing how the structure *supports* creative unfoldment rather than *restricts* growth. After all, Dave could have chosen goals that would have allowed him just enough structure to realize all of his desires. But respect for goals/Saturn needs to be the fundamental approach to life, for even though Uranus rules creative unfoldment, that unfoldment will always abort without the support of Saturn.

FOUR

The Uranus Principle
in the Cycles of Life

MYTHOLOGICAL SOURCES ARE fertile ground for astrologers, since mythic archetypes are their tools for understanding our unfoldment of consciousness in space and time. In mythology, Uranus is the ruler of the universe, the usurper of power from the primordial triple goddess of the three phases of the moon. This myth signals the time of separation from the feminine, a time when the ancient world of primal waters and chaos of the Goddess gave way to the first emergence of ego. This was when we first became self-reflective and separated from our source.

Uranus is a son of Earth. Robert Graves notes in *The Greek Myths,* "At the beginning of all things Mother Earth emerged from Chaos and bore her son Uranus as she slept."[1] Uranus was also the Earth's lover, her co-creator, and he *greened* the Earth: created rain, life-forms, lakes, and the sea. This co-creation by Uranus is a marriage to Earth, a primordial *hieros gamos,* or ritualistic sexual union, with the Goddess, from whom all creation is derived. It is the source of sexuality, of eros, of all life.

The most significant myths are always multilayered, and during a last attempt to merge with the Mother Goddess, Uranus created the Cyclopes, primordial monster-human creatures, only to banish them to the center of the Earth. Then Mother Earth persuaded her other sons, the seven Titans led by the head Titan, Saturn, to castrate their father, her lover. Finally, Uranus became a sky god; he separated from

70

Earth, and in that cleavage lies a wound that we are only beginning to heal.

This is not a happy family picture. There isn't much harmony between the sexes here. Although father Uranus made much beauty with Mother Earth, there was also much violence and battle. And this has been the archetypal underpinning of civilization's perception of the relationship between the matriarchy and patriarchy: that the former is subjected to the power of the latter. Uranus first made water and life-forms on the Earth's surface and fathered the Titans. But once his creation powers were terminated by castration, he went to the sky. This patriarchal nightmare envisions a looming wounded male creator in the sky—the castrated father—while Earth dies in punishment without his greening powers, symbolizing a profound separation from our eroticism.

Kundalini is the Earth's natural life energy, which flows through each of us more intensely at the moment of Uranus Opposition. However, our evolution into self-reflection has resulted in profound blocks in our energy conduits: the chakras, spine, and meridians. Living beings are meant to be connectors through which energy is transmitted, due to the electromagnetic flow of waves traveling at the speed of light from the Sun. We are destined to be co-creators, existing in the magnetic gravitational field of Earth as Uranus greens the life-forms with electrical sparking. The way to facilitate our evolution now is to gently allow kundalini to rise naturally at midlife, realizing that the electrical force of Uranus maximizes our *connectivity* at Uranus Opposition. The crisis at this time signals our need to fuse Earth and sky right in our own bodies.

A fully resolved Uranus Opposition balances sexual polarization, as males integrate their inner female and women their inner male. True connection is the result of the union of positive and negative electrical energies, and the feminine principle receives, or is negative, while the male principle projects, or is positive. This is why the issue at midlife for men is to open the heart and find the *anima;* for women, it is to open the throat chakra to activate the *animus.* We need to heal the looming wounded Uranus by integrating male and female within. We all need Uranus as lover and not as father.

FATHER IN THE SKY

There are many theories about the emergence of the patriarchy, but undoubtedly a critical factor was the total dominance by men of women and the family in order to control the genetic line and population. However, in the face of overpopulation, control by the patriarch of the family must cease; the birthing process must be returned to women. The invention of effective birth control and its gradual integration into the fabric of culture mean that sex is no longer considered simply a function of procreation. Fertility is now only a part of female sexuality; after hundreds of thousands of years of survival mentality, sexuality now can also be used to raise energy and consciousness.

Uranus rules this shift because it rules all creative breakthroughs beyond necessary Saturn formative processes. When men control the birthing process for survival, it is Saturnian. When sexuality can go beyond survival, it is sensual, creative, electrical—Uranian.

The full experience of kundalini energy—critical to successful midlife transformation—requires letting go of those survival triggers and getting in touch with simple pleasure. As long as the sexual experience of our bodies is ruled by procreation, we are not yet released. We are seeing that our sexuality need not be controlled by religion, nor by empty notions of patriarchal morality.

You may say to yourself, "Well, I don't think that way, and haven't for some time." But ask yourself, "Do I still secretly believe that the angry judgmental God is going to strike me down if I do exactly as I please?" You do? Notice this! That's just what I'm talking about. Until that limitation is cleared up, we are still left with Uranus separated from Earth; still left with the male energy apart from the female; still left with judgments about sexuality that interfere with an effective experience of Uranus Opposition.

WHAT HAPPENS PSYCHOLOGICALLY
WHEN KUNDALINI RISES

Scientist Dr. Itzhak Bentov and psychiatrist Dr. Lee Sannella are two highly respected early pioneers in the field of sensation patterns generated by kundalini energy. In *Kundalini: Psychosis or Transcendence?* they both strongly suggest that understanding kundalini energy may be more than an interesting intellectual discourse—that, in fact, our next stage of evolution may be related to the activation of this mechanism, *kundalini rising.*[2] Similarly, psychologist Dr. Mary Scott, author of *Kundalini in the Physical World,* believes that our failure to fully experience the conscious rise of kundalini has had a tremendous impact on the present state of the planet:

> Our failure to recognize and live up to our full potential as essentially spiritual beings is creating increasing distress and frustration in society, especially among the young. There are too many physiological theories which amputate human nature at all its growing points; too many social attitudes in high places which maximize weakness and fail to set sufficiently challenging goals for the spiritually adventurous and the idealistic to aim at. By putting too material a value on ourselves and imposing unjustifiable constraints on nature, we unconsciously take power from the true elite and place it in the hands of those whose reach most grievously fails to exceed its grasp.[3]

In *Quantum Healing: Exploring the Frontiers of Mind/Body Medicine,* Dr. Deepak Chopra discusses the "unbounded state," which is an extension of intelligence in which every thought "creates a wave in the unified field. It ripples through all the layers of ego, intellect, mind, senses, and matter, spreading out in wider and wider circles."[4] That unbounded state of quantum intelligence sounds like what I call the "healing mind," and activation of that state, in my opinion, is deeply involved with the action of Uranus.

Dr. Richard Gerber reinforces the idea that healing at this level is very powerful when he comments, "[H]ealing a person at the mental level is stronger and produces longer lasting results than healing from either the astral or etheric levels."[5] Chopra notes further, "The unbounded state is not frequently seen in our society, while its opposite is absolutely endemic. Psychiatrists see patients every day who are crippled by boundaries, people who have programmed guilt, anxiety, and unnameable insecurities into themselves."[6]

These boundaries, these limiting mental states, are what we can blast through at midlife, for they are symptoms of blocks in the chakras that can be moved through most easily at this time. As stated earlier, I believe that these blocks to a more accelerated evolutionary process are the result of primordial separation complexes that are reflected in mythology, as well as blocks from traumatic experiences. Dr. Sannella's description of this blocking effect is especially insightful:

> Kundalini causes the most sensation when it enters an area of mind or body that is blocked. But the heat generated by the friction of kundalini against this resistance soon burns out the block, and then the sensation ceases. Similarly, just as the intense flow of water through a small rubber hose will cause the hose to whip about violently, while the same water flow through a fire-hose would scarcely be noticed, so does the flow of kundalini through obstructed channels within the body or mind cause motions of those areas until the obstructions have been washed out and the channels widened.[7]

Research on spiritual crisis and the psychospiritual apparatus of spiritual energy in the body is still in its infancy. Sannella, Bentov, Scott, and others emphasize the importance of unobstructed kundalini flow and the tremendous openness and unboundedness that are possible once the blocks are cleared. They also describe physical symptoms that are identical to the bizarre reports that clients were giving me during their Uranus Oppositions. And when I first read *Kundalini: Psychosis or Transcendence?* in 1982, I was in the early stages of Uranus Opposition myself and had been mystified by the physical sensations I was experiencing, symptoms that were nearly identical to those Sannella describes:

> The signs and symptoms usually described [by meditators], such as alterations in emotions and thought processes, visions and voices, appear to be largely personally determined. But the sensations such as itching, fluttering, tingling, heat and cold, perceptions of inner lights and sounds, and the occurrence of contortions and spasms appear to be quite universal. It is this universality that leads us to postulate that all spiritual practices are activating *the same basic process,* and that this process has a definite physiological basis that gives rise to these specific bodily symptoms [author's italics].[8]

Once I noticed that the symptoms of kundalini rising peak dramatically during the three stages of Uranus Opposition, I began to gather exact descriptions of symptoms during those times by asking my clients very pointed questions about what they were experiencing. Since then, through years of client counseling, I have found that the personalized kundalini pattern is revealed by the nature of the symptoms and the content of dreams, relational experiences, memories that surface, and new life agendas that are created during midlife. That is to say, it is possible to identify *where the client is blocked*!

As the energy rises and begins opening the blocks, the obstructed chakras can be determined by observing the physiological and psychological symptoms, which actually often manifest *exactly* during the Uranus aspects. Naming that block produces clarity, offers potential therapeutic advice, and, most importantly, offers the client the power to activate the "healing mind," the more potent mental skill we all can utilize to activate the will in order to change our physiology, emotions, and judgment, once we can see clearly what is amiss.

Mary Scott notes that "the answer [to kundalini flow blockage] seems to lie in discrepancies between the objectives of surface and subliminal selves which cannot be avoided while these two vital personality structures remain unaligned."[9] As long as these vital personality structures are not aligned, the surface self, which exhibits the "acceptable" cultural suit of clothes, always resists the agenda of the soul, which is enlightenment.

Dr. Scott's observances correlated strongly with a pattern I had been seeing in my clients. Those who suffered most during Uranus Opposition were the ones most invested in the surface self, while those who grew the most during their midlife crisis were the people who were the most explorative of the subliminal self (which is the same thing as the subconscious or unconscious mind) or who otherwise opened themselves to spiritual evolution.

WHAT HAPPENS ASTRONOMICALLY

For about 90 percent of us, midlife crisis unfolds in three parts: it is a "one step forward, two steps back, three steps forward" process. It's like a car going over a point, backing up and going over it again, and then pulling forward for the last time, thus crossing the same point three times.

In the first phase, Uranus passes across the point that is exactly opposite its place in the birth chart. As this first opposition approaches, we begin to feel acutely disturbed. Physiologically, kundalini energy has awakened and moved out of the root chakra, has rushed up through the body, and has gotten stuck in whatever chakra is blocking our spiritual evolution.

Our job during Uranus Opposition is to clear that blockage by whatever means works for us: traditional therapy, journal writing, past-life regression, and bodywork are some currently useful methods. If you have difficulty thinking about memory therapy in terms of past lives, simply image those "memories" as the inner tapes that we have gotten from mythology, religion, and culture, or from our genetic, racial memory. Whatever the source, these old tapes playing in our minds conflict with the contemporary moral environment, or conditioning, up to midlife, and the inner memories function as blocks in the chakras and subtle-energy systems of the body.

Once someone has done all the work on the chakra that was activated by the first rise, the energy will flow through the chakra previously blocked and get stuck in the next obstructed chakra. In the following chapters, we'll go through the chakras specifically and individually, examining the issues that are presented by blockage in different places. For our purposes here, it is enough to note that as the first opposition hits, many people feel extreme anxiety, shake, or have hot flashes—they feel like an earthquake is happening in their bodies. What happened to my client Jane is a classic example of this process.

HOT FLASHES
(AND IT ISN'T MENOPAUSE)

At 39, Jane had a good job as a financial counselor, was in the midst of a reliable marriage, and was the mother of two teenagers. One day during a meeting with three male bankers and two male corporate executives, she felt herself getting hot, and her face turned bright red, which was acutely embarrassing to her. A few nights later, she found herself unable to sleep because she was worrying about her daughter, her mother-in-law, and the piles of financial reports she had to file. She lay in bed awake for hours thinking about these things, and then she came to the conclusion that something was "terribly wrong." The first phase of her Uranus Opposition had struck!

In the next few weeks, Jane found herself compulsively watching the news searching for what was the matter in the world, but her feelings of unease were actually sourced in inner anxiety attempting to get her attention. (Excessive fear about the economy, weather, political situations, and health scares is a common symptom at midlife crises, though of course often these worries are also legitimate.) Progressively she was becoming unhinged, and she didn't know why. Then mysteriously, the heat went away in her body, everything felt okay, and she thought she was back to normal. This was because Uranus had moved further along and moved off the exact opposition point. Jane's symptoms are very typical of the reports I have gotten from clients at midlife crisis who exist in what some would call the "normal" world or from people who have never explored energy-raising techniques such as meditation or guided imagery.

To understand Jane's experience, we need to look more fully at what happens during Uranus Opposition. After Uranus first passes the point opposite its natal position in a person's chart, its orbit *appears* from the perspective of Earth to come to a stopping point and then move backward. Of course, the planet does not literally go backward in the sky, although its electromagnetic influence reverses due to Earth's orbit around the Sun, and this perspective from Earth is what is important to astrology and the key life passages.

The second phase of the opposition occurs, then, when Uranus appears to be moving backward, and astrologers say the planet is "retrograde," but understanding such complexities is not really needed. Just know that at the exact second opposition, the planet in retrograde motion will cross over that opposition point again, then turn direct "behind" that position and cross over the point once more during the third opposition.

Physiologically, kundalini energy ceases to rise when the planet moves off its exact opposition point, causing the transformation pressure to lessen for just a while. This period is a resting point before the next rise, which occurs when the planet actually retrogrades back over its exact opposition position. During this resting phase, hopefully the individual has realized that a whole new understanding of life is coming, has accepted that this change is coming, and is attempting to be open to this new information. However, many use the relaxation of pressure to deny the reality of the force just experienced, and they just heave a sigh of relief, thinking it was only a random and weird occurrence.

Because of this temporary reversal of energy, this is the phase in midlife crisis when deepening and reflection need to occur. The retrograde period seems to activate very deep, past-life genetic and racial memories as well as memories of buried childhood traumas in whatever chakra is blocked, which greatly deepens perception about the central

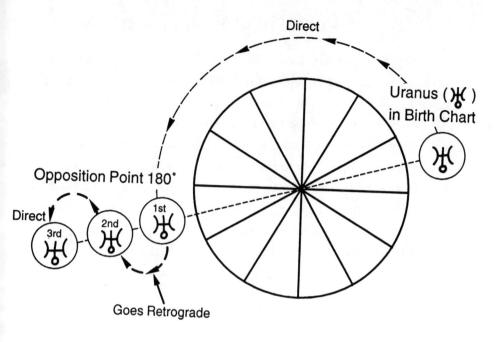

*Figure 4.1. Three oppositions of Uranus—
direct, retrograde, and direct again*

spiritual crisis. This can be a marvelously philosophical period for those who are doing their work; it shines light into a deep chasm that has opened into the inner self.

It is not necessary to believe that this deepening involves integration of actual past-life memory, but that construct is very useful to many people. What matters is that something that is buried inside, that lies deep within, is surfacing. If some power issues have been faced, you will probably be feeling almost overwhelming love for yourself and others. Many cease to shake now, but the heart opens so intensely that some clients report a burning on the chest that others can feel. Heat may also be felt in the hands, and if it is, please use those hands on those you love! As you will see in the next chapter, taking certain therapeutic actions at this time greatly alleviates stress and confusion, and a directed program almost ensures a radical level of spiritual evolution.

WHOOPS! HEAT'S ON AGAIN!

Not surprisingly, then, Jane's relief was due to the fact that Uranus had just passed its first opposition and was going retrograde for the second crossing. As Uranus moved off direct opposition, Jane was sure everything was going to be fine again. But once it came close to a second opposition, things heated up again, and Jane dreamed of a terrible fire. She was trapped in a room with smoke seeping through the baseboards, and she awoke when an eerie red glow appeared in the window. In the dream she was paralyzed in her bed and could not move as smoke filled the room and caused her to choke.

Jane awoke in terror, sniffed the air to make sure the fire was not real, and lay back, her heart pounding with terror. Suddenly, she remembered being 4 years old, when a fire consumed her cousins' summerhouse. Her uncle, two older cousins, and her 5-year-old-cousin, Mike, died in that fire. For the rest of the summer, her daily companion no longer came every day to walk and swim with her. Over time, that memory had faded.

Jane was blocked in the solar plexus chakra. She had married, had her own children, and built up a very safe life, but deep inside she was very afraid. She carried a selection of subconscious tapes that always repeated, "Everything is okay now, but at any moment disaster can strike." She thought she had controlled the problem by following extreme fire safety measures, but with Uranus Opposition pushing energy up her body, the time had come to face her deeply buried fear. Jane's pattern is typical: many compulsive behavior patterns and compulsive protective habits that block growth are the result of buried childhood complexes.

Jane came to me for a reading during the retrograde phase. The astrological timing analysis helped her to look at the root of her fear, and she did some past-life regressions to see if she would recall past-life themes of fire and/or death. Sure enough, in her third past-life session, she recalled a Roman lifetime under Nero at a time when Rome burned. She had suffocated in an aqueduct as hordes of people piled up and blocked the tunnel. Under hypnosis, she could smell the burning flesh, which she had again smelled in her uncle's cabin in this lifetime. Uncovering these memories helped to release their grip on her.

Another past-life memory that helped Jane was a life in which she died falling out of a carriage. As she was seeing her body get crushed against a curb, she remembered watching from above and flying ecstatically to a beautiful blue light. She looked back to see her crumpled body and registered the horror in the faces of the people in the street—they were suffering as they looked at her twisted body, while she was in ecstasy! Then she realized that her cousin Mike had gone to heaven while she was left to grieve. For the first time she cried for the loss of her adored companion, now that she knew he was okay. She finally experienced the convulsions of grief she had so long repressed. Her locked solar plexus opened and energy rushed past it into her heart.

Unreleased grief is one of the most common sources of chakra blocks, and it will just lie in the solar plexus chakra until kundalini rises. Once the energy activates the grief, it will manifest as seemingly sourceless anxiety. Sometimes the blocked grief will express itself in a dream or nightmare, so it is always wise to pay acute attention to dreams during midlife crisis. Therapy in childhood could have cleared Jane's grief more easily, and this is why therapy for children who have experienced a trauma is *always* advisable.

The third opposition occurs when Uranus has retrograded back as far as it will go, seems to stop as viewed from Earth, goes direct, and then moves back over the birth opposition for the last time. This phase is often less physically symptomatic for those who are progressing; the shaking and heat in the body have lessened because many of the blocks have already been cleared. For those who are not progressing because they have been blocking the whole process by massive addictions and avoidance, trouble starts now!

Jane, however, had done most of her work during the first two hits of Uranus Opposition: she cleared the fear out of her solar plexus. As a result, she became even more successful on her job, for she had gained personal courage. She also began to experience a whole new level of family joy. Her love for her husband deepened greatly when she stopped fearing that she'd suddenly lose him. But the best result could be seen with her children. They were having difficulty during adolescence because Jane had sheltered them too much due to her own fears. She found herself now able to entrust them to the world, and her increased warmth was just the support they needed at this critical time. It was exquisite to observe such growth in the whole family. As can be seen here, when one family member has the courage to clear his or her blocks, often the whole family heals.

WHY ME, WHY NOW?

Midlife crisis is never easy, but it is even harder if we resist. It is our most intense phase of personal evolution, and careful attention to the exact timing of the process offers us tremendous powers of understanding. I have counseled quite a few clients who were referred to me because of intense kundalini crisis. Usually their Uranus Opposition has already occurred, and they have had an unresolved experience. By gaining insight into what *was* going on and using techniques to open some of the chakras still shut down due to their not knowing how to let energy flow, they have been greatly helped. Nevertheless, once the transit has passed, the degree of opening that is possible is just not as great, the work is not as effective, as when the person does a great deal of therapy and clears a lot of inner blocks right at the time of Uranus Opposition. It is similar to psychotherapeutic work as adults, when we attempt to resolve issues due to trauma caused by lack of parental love. It can be done, but it is easier to be loved as a child.

It is important to add that some people manage to repress themselves and stay very dormant during midlife crisis, but then go through a very stressful and intense opening triggered by a transit of another planet to their natal Uranus position. Any opening is better than none, and these unusual cases would be better off moving through a lot of the blocks right during Uranus Opposition.

The clients that I have been able to counsel through midlife crisis have often accomplished startling levels of spiritual growth. Sure, it may not be easy and it may involve a lot of "acting out," but our actions surprise us so much as we do it that we get jolted into observing our own behavior.

Mark was a skilled accountant who was married to a gossipy, controlling wife who loved his money. From Saturn Return to the first hit of Uranus Opposition, Mark milked his clients, as he felt no concern about their welfare. As long as he brought home a fat check to his hovering wife, he worried about little else. In his late thirties, he discovered that his clients actually knew very little about what he was doing, and he even found ways to pad hours.

Then, as Uranus Opposition approached, he found himself imagining murdering his wife! For fifteen years he had put up with her flapping gums and financial control, but now he felt enraged every time she opened up her mouth. He saw himself striking that yapping face. He went out and bought a red pickup truck without telling her, and he went around town feeling great powers in his legs and groin as he drove his truck. At his exact first hit of Uranus Opposition, he told his wife to shut up, or else.

As the second rise of kundalini energy occurred when Uranus hit again, Mark felt ecstatic clearing as the energy rushed through his solar plexus. He felt magnificent pure power, but then the energy flooded into the heart and got stuck, since he had so little feeling for his clients or family. He was afraid of his desire to just smash his wife, and some of his clients left because they got tired of his lack of concern for them.

Mark came to see me mainly because he was nervous about his violent feelings toward his wife. With the reading, he actually could see that his own blocked solar plexus was manifesting through his wife's obsessive control of him—an energy function that will become much clearer in the next chapter—and that he was using money for control instead of as a free-flow use of energy. I suggested that he attend a "Stalking the Wild Man" workshop with Robert Bly, which he did, and I have not seen him again.

Just as the transits of Saturn gradually help us discover processes for living that enable us to consciously manifest goals, the transits of Uranus take the newly formed, structured identity and spiritualize it. And just as the mythologized Uranus greened the Earth and made water and life-forms, Uranus transits wake us up to remembering our story, our own unique spiritual potential. Saturn teaches us who we can be on the practical level, and Uranus teaches us how to create and expand based upon the gifts the Earth offers each person who incarnates. Kundalini rising does not attain its full potential for people without their conscious perception of the full range of the dance of life on Earth.

The alternatives to active participation in the potential growth available at Uranus Opposition are potentially traumatic. You can begin dying in spirit at midlife, or the uncleared blocks can create confusion and pain as you approach age 50. Take Tex: He shook and had acute anxiety during the first opposition. Not only that, as kundalini shot out of his root chakra, he found himself partially impotent at times.

Most men whom I have counseled experience some decreased sexual potency during midlife crisis, as kundalini moves out of the root chakra, where it was an easy source of erectile strength. So Tex, who was already totally freaked out by the shaking in his body, also started having a sexual crisis! The energy was attempting to open up his root chakra—the sexual center—and his solar plexus chakra—the power center.

To regain some of his former performance, Tex had an affair with a wildly sexual woman. She was a woman he couldn't have seduced when he was younger, but now that he was making a lot of money, she was willing. He was abusing his power by cheating on his wife, who was dependent on him while she mothered his children, and he paid plenty for his time with the wild woman by indulging her frequent shopping needs! This is, of course, the classic male midlife crisis pattern. The movie *10,* starring Bo Derek, is an excellent portrayal of this pattern, in which the older male becomes obsessed with a younger woman who temporarily engages his sexual fantasies and restores his sexual potency.

Tex carried on his affair while Uranus moved past the first hit and retrograded back. But on the second opposition, he had sexual dysfunction and anxiety attacks with the wild woman as well. All his energy was stuck in his solar plexus, because he couldn't be honest with himself in the face of his performance fear. Nothing was left to do but drink and utilize pornography, and he effectively avoided purifying his root chakra so as to open his solar plexus. Tex's story is a prime example of a pointless and unsatisfying journey through Uranus Opposition—the alternative to consciously taking on the opportunity of a lifetime.

DID I MISS MIDLIFE CRISIS ALTOGETHER?

These stories about Alice, Tex, and Mark are very interesting, but, you may say, "I've checked the tables in the back of the book; I've already passed my Uranus Opposition and nothing happened to me. Is this all useless to me then?" Be assured, all is not lost. First, this book focuses on Uranus Opposition because it is a universal growth stage at midlife. Of course, it is remotely possible that you are a *nondysfunctional human and truly have not experienced the crisis that this planetary pattern usually triggers!* I strongly suspect that all this tension at midlife would not be necessary if people came from functional childhoods and lived in a functional culture. (In later chapters, we will be looking at the possibility that the whole world is in the midst of midlife crisis.)

Aside from this scenario, an explanation for your situation may be the fact that some individuals become consciously aware of the energy released physiologically during Uranus Opposition within a few years *after* the exact Uranus Opposition instead of when it is actually occurring. The resistance to Uranus transits can be so high, as already mentioned, that a person's ability to identify what has been happening may be blocked until he or she encounters the reaction set off by other planetary aspects later on. Nevertheless, such individuals will usually still show signs of heat in the body, have high anxiety, and experience shaking at Uranus Opposition, though the conscious awareness of the transformation comes later.

Secondly, now you may be in your forties and may have experienced a lot of the symptoms and life changes described in this book, but you were not in a position to do any therapy or process what was happening to you at the time. Hopefully, your reflections triggered by this book will help you understand yourself a lot better. You may even opt for some therapy.

It is important to note that blocks that are not effectively processed at Uranus Opposition will continue to exert pressure all the way through your forties, and they will manifest powerfully again as you approach 50. However, although it is best for the body to move the energy during Uranus Opposition, you can still accomplish a lot of growth after the transit is over by understanding later what was happening and shifting yourself by means of the healing mind; it is just easier to accomplish transformation when the pressure is on. For those going through kundalini rising after the dates given for the month of birth at the end of the book, the therapeutic advice and chakra analysis is the same.

BUT I'M HAVING KUNDALINI BLOWOUT AT AGE 23!

If you think you are having kundalini rising before midlife, which can be set off by an unusual configuration in your natal chart or by meditation techniques, *I strongly advise you to attempt to slow the process.* It helps to get lots of rest, stop the meditation technique that triggered early kundalini rising, eat red meat, be soothed by swimming and walking, and use acupuncture to balance your body. Dr. Sannella's advice about how to slow the process offered in *Kundalini: Psychosis or Transcendence?* has been a lifesaver for many. Also, Mary Scott's *Kundalini in the Physical World* is loaded with helpful advice about handling the incredible powers of this fire in our bodies. She wisely comments about tampering with kundalini: "Only those who are not ready will try to force its pace, and only the unwise or unfortunate will raise it prematurely."[10] She notes that in India, "only after fulfilling one's role as a member of society is one free to withdraw within the world of the psyche."[11]

For the most part, few have fulfilled their roles in society until age 40. Kundalini rising in the immature body—before age 38—is very dangerous, and if you must pursue it, remember the techniques for slowing down kundalini offered in this book. It is not necessary to hurry to become enlightened.

Uranus Opposition is the most accelerated integration point of a person's entire life. It comes at midlife, goes through its process, and then its force is gone. What you do during this transit determines how far you may evolve; the openings you create are the places where you can grow in the future. I suggest that it is dangerous to not go all out at Uranus Opposition because it is often the ideal opportunity to broaden as much as possible, and this does not come again. Spiritual breakthroughs may come later in your life, but the potential for growth that you will possess then is established now.

FIVE

Uranus and Personal Empowerment

....

The Lower Chakras

THIS CHAPTER DESCRIBES ways to open each chakra, move kundalini energy the most effectively, and make conscious use of the great transformative powers of Uranus. If you haven't done so already, be sure to note at this time the timing of your midlife crisis in the tables at the end of the book.

As we go through all of the chakras and their various archetypal contents, you may find you instantly recognize your personal blocks. Possibly you can access your healing mind, since the entrance to potential unbounded states of consciousness is so open at midlife. A number of my clients have actually managed to discover their healing mind's unbounded knowledge about their own transformation needs at midlife just by means of contemplating the messages being given out by the various types of chakra blockage. Some of the case-history descriptions may seem bizarre, but they illustrate the sometimes dramatic qualities of symptoms.

There are seven chakras in the body. The heart chakra sits in the middle and acts as a compassionate gateway between the three lower and three upper chakras. In the lower chakras—Earth, root, and solar plexus—having and using power are primary issues. In the upper chakras—throat, third eye, and crown—the acquisition of enlightenment, the infusion of light, and our bodies' attunement with spirit are the primary issues. The more the heart chakra opens, the more there is balance between the pull within ourselves to the lower and upper realities.

Conceptually, it may work to think of the Earth and crown chakras as the points that connect us to Earth and sky respectively, and the other five chakras as inner centers that organize the energy fields of our physical bodies. The root chakra governs sexual response; the solar plexus rules gut, where we process all our relationships; the heart rules love, where we magnetically draw and hold existence; the throat rules the gateway to communication to all that exists; and the third eye governs sight of the nonphysical. Since opening the lower chakras differs from opening the upper chakras, this chapter will focus on the lower chakras, and the next chapter will cover opening the heart and the upper three chakras, while showing how these openings purify and further augment more potent and complete opening of the lower chakras.

For anyone beginning the time of midlife crisis, I strongly recommend a complete physical; it can be helpful to rule out any actual physical cause for symptoms *before* it is assumed symptoms are generated by subtle energy. All body processes are accelerated during the opposition of Uranus, and if there is a physical disease, it is likely to progress faster at midlife, so the earlier the diagnosis the better. However, even if there is a physical cause of symptoms, subtle-body work is still useful. For example, those who are struggling with cancer, AIDS, or other life-threatening conditions will find that doing Uranus Opposition therapeutic work can complement radical medical programs.

On the flip side, knowing that there is no immediate physical cause for a symptom leaves open the consideration of whether kundalini energy is the real source opening a person to subtle perceptions. In fact, I believe (although I have not yet proved it) that the genetic predisposition to many of the diseases of aging—such as Alzheimer's disease, arthritis, and cancer—is triggered in cells, bones, and muscles that were not regenerated during midlife crisis. Kundalini rising rejuvenates the body for the second half of life, and if this energy is blocked and never released, the aging process will not be as healthy or meaningful, and emotional dysfunctions will be more likely to occur. Senility, from this point of view, is caused by inadequate kundalini or erotic energization of our bodies. From the astrological point of view, the ideal human life span would be 84 years—one solar orbit of the planet Uranus—in which the first half of life up to the mid-point would involve mastery of physical or emotional realities, and the second half would consist of the attainment of wisdom while enjoying good health.

For most symptoms during midlife crisis, certain forms of therapy will assist the process. Dr. Sannella's *Kundalini: Psychosis or Transcendence?* contains much good therapeutic advice in this regard. Massage, long walks, hot tubs, yoga, and acupuncture will balance the body, and such forms of therapy even seem to slow kundalini rising. They balance the flow from left to right in the *Ida* and *Pingala,* the channels of subtle energy according to traditional Indian wisdom. Frequently, severe imbalances during midlife crisis are a result of energy imbalances from side to side in our bodies. Traditional psychotherapy such as Jungian analysis, dream therapy, journal exploration, a long walk with your favorite old friend—even past-life regression work—will be unusually fruitful at this time of heightened awareness. Every dollar you spend on yourself now is worth a hundred because your accelerated energy fields focus your healing mind on regeneration of your body, emotions, and mind.

As for which therapy is most appropriate, an astrological analysis can be a terrific guide, but I have noticed that most people are able to intuit what is best for them. This is also a great time to eliminate addictions, since heightened kundalini energy in our bodies seems to cause us to feel more acutely than usual the progressive physiological and mental damage that is the result of addictions. Addictions reflect our deep-seated death wishes, and *eros*—the primal life force—is the antidote to this pull toward death—*thanatos.* Tune in to what you need, then go out and get it; do not ignore any of the signals you are getting. Allow your body to be inundated by the flow of electromagnetic healing power being channeled through each of your chakras. A vital, *bioelectric body,* a body enlivened with kundalini, is the key to resistance to environmental pollution and stress, and it is a necessary vehicle for a healthy and productive second half of life.

EARTH CHAKRA

"Earth chakra" is my own name for the lowest chakra, the energy center that is located below the root chakra/sexual center. Mary Scott places Earth resonation *in* the root chakra, but I find these two energy forms to be radically different. She notes, "The fact that the root Chakra is associated with the Earth is less well known than that it is the resting-place of coiled Kundalini."[1] I suspect that the energy center of the Earth chakra is located below our feet instead of at the base of the spine, which is the traditional location—that it resonates with the Hertz frequency of the Earth, 7.5 Hz. Other healers with whom I've discussed this issue also report that they sense this chakra is about eighteen inches below the feet.

The Earth chakra exults the body, and I think our awareness of this chakra has been dormant, except in pagan or indigenous cultures, for two thousand years because Christianity has tended to emphasize spiritual ascension while being negative about earthiness. Actually, this tendency began much earlier, when the patriarchy took control of culture thousands of years before Christianity and denigrated female Earth religions. The malfunction of the Earth chakra in modern times is specifically caused by our alienation from the pulse of the Earth. This is the result of ecological desecration and the confusion of so many people who were not effectively grounded at birth.

I sense that the dormancy of this chakra is deeply related to the early mythology of Uranus being castrated by Saturn, then Saturn banishing the Cyclopes to the center of the Earth and taking control of the Earth. For those who would say that these ancient myths do not influence us, Jungian analysts and past-life regression therapists insist that

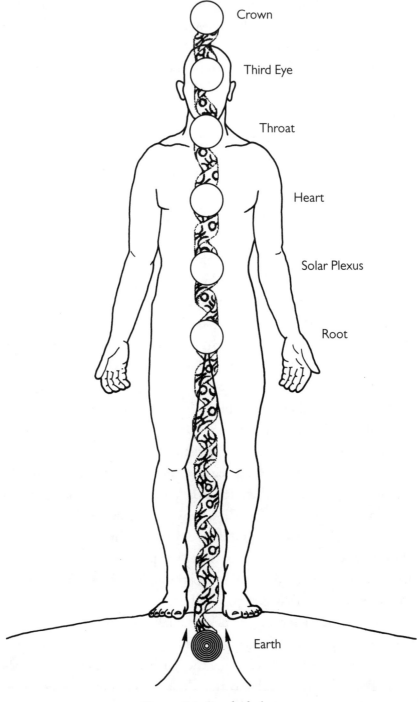

Figure 5.1. Earth chakra

the deep mind consistently reports such contents when probed. We are profoundly cut off from our erotic nature whenever there is too much control/Saturn; we cannot then resonate with the pulse of the Earth. It is as if we have been castrated, and the existence of female circumcision shows that this is not just a male issue. This chakra is the energy center that holds us in our bodies, and when it is blocked we are not grounded.

To be truly grounded, the Earth chakra must open fully at birth; it is the basis of incarnation on Earth. Our first connection must be to the Earth, our Mother; and in mythology, the Earth bore Uranus. When this occurs, the infant does not separate from its environment and become fearful or sad. The child has courage and becomes comfortable in its world by means of creative exploration. He or she does not become emotionally alienated and knows how to put up boundaries against negativity when it inevitably appears. This is a child who knows how to get what it needs by being able to ask the right questions and who demands adequate respect, affection, and the opportunity to grow.

Often in our modern world, however, birth is in sterile hospitals and the baby is separated from its mother almost immediately. The tendency to die and return to the source is intense at birth as the child has just left the multidimensional spirit realm, and this pull needs to be counteracted by sucking on the Mother Earth—that is, by breastfeeding. (As the Earth bore Uranus, every mother bears the divine child.) Instead, a hard, plastic, "man-made" nipple is thrust in the tiny mouth seeking primal connection, and the eyes of the infant seeking to identify its new location in this third-dimensional, or solid, place are not met with eyes that understand.

As a result of this shock at birth, the connection to the multidimensional spirit realm—the crown and third-eye chakras—stay open to help the infant locate itself, or else it will die. What this means is that the baby is not really in its body for a while, is not really interested in being in the solid dimension in a cold hospital where there are not healing hands and reassuring eyes. It begins life with a sense of alienation to the Earth plane.

Then, during early childhood, this feeling of separation is

compounded by a culture that rarely encourages attunement to spirit. As a result, the child learns to shut down. It is this profound alienation and ungroundedness that I think may one day be determined to be the cause of schizophrenia, psychosis, and acute manic depression. Midlife crisis can surface many symptoms of these horrible, disconnective disorders, and this is why Earth chakra blockage is so intense.

This may explain why those with blocked Earth chakras often are exceedingly spiritual. Spirit has opened upper chakras at birth to protect the baby's connection to its soul in the spirit realm and to keep the baby alive in the third dimension in the midst of the harsh hospital environment. This method of staying in the body ensures time for that soul to gather its lessons in the physical body, which is the reason for incarnation.

Indeed, in indigenous cultures, children with powerful connections to Source are identified and trained, for they are the future seers and shamans of the tribe. The elders know that the lower chakras in these children must be opened as well in order for them to have power, and that higher-chakra skills such as healing, having "the sight," and seeing visions are difficult to recover during adulthood if the power centers of their physical bodies have atrophied in childhood due to denial and lack of encouragement and enlightened birthing.

A blocked Earth chakra may indicate a childhood of little parental love, because many parents in the twentieth century have been afraid of such children. This lack of primary bonding creates children who cannot picture ever being a useful part of the planetary experience. As a child, for instance, did you have extraordinary visions of spiritual light? Did you have difficulty expressing what you saw and knew? Did you exhibit extraordinary healing and perceptual powers as a child, and were the people around you afraid of this?

At worst, such "unusual" qualities may have caused you to be violently suppressed, making it impossible for you to establish normal *boundaries* between yourself and those around you. Boundary difficulties occur when you have open upper chakras and closed lower ones. You may have forgotten about this because the perceptual skills of the upper chakras atrophy at about age 7, unseen and not named, unless you are born in an indigenous culture in which magical skills are developed in children. If you cannot remember much about your childhood before age 7 and are experiencing a chaotic desire to leave the planet at midlife, this description may fit you. One thing is certain: you carry a deep sadness within that is hard to penetrate. You have not been welcomed here. Often such clients say they feel like they got dropped out of the sky and just can't figure this planet out.

Some clients who seem to have this difficulty report obsession with extraterrestrial-contact questions. This strongly backs up the esoteric tradition that these individuals actually are from locations beyond Earth. This tendency to be more in the sky than on Earth shows up as fascination with "contact," and the best antidote is grounding oneself in ordinary reality. ET contacts are real, as far as I know from my own experience, but people who have such experiences who are also not well grounded can end up being very disturbed.

Whitley Strieber brilliantly and bravely describes his terror and psychological disintegration from ET contact experience in *Communion*. Then, in his subsequent book, *Transformation*, he seems to have gone beyond his own great fear of the "visitors." As we contemplate the implications of ET interference into our lives, says Strieber, "we must learn to walk the razor's edge between fear and ecstasy—in other words, to begin to finally seek the full flowering of our humanity. . . . Really facing the visitors means accepting that one may also endure great fear . . . and become free of all fear."[2] The only opportunity I've had to discuss ET contact questions with people who *are* grounded has been with Yucatán Mayans such as Hunbatz Men. They are not seriously disturbed by contact with the visitors because they also feel safe on Earth.

Paralyzing fear is the key emotional symptom of a blocked Earth chakra, and that fear evolves into unnamed, irrational, and totally unexpected deep inner terror at midlife crisis. People report acute panic, obsession with the end of the world, suicidal thoughts that seem to have no basis, and a distressing loss of feeling for any meaning in their personal lives. Sound familiar? Then some of the following description might also be true for you: You don't know why you're here, and you're not sure you actually want to bother with any of it. People talk about how they enjoy life, but there is little enjoyment in your own. You may think, why bother about sex? What is happiness? What could joy or ecstasy be? Why did your soul choose for you to come to this planet?

Susan, a famous and brilliant therapist who is shockingly open in her third eye and crown chakras, was obsessed with suicidal thoughts during midlife crisis, which hit at the peak of her professional career. She reported recurrent panic attacks and was afraid of what she might do to herself. However, once Susan got the description of a blocked Earth chakra in counseling, her healing mind got insight into what was going on for her, and she made a choice to stay on the planet. The intensity of this crisis results from the lack of grounding throughout one's entire growth pattern up to midlife, because being grounded is what makes us safe here.

At midlife crisis, this fundamental lack of connection to the Earth plane causes the symptoms of a blocked Earth chakra to manifest. Not facing it can actually cause teeth to crack and the spine to freeze. Another of my clients, Elizabeth, developed severe cracking teeth and had many root canals and tooth removals, which greatly taxed out her immune system.

In the midst of her health crisis, Elizabeth got in touch with other lifetimes in other star systems during a hypnotic session. She next embarked on an obsessive investigation of ET interferences, such as cattle mutilations and reports of people being taken up in ships and implanted with mechanical devices by ETs. She just could not stop compulsively searching for the "real truth," and during midlife crisis, such compulsive behavior may be masking the real issues to be faced. In Elizabeth's case, she needed to face her own fears and lack of security within and forget about "knowing" for a while. She got sicker and sicker; her body was giving out under the physiological pressure being generated by her neurotic fear of life and her constant dental surgery.

Until I figured out the cause I was amazed by clients such as Elizabeth, who reported violent shaking, acute adrenal imbalances—

such as ringing ears, vision deterioration, and exhaustion—cracked teeth, and even spinal paralysis! When the Earth chakra is blocked, you will know it by manifesting some or all of these symptoms as you approach age 40. You can go to doctors with the above symptoms, including acute anxiety and panic attacks, but even a battery of expensive tests may reveal no physical cause. Western medicine can do nothing for kundalini rising, since it does not yet recognize the existence of subtle energy.

Sally, who had an unusually intense reaction to blocked Earth chakra during Uranus Opposition, said to me in a letter:

Earlier this year starting in March, something happened, which I still can't describe or explain, but I'm sure I almost left. I experienced the greatest influx of kundalini energy—like an eight-inch undulating river up my spine and into my head and over. All boundaries receded. I became aware of the energy of *everything,* including electric lights. I was totally overwhelmed. I went to the emergency room with chest pains, I went back *in utero,* I was drunk and unable to stand, and I got stuck in a 3-year-old state for months. I had *grand mal* seizures, felt all the energy systems in my own body. I lost my mind, could not think, remember, read, write, walk, or talk at times. Even now I cry to remember the horrors of that experience.

I think individuals who report such extraordinary physiological patterns at midlife should be tested by scientists. Instead, attempts were made to commit Sally into a mental facility for electric shock treatments, which is the *worst* thing that can be done during Uranus transits, since the nervous system is acutely sensitive. Luckily, her husband sensed that something else was going on and protected her from the "great healers in white coats."

Of course, it makes sense to go to your dentist if your teeth start cracking—how could you respond otherwise in Western culture? But if the cause is kundalini rising, the faster you get the energy to flow through and burn out the blocks, the *less* permanent damage you will have to your teeth. A few clients of mine may have prevented some damage to their teeth by wearing dental guards at night that prevent grinding.

At Uranus Opposition, the goal is to find a safe way to allow the healing power of the Earth to flow through your body while observing your own physiological and emotional symptoms to see what needs to be changed. Again, many clients experience great relief just by realizing that there is a real process going on. They understand that they aren't getting sick or going crazy, and it is easier to evaluate whether symptoms do require medical attention or whether treatment should be sought from alternative medical and/or healing sources.

What can you do about the physical aspects of Uranus Opposition? The shaking, heat, cramping, and aches, even the paralysis and seizures, are greatly alleviated by acupuncture. I advise one or two sessions a week until the quaking ceases. Acupuncture aligns the human body with the *telluric forces,* the natural electric currents flowing near the Earth's surface, allowing energy to move through the blocked chakras more easily. For severe muscular and bone problems, your best bet is to see a chiropractor, have massages and acupuncture, and go walking and/or swimming. Vitamins and minerals are an absolute necessity, since people become extremely depleted by the electromagnetic power of kundalini rising. For those who have severe symptoms such as seizures, paralysis, or tooth cracking, I advise the most aggressive forms of natural medicine, such as acupuncture, Rolfing, and chiropractic, and it is very important to rest, eat well, take vitamins, and consider the methods already covered for slowing kundalini rise.

With a blocked Earth chakra, psychotherapy is extremely useful in order to recall and process early environmental lack of bonding. You need to *experience and feel* your primal ungroundedness. Psychosynthesis and transactional analysis can be effective, but be sure your therapist is grounded and not working only from the mind. Past-life or rebirthing therapy is advised in some cases, because reexperiencing a past life when you *were* grounded will often open the Earth chakra. I have seen clients totally heal their crippling separations by means of past-life regression, a "re-membering" of the soul. Rebirthing is also a very powerful grounding tool, but it would be wise to first balance the body with massage and/or acupuncture. Rebirthing can be a "first birthing" for those who were not grounded as newborns, and it can be a very intense experience. Follow-up therapy is always necessary after rebirthing.

But perhaps most important is creating a relationship with the Earth herself. Although telluric force—such as the magnetic force of underground springs, ley lines, sacred places, and stones—is not officially recognized by conventional science, in sacred-site research telluric energy is another subtle energetic force that is real and can be felt. James Swan says in *Sacred Places,* "According to traditional culture wisdom, sacred places in nature are unique because they have a power which can more readily move us into spiritual consciousness."[3]

According to those who investigate telluric forces—Janet and Colin Bord, Lewis Spence, Francis Hitching, John Michell, and others—the Earth has power points that correspond to human acupuncture points, and both can be "needled" to activate energy flow. I am sure this is the reason for mysterious megalithic stone circles and monuments all over the planet. When ceremony, or even simple meditation, is done at sacred sites—such as Mayan temples or megalithic sites in the Aegean or British Isles—it activates or "needles" these power points, and the Earth energy flows in response.

This flow can in turn be utilized by people who are ungrounded to resonate with the pulse of the planet by simply being still and meditating at sacred sites. Use of these power spots is one of the ways that indigenous people ground infants. It is also why millions of people went to sacred sites during Harmonic Convergence in August 1987. A generation of ungrounded youth who felt like Cyclops born into an unwelcoming, overpopulated world felt mystically called to rediscover the powers of the Earth.

Walking barefoot in sand or dirt and imaging the powers of the Earth can also really help, as can sweats, dances, and meditation with teachers using Native American teachings. Balance yourself by means of swimming in a river, soaking in hot springs, or hugging a tree, as the ancient ones did. Lie on the Earth as if lying on your mother's belly at birth. Tune in to the powerful lower chakras in the root system of a giant tree, sense the heart beating in the trunk, and share the glorious reaching to the sky of the branches and leaves.

Let your energy flow—do not fear. When you let go, you can feel the Earth and synchronize with her energies. You can know what it is like to be wanted, to be a child who was asked to come here and create.

ROOT CHAKRA

As the *root chakra* opens, we are challenged to seek life without judgment, to simply enjoy—just what you might expect from the chakra in which we awaken our creativity and sexuality. Sexual energy must be released by humans, and full development of the energy of the total person comes with movement of kundalini energy through the body by means of sexual release and/or meditation techniques. Wilhelm Reich's orgone research—study of the human sexual force as the vitalizing principle—demonstrated in the 1950s that sexual release is as necessary for health as eating.

Sexuality is not just for procreation—it is a biological urge coiled in the body. It lies dormant, waiting to burst open to joyful communion with all life. This life force is always vibrating within electromagnetic fields that are continuously sparked by the electricity of sexual attraction. Many indigenous people are still able to resonate with the life force and generate electrical energy. I have observed Pueblo rain dances in which huge electrical storms were created on completely cloudless days to cover localized areas; within miles of the dance, there were still no clouds.

Unfortunately, this feeling of reciprocity with primal life forces has been nearly obliterated for many individuals because of lack of contact with raw nature. When this energy is internally repressed, it often externally manifests in excessive violence and abuse, much like an electrical storm, volcano, or hurricane in the atmosphere.

Paradoxically, those who are grounded but blocked in the root

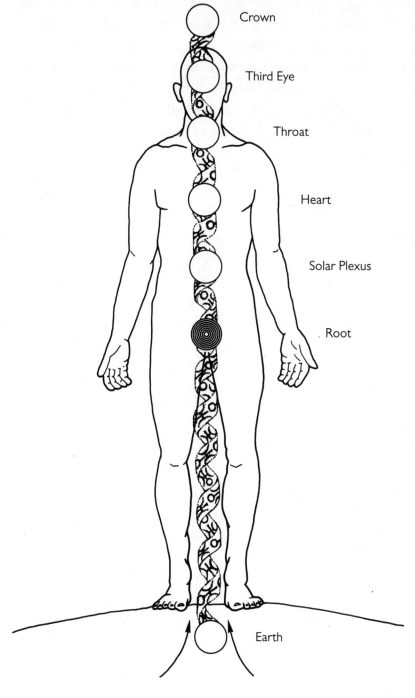

Figure 5.2. Root chakra

chakra often had very controlled and loving childhoods. Religious households are often very grounded, since such families tend to be more conservative and stay in one place for generations. But these parents tend to be sexually repressed themselves and project their own moral systems on their children, thinking, perhaps, that they are protecting them against danger. Conversely, a child may be sexually abused; in either case, the sexual center will shut down.

However this happens, children learn to control themselves based on a judgment that harm will result from sexual experience. Instead they need to learn inner self-control in the root chakra by means of a courageous exploration of sexuality while growing up. There is no reason that sexual development should be different from any other skill attained during the maturation process.

Those blocked in the root chakra are always sexually dysfunctional, whether it is obvious to the world or not. Marriages may hold together out of convenience, but a wife may be nonorgasmic and a husband may have intercourse quickly, just for relief like a teenage boy, or there may be almost no sex at all. Whatever the pattern, once midlife crisis comes, the tension builds dramatically.

Some people manage—at great cost—to appear to keep it all together. The frustrated wife, pent-up husband, or celibate may do everything possible to avoid the stress of releasing, since that would involve breaking through adeptly created patterns of repressed sexual response or opposing repressive rules superimposed on them by others who wish to control them. To avoid some nasty discovery, many intuit that it's just not worth it to mess around with sex or dig for too much self-knowledge.

But that's not the case with most people, at least not since the 1960s. As the energy of Uranus Opposition flows into their root chakras, many people separate from the moralistic reality around themselves. Those with a blocked root chakra avoid parents, spouses, and other judgmental people as much as possible during midlife crisis. People who are heavily invested in having them continue to be "good old Sue or Joe" get nervous around their inner urge to act out. Most of those blocked in the root chakra are invested in a lifestyle set up to avoid sex; at the same time, they feel a need to experience satisfying and pleasurable sexual feelings.

Nancy, for example, reported being unable to tolerate social functions and church activities that she used to enjoy. Not coincidentally, she also reported strong distaste for sex with her husband. Their sex life had always been just a necessary task, but now she longed for something more. She was spending a lot of time remembering being a teenager when there was the chance to do something risky.

Nancy had been promiscuous during her twenties. This is a common pattern in those with blocked root chakras because they experience a deep-seated separation between sex and love. They cannot tell whether someone pursuing them feels love, they have lots of sex without love, and then sex becomes a lonely act, while what they perceive as "love" is sexless. During midlife crisis, Nancy felt like reconnecting with an old boyfriend. The energy trying to move inside her made her feel like she had felt when she first attempted to have love and sex together.

Often in the late twentieth century, individuals who have become priests and nuns have done so partly to avoid confronting their own inner repressions. A very beautiful red-headed nun was having a relationship with a priest in another city who was always out on the lecture circuit. As far as I could guess, he probably had relationships with nuns in quite a few cities. The nun described the culmination of her buildup of energy during midlife crisis, generated by the fierce fires of repression, in this way:

> We had touched every part of each other's bodies, but he had not yet penetrated me. I had never had sex, although I did everything short of giving up my virginity before I entered the convent. The desire to be pierced built up as if it would burst my heart. During heavy petting, he finally reached the point where he could not stop himself in spite of my desire to remain pure, and yet we felt so guilty. So he brought out his Holy Communion Chalice, we celebrated the Mass together, and at the Consecration, he penetrated me as I felt ecstatic fusion with the cosmic dimension for the first time.

Juicy? This is a graphic example of how the root chakra opening can break the blocks of sexual repression.

This urge is a powerful one—the energy feels like a survival instinct to many blocked in the root chakra. At midlife, disturbingly, suddenly the body seems to be on fire with a quaking energy that has no outlet. This is similar to the pent-up feelings many of us felt in adolescence before actually experiencing sexual intimacy.

As during adolescence, many people fantasize intensely during midlife crisis. Some, like Nancy, yearn for a previous, more sexually active time, instead of the perfunctory physical contact necessary to keep a husband content and have children. Others explode their repression, and the twentieth century has seen a terrifying outbreak of violence and sexual abuse, partly caused by people trying to get beyond the repression of the Victorian era. On a more mundane level, many with a blocked root chakra seem to be wound up in a swirl of activities designed to keep them from being alone and facing themselves. Those who are sexually dysfunctional become irrational, very panicky, very likely to act out; yet for these eighteen months of Uranus Opposition, they have the greatest opportunity to access their sensuality. It is time to become vulnerable.

A central issue for those with a blocked root chakra is trust. Once the Earth chakra has opened and we have conquered our fear of life, we need to trust others so that we can surrender to sensuality. That means becoming comfortable with ourselves and being able to reveal ourselves to another without feeling like we will be invaded or judged.

Don had an especially difficult time trusting women. He told me that he had closed himself down at age 12 and had shut his parents out; whenever he had revealed anything about his feelings, they had used it against him or used the information to figure out what he was doing. Then he married a cold, manipulative woman who took advantage of his feelings to get what she wanted all the time. At midlife, he had a series of affairs just to see if he could feel anything within himself. Don began to feel a true closeness with another woman, and that was the end of a cold and loveless marriage.

At midlife, if you can totally trust just one other human, you will have begun to penetrate the repression that creates the block to sexual releasing. Our only access to the experience of trust is through other humans, and that experience may or may not be sexual. Do you trust anyone? Is there one person before whom you can be naked, emotionally and/or physically, knowing that he or she accepts you no matter what? Now is the time to stop spinning through the day like an idiot, stop fantasizing to the point of mindlessness, and realize you need to expose yourself to another human, be vulnerable, and just give in—*let go*.

As the kundalini energy rises, the extreme levels of sexual obsession, fantasizing, and acting out engendered by a blocked root chakra seem to force people to action. This is when counseling is needed, because taking action may often be the last thing one should do at this time. I advise all my clients not to divorce, move, or make major changes in their lives during midlife crisis. The more that people can keep their reality stable, not break away too quickly and intensely from emotional structures with which they have been living, the more they can avoid destroying access to the life systems that may be needed for growth.

One sure way to avoid transformation at midlife crisis is to create a flurry of distractions, such as building a new house and decorating, getting another job, moving to another city, or getting a divorce and fighting your family. Examining the inner issues will have been avoided the whole time! For example, rather than pursuing sensuality with her husband during midlife crisis, Nancy filed for divorce (against my advice) when Uranus came to its first opposition, was involved in costly legal entanglements throughout the whole transit, and then, as soon as the last opposition moved off, reconciled with her husband because of the children.

On a physical level, clearing this blockage involves dealing directly with the sexual energy, either through sexual relations or by means of other disciplines like the various yogic forms that work with tantra and kundalini in meditation. The energy needs to be moved through the root chakra one way or another, or else people become bitter, distrusting of life, angry, compulsive, and/or abusive years after their midlife crisis passes. For example, celibates seem to need meditation techniques for raising kundalini after age 40, since they are not involved in sexual partnership.

For those who have a sexual partner, now is the time to explore sex in a more creative way so as to find ways to break down repressive patterns. Experimentation with high-quality sexual films, literature, or devices may be useful. Sex therapy may be appropriate. For those who are partners with people blocked in the root chakra, take time with them, be loving and sensual, because now is the time for them to realize what life is all about, as they push out of one repressive pattern after another. Lots of talking about how you are feeling during sex also is very helpful. Take time together, such as long weekends away from the family, which may save a twenty-year marriage and prevent heartbreak for yet another generation of children.

Psychologically, past-life regression under hypnosis is fantastic for a blocked root chakra, because a past-life pattern of being sexually abused and/or abusing others is almost always found.[4] This is especially true for those who have suffered sexual abuse in their present lifetime. Many of my clients have spontaneously remembered the contents of early childhood abuse at midlife; even though readings in previous years had revealed signs of much abuse, they couldn't hear about the issue until they were ready to face it. It is obvious that they were armored against the contents of their own subconscious minds, which they successfully repressed until midlife. Recovering memories of prior events allows us to see how inner blocks relate to present blocks. It allows us to reexperience traumatic moments for the purpose of releasing repressive memories, thus helping us to clear the pain of abuse from our present lives. Even if what comes up during these sessions is not really the past, this type of therapy creates a *distance* from the traumatic contents that leaves us free to dissolve the blocks.

The resolution of a blocked sexual center is, as I said before, trust. The soul is always pained over abuse and the inability to be loving, and it begs us to see that disconnection. There is space for our wounds on this planet. Mother Earth does not reject our pain; she absorbs it so that we can be at peace again.

SOLAR PLEXUS CHAKRA

Nearly everyone except highly evolved masters of human consciousness has a blocked solar plexus chakra until midlife, since most people don't get or need much power until about then. Midlife is the time to take on power without abusing it. At this time, by means of a series of relational dramas, the solar plexus can be cleared and purified by assuming our personal integrity and ending all manipulation of others. The key to successful opening of the solar plexus is to find a way to take our power without harming other people, thus creating negative karma. Like love, power is unlimited, and only by holding it or trying to control another with it does it become destructive. The trick, scary though it may seem at times, is to freely offer power, not hold it or give it in a way that lacks integrity.

The solar plexus is the personal power center, the seat of the emotional body. From this chakra, we size up other people, and as it opens we become honest and discriminating. The more we are clear in the gut, the more easily we can see the truth or degree of manipulation in the motives and actions of others. As the solar plexus opens, it raises questions of what do we want to *get,* to *grasp,* and how do we feel in the *gut?* It is time to build our personal power without abusing others.

Outrageous dramas are created to better understand "power over" versus "taking on our own power." Individuals who have successfully taken on power always use it in league with others. In learning about taking on power, all power-abuse tendencies must be looked at, and they can be very subtle and graphic. These dramas are relational, meaning that the person who already has power may feel invaded by a person who envies that power. Those who feel powerless are naturally drawn to individuals who already have taken some power. When the solar plexus is blocked, people are either too defensive or deferential, or they are busy trying to control and abuse others.

A person tends to pair up with another who permits the drama to be played out. We see such dramas incessantly in the media, and such tabloids as the *National Enquirer* have become experts at showing us

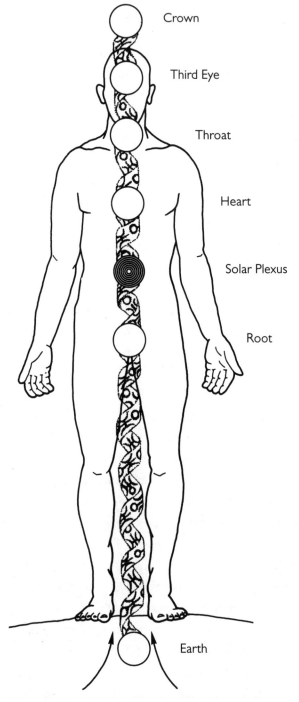

Figure 5.3. Solar plexus chakra

the abused/abuser paradigm. A deferential person might be involved with a control freak. It doesn't occur to the meek one to take care of him/herself. Meanwhile, the control freak, unable to believe that anyone could be such a wimp, pulls out the whip. Crack! The curtain is up for Act One. Seeing these dramas gives us opportunity at midlife to attain more sophistication and honesty in our relationships, so that we can handle authority with joy and integrity.

During midlife crisis there also are many frustrating encounters with others that involve dramas of "grasping and getting." As these are played out, we begin to develop discrimination about the intentions of others. Disturbances are felt in the gut that are caused by *projections*—energy invasions from others. Inevitably, somebody appears who creates a lot of stress and pain because he or she got right into our gut, totally penetrating our energy field. Maybe they want money, maybe they want sex, maybe they want to swindle us, maybe they want love. Whatever it is, instead of approaching us in a way that's safe and honest for us, they invade our boundaries. They seem to take whatever they want, even if it is under the ownership or control of another.

On the other hand, we may see something and envy it, and begin an overt or covert effort to grasp it and take it away from another. Envy surfaces now as we watch another person who has actualized our own desire. It reveals where our dissatisfactions lie. What is envied in another at midlife reveals that which is desired the most. This great teacher is activated during midlife because we feel urged to merge instead of being separate.

Identifying inner wishes by projection—seeing what we desire in someone else's lifestyle or possessions—triggers people into the creation of dramas that distract from the real issue at hand—taking our personal power so as to create the reality we desire using only our rightful resources to manifest our needs. It is not necessary to get the power by taking it from anyone else, but many people need to try that one for a while, until they learn that the source of power is within *the self*. Opening the solar plexus involves the use of discernment and discrimination. The more we can detach ourselves from the drama and observe our relations with others at midlife, the better.

I watched clients Shawn and Veronica, who were close friends as well as business associates, play out an incredible solar plexus chakra drama. In spite of their friendship, Veronica began to exhibit jealousy and envy over Shawn's professional and personal success. In an effort to salvage their professional relationship, Shawn ended their personal relationship. But that didn't stop Veronica's frustrations. Soon, she initiated a lawsuit against Shawn and the company for which she worked. As a result, both women got the chance to learn a great deal about clearing the solar plexus during a long, drawn-out battle, and the lawyers were smiling all the way to the bank. Planetary transits helped trigger various aspects of the power complex here. Shawn saw for the first time that the power she wielded often attracted envy and power attempts by others. Veronica had to struggle with the unsatisfying effects of her envy, since she lost the lawsuit. She had to come to grips with the fact that the only way she could have the reality she desired was not to take it from someone else, but to create it herself.

Midlife is the time to take on power and to observe carefully any power issues or personal desires coming forth during your first exact Uranus Opposition. Various kinds of power games going on can offer awareness on how to end the invasions and cut the projections from friends and associates. If you happen to be a leader and responsible for the fate of others, you may experience some invasions from those who envy you. It is possible to lead people without victimizing them, but this requires careful observation of the self in all your relationships.

Ask yourself, why do you want that? Ask yourself the following series of questions about your power:

- Have you always felt you had something big to do in life and now is the time? If you're so great, why aren't you doing exactly what you want right now? Why are people opposing you? Do you feel as vigorous as you think you should? How is your gut feeling?
- Are you planning on taking your power in the near future? Can you use it honestly, with integrity, and without damaging anyone

(including yourself) or anything? Remember that solar plexus complexes are about power and abuse. Who says you would not abuse others? How would you get the result you want with that power?

- Perhaps you are a teacher of some kind. Do you go out there just to get ego strokes and power from those who need to trust you, or do you go out to create and learn with every one of them? Can you freely offer your power, and can you tell whether those to whom you offer it will use it or abuse it?

- Are you a mother who has found her power raising a family? Do you bask in this blessed sharing and spread it as widely as possible? Or are you a tyrannical, avenging mother with your long nails in the backs of your children? Do you resent any of them? Do you wish they would obey you more? Do you resent the time they take from your life?

- Are you ready to admit that you have some enemies? Are they a teaching for you, or are you teaching them? Are your enemies your worthy opponents, or are you standing in your power and teaching them a lesson they came to you for? (Careful, the ego's need to identify, separate, and judge here can become a constriction.) Is that "other" your teacher? Or are you holding yourself back from the learning because of your judgments of being separate from these adversaries?

- Even if you are a fantastic boss, is your company polluting the Earth? Is there an employee to whom you have been unfair? Do you feel vigorous and creative as you work with your employees, or are you drained by them? Do you have stomachaches while running meetings? Do you ever find you hate the people who need you?

Watch out! For those of you who are playing "power over," remember that the humble servant always wins against the foolish master. You will be another master fooled by the humble servant.

Ted, age 40, was in a high position as a scientist in a laboratory working on radiation research when he dreamed he had a huge hole in his stomach. In my reading with him, he was able to begin looking at the environmental abuses he was in the midst of creating on his job, which resulted in his changing professions. Ordinarily, changing one's profession during midlife crisis is unwise, but Ted's profession was his problem. He also was such a prominent scientist that he had no difficulty getting an excellent job in another field, so for him, changing professions was in no way an avoidance of reality. From my experience, I believe that if he hadn't done so, he would have started developing a disease of the solar plexus organs. Ted knew that his dream of a hole in his middle was a big warning that he was afraid of something he was doing, and his terror of it probably saved his life. It is important to ask yourself questions at midlife with the deep intention of being honest about your answers.

On the physical level, this chakra is in the middle section of the body where the organs of digestion and elimination lie, so all the diseases and conditions of the solar plexus area need to be watched. What is going on in the bowels, liver, pancreas, and other related organs can be a great source of knowledge. It is a good idea to notice how your body feels, especially in the gut, when around other people. Shawn commented that her stomach always hurt when Veronica was around, and after that experience she learned to check her gut feelings in a working relationship.

Deep massage of the bowels and other central organs will speed up clearing in that area. One of my clients did a long past-life regression during which he took a long trip beginning in the pancreas and moving through much of the digestive system. As a result, he processed about twenty people he was involved with in various ways by digesting them all and then moving them out through the bowels! I thought this was really amazing though weird, but when I mentioned this to a few past-life regression therapists, they told me that this kind of session is a thrill because it means that the person is really doing his or her inner work.

The general advice for midlife-crisis therapy also applies to solar plexus clearing, as do various forms of warrior and initiatic teaching, leadership work, and goal setting. T'ai chi, for example, is an ancient mastery teaching that was created to help mature the solar plexus. Past-life regression is also extremely useful for opening a blocked solar plexus, with clients recalling absolutely incredible stories of violence and abuse under hypnosis. The media offers movies and videos that give people easy opportunities to play out all kinds of dramas forbidden in every-day life. Often we easily conclude that we'd actually rather not do this or that even if we were given the chance. The more we can move such power dramas into the realm of the imagination and off the street, the safer we will all be.

In the next chapter, we will investigate the opening of the heart and the upper chakras. As the solar plexus opens and integrity is established, the throat chakra refines. For example, Shawn's throat was blocked when she ran into Veronica. After clearing her solar plexus to a degree, she began to unblock her throat chakra, and, as a result, she became more adept at speaking her truth. I knew she had really made it when she told me about a lunch she had with a very pushy doctor selling her a proposal. It all sounded great, but she noticed that her bowels had turned to liquid while she was eating sushi. So she simply told him she wasn't interested in working with him, and he moved on to con some-body else.

The open solar plexus is alive with the greatness of self-expression and physical joy, and it seeks to create more and more energy. The clear solar plexus has integrity, and its carrier expresses Earth-shaking energy from the gut. With the hard work of the opening of the lower chakras accomplished, life becomes a fascinating journey into deep emotional response, clear verbal expression, psychic realms and the dreamtime, and, lastly, the spirit world.

SIX
Uranus and Enlightenment

....

The Upper Chakras

WITH THE OPENING of the heart and the upper chakras, we encounter consciousness-raising experiences that are more subtle and are deeply rewarding. However, after four hundred years of a left-brain, analytic mode of consciousness in the West, most people are not accustomed to subtle states of awareness. The upper chakras and the heart have a tremendous impact on ordinary reality, but most discussion of their impact on consciousness in Eastern sources, such as Buddhism, has been from a very spiritual and nonordinary viewpoint. To put it simplistically, Westerners have focused on practicality while inhabitants of the East have pursued spiritual awareness above all else. Therefore, the first approach to the upper chakras needs to be practical for primarily Western readers.

Much of what is known about opening the upper chakras, particularly the third eye and crown, comes from the wisdom of the East; it is very esoteric and may seem bizarre to readers who are unfamiliar with this material. But just as it has been a custom to go to church on Sunday for hundreds of years in many places in the West, opening the upper chakras or access points to subtle awareness has been a regular practice in the East. Meanwhile, even though these experiences—such as psychic communication, ecstatic spiritual visions, and channeling—are actually quite universal, they were almost never spoken about in Western cultures until recently. Often someone who had such experiences was a candidate for pickup by the men in white coats.

It is obvious to me that medieval saints and mystics were experiencing classic kundalini rising when they had visions. But this type of comparison between saintly states of consciousness and kundalini rising by Eastern mystics has been made only recently in theological schools such as Creation Spirituality, as developed by Matthew Fox. From my point of view, the ecstatic religious experiences of Shakers in the nineteenth century or speaking in tongues by Christian charismatics are clearly the same as the classic symptoms of kundalini rising.

There is little information in Eastern literature on the more ordinary aspects of the upper chakras, to be discussed in the following sections, except in Zen sources. From my own experience as well as from my research on the newly sighted planet, Chiron, I've realized that even the most esoteric and subtle states of human awareness can be easily comprehended with accessible examples drawn from real experiences. Now it is time to expand the definition of the human, because the planet is becoming global. West is meeting East, and the thousands of years of wisdom about the upper chakras hold incredible keys about subtle consciousness for the West. The pursuit of spirituality just in the monastery is over, and the time has come for us all to exist in states of ecstasy and bliss in ordinary reality.

HEART CHAKRA

Because the heart is both a cosmic center and an Earth center, since it resides in the middle of the body where the spiritual and physical unite, once it is open the full participation of the "higher self"—guiding soul—in our actions is ensured. And it opens once we have learned honesty and integrity through clearance of the solar plexus chakra, which allows *feelings to originate directly in the heart*. Before this time, feelings are actually coming from the lower chakras—the heart does not open if

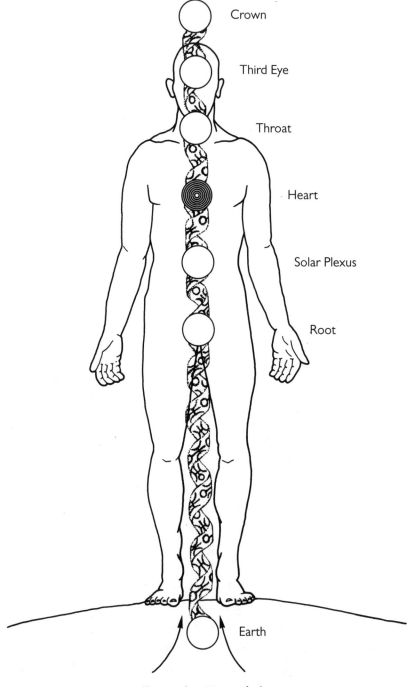

Figure 6.1. Heart chakra

one is lying to oneself or others, is manipulating or controlling others, or is separated from other people.

If we have been able to allow kundalini to rush upward from the Earth chakra (grounding), through the root chakra (trust), and through the solar plexus (power), then the energy begins to accelerate as the heart burns and purifies the last of our resistance once kundalini fire consumes the heart. This process imprints the spirit into every cell in our bodies. With the opening of the heart chakra, the telluric energy of the Earth actually can be felt sucking up through our lower bodies to reside in the heart center. The heart chakra opening is the signal of "radical embodiment"—the soul totally in the body—which is the most exquisite experience available on Earth. The integrity of a person with an open heart is always astounding.

The solar plexus and root chakras are the seats of present-life abuse complexes and past-life uncleared trauma, the contents of the *subconscious* mind. Those lower chakras, the primary location of physical response to life, purify if we can explore the subconscious. Then the location of "feeling response" moves into the heart, and we are able to feel more freely and to respond exactly in the moment. Since the solar plexus is the seat of emotional-body complexes that need to be cleared before power can be accessed, these complexes cloud an individual—and hence a relationship in which that individual is involved—until they are cleared. People with such uncleared sexual and solar plexus complexes respond strongly to pornography, abusive sexual practices, fantasy, and manipulative relationships. As the root and solar plexus chakras clear, the potential exists for relationships to be based cleanly in the heart for the first time.

The heart chakra is most intimately connected with relationship, for the issues of the heart—love, compassion, and dedication—are clearly those involving other beings. Like the root chakra, the heart chakra is experienced very physically, and it is possible to actually *feel* the heart opening at midlife as the kundalini energy flows in; many of my clients, for example, report a burning in their heart areas.

As the heart is first opening, boundary difficulties are often encountered due to the intense feelings that are beginning to flow out. One of my clients, Marilyn, was unable to be in crowds for months during her midlife crisis. She felt swirling energies flowing in and out of her heart that pierced her when she saw a lonely elderly person, an impoverished person, or an adorable baby. She would cry for no reason in the middle of the supermarket. Since the heart feels intensely, in a way that is similar to the root chakra melting during orgasm, the opening is very intense, and it is possible to work easily with it in a healing way by means of therapy and visualization.

Feelings are the only access to heart chakra blockage. Generally speaking, most women are not severely blocked in the heart because as girls they were allowed to exhibit their feelings—to laugh, cry, get mad, or be ecstatic without a reason. I don't suggest that they are allowed this freedom for their own good; in fact, they are often allowed this space because they are being ignored, except by other women. "It's just the way women are" is a common refrain that discounts the emotional processes of women. Women who are blocked in the heart tend to be very cruel and manipulative, but even then they do *feel* a lot. In my experience, it is men who are actually blocked in the feeling process itself.

Boys are taught that crying is sissy behavior, and they are heavily conditioned to show their feelings in certain situations only. For example, it is "acceptable" for a boy who under normal circumstances "shouldn't" ever cry to cry for up to a month if his mother dies. Of course, as the "boy" gets older, even that one month gets reduced, until as a grown man maybe all he'll do is take off from work for a couple of days.

Brian expressed this condition exquisitely during his midlife crisis. His relationship with his father had always been exceedingly restrained and frustrating, with little if any discussion of feelings. But when Brian's wife got pregnant, he got a letter from his father that caused tears to well up from the very center of his heart. For some reason, by his becoming a father, his own father was able to communicate with him *from the heart* for the first time. In the letter, his father said that in his day, men about to become fathers sat in the waiting room with a box of cigars, dressed in a good business suit. Still, the father wrote, when Brian's safe arrival was announced he went into the hospital bathroom and cried tears of joy. Brian now knew for the first time that his father had felt something when he was born!

The male who has been cultured to ignore feelings often finds himself at midlife earning a substantial living, but he is often overworked and freaks out every time another hair falls out. For my client Steve at age 40, the battle with the roll at the waist was a source of great concern, and the frequent passes from younger women at the office were a major buildup for his sagging ego.

Steve was bored with his wife, Barbara, and his children, and he found everything at home oppressive. His wife's mother always seemed to be observing him like an eagle, and he wondered why he hadn't ever noticed that she was such an old bag. Steve feared that Barbara might end up having the same bad habits and hideous scowl on her face as her mother did. Anything "old" he saw in the women around him made him feel like he was aging himself. He stewed around in the domestic swill feeling most unappreciated, and then one night, he couldn't get an erection! This disaster had been preceded by months of shaking, heart palpitations, sweating, heat flashes, and anxiety attacks, and when he couldn't get it up, he panicked.

As was the case with the lower chakras, clients who felt they understood exactly what was going on at this point have fared much better than the typical uninformed 40-year-old Western male. This temporary sexual dysfunction is the natural result of kundalini energy moving out of the root chakra, where males have learned to hold it for erections. Remember, the first feeling centers for most people are the root and solar plexus chakras. Faced with the need around age 14 to create an erection in order to perform sexually, males tend to activate the root chakra for this performance need. They also activate the solar plexus chakra to create erections; this is why fantasy can activate the penis. Unfortunately, this mechanism is also the source of rape—sex used for violence—since the solar plexus chakra is the seat of anger and frustration, which can erupt into violence.

Thus, at midlife, as the heart becomes the feeling locus, it is natural that the penis can become initially less responsive. But when the feelings come from the heart sourced in the feet, genitals, and gut—that is, once the energy has reorganized—responsiveness returns, even more enhanced as a total-body reaction. This pattern of mild to severe impotency is reported by only about half of my male clients—possibly some of the others just cannot handle talking about such an intimate subject or possibly quite a few men just do not lose erectile powers as the energy is rising. *All* male clients, however, report a feeling of more sexual energy in the whole body after about age 42.

For women reading this book who have a husband or lover experiencing midlife crisis, you might try getting the exact timing of his Uranus Opposition by consulting the tables at the end of this book and then explaining the paradigm to him. Everyone is relieved by the insight that *a process is going on*—as opposed to a seemingly isolated event—and they are even more relieved to find out it has an end.

A few years ago, I counseled a 39-year-old man from Texas who had a wife and three children whom he adored. He was so distraught about his "failing manhood" that he was contemplating an affair. When I described how the male physical body readjusts energy during midlife crisis, he relaxed and quit worrying so much—in fact, he was so relieved that he tried to get me to accept a thousand-dollar bill!

This readjustment does not have to result in tragedy; it will be over soon enough, and most men at midlife do not really want to have an affair at all. Rather, they want to understand what is happening to them, and they sense that they need to address major inner issues. *Men truly do sense, as midlife crisis approaches, that they cannot continue to ignore inner urgency.* The tension is often so little understood and the anxiety so high, however, that the result is an affair. The family responds with fear and low self-esteem, and the wife may even seek to control the "wild and woolly male stag," which is the worst possible reaction since all he is trying to do is to *feel* in a new way.

Since midlife crisis is a process that ideally results in a person's learning to seek life energy over giving in to deathly tendencies, it is an aging crisis, and keeping parents at a distance during this time is almost a necessity for some couples. It is better to face at a less person-ally volatile time the fact that we all learn much about the aging pro-cess by observing the experiences of our parents. It is very important for couples to rekindle romance during midlife crisis and avoid having family needs destroy their love affair. Parents and children are the win-ners when a marriage survives.

Let's get back to Steve. . . . Being unaware of the cause of his low-ered sexual interest, he immediately signed up for an aerobics class, got some new clothes, and bought a two-seater red sports car, which his teenage son constantly tried to borrow for dates! His communications with Barbara were at an all-time low, and she was afraid he was having an affair. She bought ladies' magazines and filled out questionnaires on how to identify the sure signs of a husband's affair. What no one did was ask Steve what he was *feeling*.

Given the cultural bias against men integrating their female sides, it's amazing that men are ever able to discover how to feel from their hearts. Before trying this, my advice to men at midlife crisis is to get a physical. If you are a man who has been plagued with extremely locked-in feelings, the rushing electromagnetic flow of the heart opening *can* trigger heart trouble at midlife. So take a moment to breathe, and then read on.

The statistics show that heart attacks increase markedly between ages 38 and 44, especially for men. If minor heart weakness is detected, it is important to slow down, walk, swim, pay attention to your breath, lose weight gradually, drink less, and do acupuncture. If major heart weakness is detected, be sure you are monitored regularly by a physician. Undertaking a demanding aerobics schedule like Steve did could be life threatening. If you have gotten a physical and your heart and circulatory system are healthy, then when you experience angina or fluttering in the heart as the kundalini energy rises, you won't necessarily go running off to the emergency room. Or you may run to the emergency room the first time it happens, but you may find that your understanding about the subtle-energy shift going on will allow you to avoid a whole lot of expensive and potentially dangerous testing.

At this time in their lives, men are getting older and are often wondering if they've lived and felt enough in the midst of a culture that devalues true feeling for others, meaningful work, and deep spiritual seeking. Now is the time to take a long trip alone or with your wife or lover, and allow yourself to think deeply about your whole life. It is a good time to reconnect with a distant aging parent and join a men's group. If there is sexual tension in your marriage, going camping with one of your children or with a close friend may help to relieve it. Seeing an old friend or returning to your childhood home may help you get in touch with memories that trigger old feelings that were left behind as you rushed along through life.

Jungian psychoanalysis, past-life regression, and encounter therapy are useful tools to help you open your heart. The more you can feel intensely, the better, because once the energy really flows through your solar plexus and heart, you will spontaneously process childhood trauma and past-life issues locked in the lower chakras. Getting a dog at midlife crisis can be a fantastic heart opener for men, because many men felt love in their hearts for their dogs when they were children; having another dog to love now can pierce the heart to an amazing degree. Most importantly, it is time to cry and allow yourself to enjoy all of your new feelings. Tears release the heart and reenergize it, and the extra water flowing in the body keeps the heart cool enough so it can process the spiritual fire.

You may find yourself receiving sudden new, creative insights; acute feelings about nature; or religious or mystical ideas. You are on the verge of a whole new life if you can just let go and allow the energy to course through your body without resistance. After years of control, *now it is time to let go.* It is worthwhile to negotiate this crisis with awareness; the rewards for feeling from the heart are expansiveness, freedom from ethical dilemmas, and freedom from emotional murkiness.

Pay attention to the love you are receiving from those around you. In *Quantum Healing,* Dr. Deepak Chopra makes a profound comment about the need for men to have love in their lives as protection against heart disease.

A study with adult male victims of heart attacks showed that the most significant factor in their recovery—meaning whether they lived or died—was not anything to do with diet, exercise, smoking, or the will to live. The men who lived felt that their wives loved them, while those who felt unloved tended not to survive; no other correlation the researchers could find was so strong.[1]

If you are the wife or lover of a man in midlife crisis, you have much to gain at this point if you can attain the ability to trust, maintain self-esteem, and support your man's doing therapeutic work. Assuming you are somewhat close in age and thus are both experiencing midlife crisis at the same time, your own issue now may be to learn to really take on your own power. What you need for yourself is often what will help your partner's critical passage, for a much more free and spontaneous bonding is available now through realizing you really can *trust* your partner without always needing to control him. In Steve's case, ultimately, it turned out that his wife did love him very much, and she was able to work with him in a positive way. A new and deeper relationship is not an uncommon result for partners of men with blocked heart chakras, when the woman genuinely loves the man and helps him through this critical passage into a mature and loving marriage.

Barbara watched Steve for a few weeks and concluded he was not having an affair, even though her mother was sure he was. She realized (accurately) that he was having an aging crisis, and she supported his attention to appearance and health by going shopping with him and finding him a few sexy shirts herself. She was marking him, and subconsciously he was getting the message that he was her territory. She bought him a decorative ring. She fought to keep the teenage son away from the red sports car, and she went for rides with Steve. They even went cruising one night and played their favorite songs on tape.

She came to me for a reading at this point, and I loved her extreme alertness, which was being activated by her own midlife issues. In Barbara's case, her low self-esteem from childhood, when her father strayed occasionally from her mother, had caused her to always fear that she might eventually lose her own man. Now, faced with this danger, she discovered a great jungle cat within herself, and she allowed this inner cat the opportunity to teach her a new dimension of femininity. She realized that instinctually she knew how to protect her territory. I suggested she still watch the women around Steve like a hawk and be sure that he knew he was her territory while he sought his new identity.

The "other woman" seems to be magnetized to men going through midlife crisis. She senses his vulnerability at this time in his life, and often such men carry substantial incomes, making them a good target. Or she may just want to toy with him: his marital status means he is not easily available, and he could be just fun with no commitment. If Steve were to fall into such a trap, however, his feeling center would probably plunge back down into the lower chakras and he would lose this chance to open his heart!

Barbara really loved Steve. She had lived with him for years and had given birth to his children, and here she was right in the midst of midlife crisis, too! Like Artemis, huntress of the forest, she defended her territory by supporting Steve's needs, which were really her own needs, since she needed to open her throat chakra—integrate the inner male—which we will see in a moment is the work for most women at midlife crisis. I noted in my reading with her that she could have what every woman says she wants but often does not fight for: a sensitive husband. She built up his self-esteem at home. They even had lots of fun attending Jungian lectures and workshops on anima/animus, which emphasized integration of the *inner male* for women and integration of the *inner female* for men.

Many good things can come to women as a result of their partners' heart openings. Up to midlife, males find that their sexuality is strongly sourced in the root and solar plexus chakras. Since the issue of the root chakra is sensuality, males tend to want to "possess" their wives in order to maintain a constant sex life. This possessiveness inhibits deep relating and tends to base a great deal of the marriage on separation and distrust. However, for a healthy relationship, sensuality cannot be contained—it must simply be released, which is what creates merging.

This raises a parallel issue: what about the woman who is tempted to have an affair during midlife crisis? Since her need is to develop her inner male by opening the throat chakra, she will be tempted to find a lover if she is blocked from learning how to express her most important needs. As previously stated, midlife crisis for women tends to be less of a sexual crisis than it is for men. But a woman who is repressed at this time will naturally seek a lover, often younger, who is genuinely interested in her emerging power and self-expression.

If ever there is a time for a person to be nonjudgmental about infidelity, it is now. If your partner has an affair, it may not be because he or she doesn't love you. For a man, this behavior is more likely sourced in his irrational *fears about potency,* a male issue that is as major as *fertility* is for the female. For a woman, this behavior is more likely caused by her desperation about *feeling like she is not being heard or understood.* Take time with each other now; listen to each other, and do everything you can to discover new areas of feeling and sharing with each other.

Be cautious about sexual needs, particularly during the three hits of Uranus Opposition. (See the tables at the back of the book for the exact dates.) This is a very tricky passage in marriages, especially in very passionate ones. The husband may have adored his wife primarily as *a possessed sexual object,* but now this love must broaden and deepen. And if she is in the midst of midlife crisis, too, her need to be recognized for who she really is will cause her to hate his possessiveness. Or her own need to be heard will clash with his need to find a new feeling process. Jungian analysts tend to be very wise and sophisticated about the fundamental male/female crisis at midlife—integration of the opposite gender polarity. Seeking the help of a Jungian counselor to deal with feelings of anger and betrayal at this time has saved many relationships.

At midlife, we are each integrating the opposite sex: men finding the *inner female* and women the *inner male*. For men, the process involves realizing that their inner female is a great gift available from their mothers, lovers, wives, and daughters; it is softness. Gay men and lesbians also need to integrate the opposite polarity, and true and deep friendships with people of the opposite sex are useful at midlife to resolve tricky gender-polarity issues.

For women, at first, integrating the opposite sex is potentially more complex than the male integration of the female. After thousands of years of patriarchal culture, most women are still experiencing much denigration of their potential power from events with their fathers, brothers, and male authority figures, and the inner male in women is charged with negativity. At this time in patriarchal cultures, female anger against the male does not tend to manifest on the outside. The angry inner male resides trapped and unseen in the solar plexus and throat of women, and it must be cleared during midlife crisis. This is why women need to *do something "out there."* This common female crisis—throat chakra opening along with huge solar plexus release—will not resolve unless the primal anger against the female condition is released. Let us focus on women next in order to understand how the opening of the throat chakra manifests.

THROAT CHAKRA

Opening the throat chakra is a very tricky process. Patriarchal authority conspires to keep it blocked, since people with open throat chakras cannot be controlled. Our inner memory banks are loaded with lifetimes in which we were hung or strangled for fighting for something we believed in, and our schools and workplaces are society's training programs to keep us from saying what we really believe. However, the opening of our hearts, which represent honesty and integrity, galvanizes us into becoming people of courage who then have the power to open our throats. The heart is the bridge between sky and Earth, between where we came from and where we live now. The resolution of the inner-male conflict—the rescripting of the original Uranus/Gaia struggle—could eliminate the looming and separate Father/Sky god as a source of inner fear and limitation. And this conflict—our individual conflict with our own inner male—is at the source of any throat chakra blockage we may experience.

In fact, *all* males and females have been fathered by males, and it is useless to hate our progenitors—our "seed source." Men as well as women have difficulty with the inner male—they have been just as abused by patriarchy as females. The male has usually played the role of oppressor, the one who has more voice, while the female has been the one oppressed, but both have lived in this battleground of self-limiting roles. As this difficulty clears on universal and personal levels simultaneously, we are able to see what we have lost, in terms of sensuality and freedom, to patriarchy.

For both sexes the throat opening follows right after the heart opening. However, most women feel as if an inner roadblock has been constructed right in their throats. As the throat begins to release, memories of previous blocking tend to cause a great deal of constriction to well up. After thousands of years of suppression of the Goddess—who represents the female with an open throat—blockage is at a very intense level. Women actually feel they will die if they express their real truth, creating an intense rage and hatred for the source of that suppression—the inner male. Ask yourself, as a woman at midlife, are you finding yourself incredibly angry at your father and husband? Do you resent your sons? Has your whole life been determined by where *he* needs to be or go, which leaves you adjusting to a community that you might not like?

Gail had a husband who wanted to live out in the country so as to separate work from home. Thus, he commuted a long distance each day and didn't get home until the kids were in bed. Gail was bored and isolated, and she thought she would throw up if she spent one more morning with another housewife talking about childbirth or what the pediatrician said at the last appointment. She felt she had nothing intelligent to say to her husband when he came home at night.

Gail started thinking that she hated her life, and it seemed to her

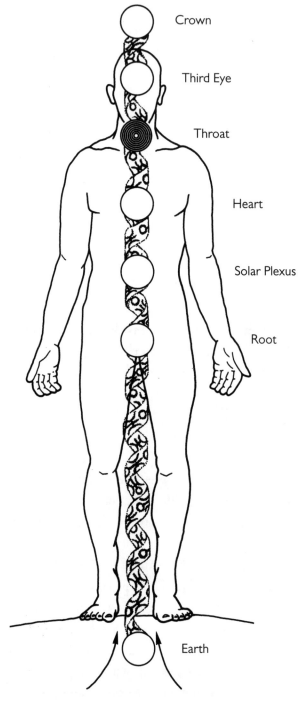

Figure 6.2. Throat chakra

that all could have been better if she'd lived her life the way she had secretly wanted to. She'd had to deal first with her father, then her husband, now her sons. They'd all kept her from following her own desires.

On the opposite extreme was Martha, a working woman not getting paid as much as the men around her, who were often less efficient. She had never married because she had wanted to succeed in a career, and now that she was getting older, she found she was going out less and less. A few years back she'd had an affair with a married man, who eventually had gone back to his wife. Then one day she looked at "anyman" in the office and felt utter contempt. She felt hot red anger in her gut; she didn't even know the guy's name, but she thought, "What a slimeball!" She stopped herself, wondering why such thoughts were in her mind. She wondered if she hated all men.

What Martha hated was her own inner male, which she had never acknowledged. It was holding all the expressive energy she'd never been allowed to explore. To clear this hotbed of ill-defined judgments and blocked desires, she had to offer her inner male the opportunity to teach her about its needs. If we hate men, we hate our own inner male, and we will always be repressed by any vestiges of self-hatred in ourselves. The only way to make peace with the inner male is to honor its needs. We must take on our power now, at all costs, and this need is the major work for women at midlife.

Martha needed to look at every aspect of her life to see if somebody else was preventing her from doing something. The facts were that she could change *herself* but not necessarily her *situation*. Martha needed to stop believing she was earning less because of female oppression and to start demanding, from a place of self-confidence and not from anger, what she felt she was worth. She had to make peace with her situation, to awaken her inner male and change it, since her repressed anger was as much the cause of her limitations as what others imposed upon her.

Gail needed to negotiate with her husband to move to another location, or she needed to accept that she, too, had chosen the country lifestyle. She had felt like nobody had asked her what she wanted, but she started to see that she had only begun to get a sense of what she wanted at midlife! I advised her to get involved in some community projects and to take a public-speaking course. She became a leader in a parent's group and was to give the opening address for a school Christmas play. Luckily, I was able to attend. Gail stood at the podium as if she was addressing the U.S. Senate; her husband was amazed at her, and I finally saw how important even small community roles can be for opening the throat. Gail felt terrific! In many cases we can initially change only *ourselves* and not other people or systems; the potential power to change outside reality usually comes after major changes in the self first.

Socially acceptable fields of expression have been determined by the patriarchy, and for expressing with the throat, male culture has created work, sports, bars, clubs, and the military. However, the universe of the patriarchy is not basically relevant to females. Basic skills of discourse are not based on the universe of the woman, which revolves around birthing, sensuality, timelessness, play, and creativity. Yet it is not normal for any reality to be based on half the human, and this distortion comes to a massive peak at midlife for both men and women.

Whether you are a man or a woman, do you feel from your place of *anima* that if you really expressed what you want, you'd be ridiculed, deserted, beaten? Do you carry around the feeling that your world would crash in if you stood up and screamed, "But I want it this way!!!" Have you felt like running away—just getting in the car and driving forever? Do you feel like your secret sense of self is absolutely irrelevant, and if you disappeared tomorrow it would make no difference? Have you been stewing for years on a very great and important creation for the world, and if you managed to get even one word out about it, you were greeted with "Prove it!" or "Why can't you explain yourself in a way that can be understood?" or "Be logical!" or "Why do you have to talk in such an irritating voice?" or "What are your credentials?" or "Why do you have to argue about everything?" or "Don't you see how stupid you sound?" This frustration often results in extraordinary creations, which if not encouraged can result in damage to a person's spirit.

Just before her fortieth birthday, Annabelle spent six months making huge sculptures out of mud brick that were like the great water storage pots of ancient Sumeria, Egypt, Greece, India, and Africa. While she was doing this, her friends and family were secretly laughing at her behind her back. She, however, was oblivious, lost in another world, as the pots formed out of her inner images of the primordial ocean, the cycles of the Moon, and mountains becoming valleys by means of volcanoes and earthquakes. When they were finished, she named them "Containers of Time," and she planned to invite many people to see this exhibition in her backyard. Her husband, however, felt he had humored her long enough and let her know that everyone would think she'd lost her mind.

Three years later, a few neighbors wondered why Annabelle muttered to herself a lot and had a vacant stare in her eyes. Most of them were happy when the rain and snow melted her crazy pots back into the soil, because they had bothered everybody. Meanwhile, another great expression of the essential female—creating without a "why"—was lost. I had watched the pots form, and I thought a lot about how Annabelle's work had been greater than every single man-hour spent making bombs nearby in Los Alamos, New Mexico.

Husbands and lovers, midlife crisis is a very dangerous time for your partner, and you must realize what a panic she is in. She has been blocked in saying what she has wanted for forty years, and now the energy in her throat is choking her. Give her the space to speak her piece. Of course, some males are also very blocked in the throat, but most men find it hard to imagine the force of the panic that builds in a woman. An apt analogy is that of the guillotine. The woman feels as if she has the hangman's noose around her neck, and she is about to be pushed off the chair holding her. She feels as if she will die if she can't express herself.

This woman in midlife crisis needs time to be alone to find herself; things she has to do must be cut down to a bare minimum, which may even include having sex with her spouse or lover. She may need to go to workshops, travel, or make new friends. The most important thing now is to *listen* to her, for she feels like nobody can hear her, and she's scared to death. She feels like she will die if she utters one more word that is not heard. Worse than that, she feels that if you knew her secret self, you would absolutely reject her as if she were a pariah.

As the woman in your life is going through this period, remember that it is the *process* of the throat chakra—using essential communication skills—that has been blocked. Just as the feeling process has been discouraged for men, the essential, operative, expressive skills of the throat have been stifled for women. For example, it has been less than a hundred years since women have been "allowed" to vote. Deep inside, women feel that what freedom they do have is being allowed by men. And in the contemporary scene of rampant rape and physical abuse of women, no woman can be sure that any freedom she has will be permanently "allowed."

Men, can you remember when your mother felt like she just could not express herself, your father got violent with her, and you weren't even allowed to cry for her? Motivate yourself to help your wife, because this conflict becomes insidious and destructive in couples who have stayed together and do not resolve it. On the other hand, as we'll see in the next chapter, a fully open throat accesses creativity, which is the doorway to the secret self for both men and women. A man who supports his wife or lover through this passage will probably gain her support for accessing his own creativity in his mid-forties, when the more subtle levels of the throat chakra opening can occur for men and women.

If a woman can find her purpose and learn to articulate it at midlife, she will have years of meaningful work ahead of her, as this crisis accelerates a renewal of energy. As hard as it is for her spouse or lover to free her, he needs to go ahead and do so—totally. She will return to her nest later, hopefully, with all the skills and powers of an open throat chakra. Be patient.

In one family with three children I counseled quite a few years ago, the mother, Nancy, walked out and literally disappeared at Uranus Opposition. She called them all at one point to say she was alive and working, and that she would return when she knew who she was! She returned a year later. Somehow her husband understood, because he knew she had to escape him to grow, and they are still a family six years later.

But, men, what about *your* secret self? What about that creative universe in you that has been even *more* suppressed than for women? Since most forms of creative expression have largely been thought to be a waste of time in Western culture, women's activities have been seen as more "creative," while men have been encouraged to pursue activities that have been deemed more "important." Where has your creativity been blocked? How can you express it?

All clients with throat chakra blockage report continual sore throats, neck locking and stiffness, ringing in the ears, breathing problems, and speech difficulties. Again, such symptoms are often more intense for women, since men break through some of the communication blocks by means of their jobs and/or education. Rolfing, neck and breathing exercises, public speaking, and simply expressing your truth can be very helpful. An open throat affords deep breathing, effective communication, and expression of your purpose.

Midlife is also a time for more men and women to move through blockage in the third eye, which rules information gathering on a very subtle level. This level of opening is rapidly becoming a *survival skill,* as people begin to communicate with more sophistication. So let us examine the first stages of opening the third eye.

THE THIRD EYE

Using the "third eye," centered in the forehead, we can see the nonphysical. Intuition, dreaming, out-of-body sight, magical awareness—all of these are the province of this sixth chakra, which rules the "sixth sense." With the third eye we can locate ourselves in nonsolid realms— other dimensions such as the "dreamtime," where we can travel into times and places outside of our ordinary reality, a state of consciousness where we can meet with people who have died but are still alive for us in spirit. These are realms that are not easily accessible during the day; however, these realms do exist simultaneously with the solid dimension.

Such movies as *Ghost* and *Field of Dreams* help us accept these other dimensions. The development of the third eye is very subtle, but the ability to access dreams, intuition, and invisible realms is becoming an essential skill as we become more crowded and "aware" on the planet, making the ordinary daytime reality too constricting for our minds and imagination.

Males and females are equally adept with the third eye. We say, "Women have better intuition," but this statement is a profound cultural devaluation of male skills, which are in fact no different. Men have tended to discount a mother's "sight," which causes her to rush to the aid of her endangered child without "seeing" the danger. "Women's intuition," they chuckle. Ha! ha! However, it is time for men to stop thinking it is silly to be psychic and to begin developing their own intuitive skills, which will open new avenues for the world besides going to war and conquering the environment.

The open third eye allows access to genius, something that men greatly value. Yet they lose 90 percent of their potential genius by devaluing and ignoring its source: the knowledge obtained in dreams and/or nonordinary insights. Most of what Einstein invented came through explosive insights, and then he later developed the scientific proofs for what he'd already seen. We should be studying the *process* by which Einstein thought instead of mastering his *proofs*. Too much left-brain education blocks access to complete knowledge, and virtually no scientists have been trained in nonordinary access to insight except in the former Soviet Union.

So how can we sharpen access to dreams, insight, and intuition? The easiest way is to think of the third eye as being similar to our physical eyes, which perceive the *physical* dimension. We value clear sight close up or at a distance, and the third eye is essentially the same faculty, except that it allows us vision into the nonphysical realm.

Opening the third eye is lots of fun and very simple; it is the same training process as that for accessing genius and intuition. First, take careful note when any unusual thought or awareness comes in a dream or during daydreams; notice whether it seems "big." Write it down,

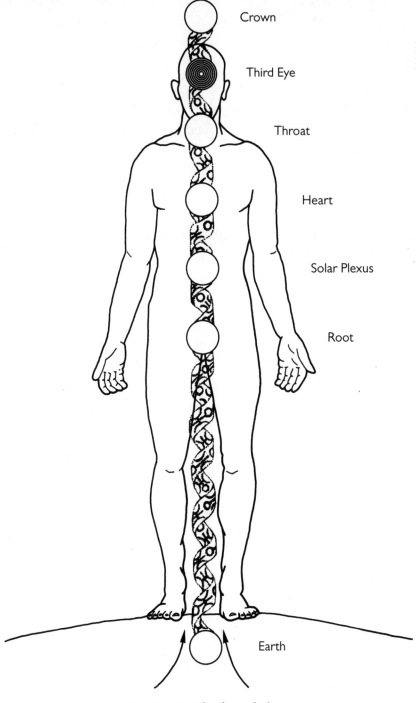

Figure 6.3. Third eye chakra

and wait for events in the "real world" to happen that will decode this insight. This is the beginning of access to the constant stream of inner consciousness that flows within all beings and is the same as the synchronicity of the universe.

Second, pay attention to a piece of information coming from another person, the media, or some odd event that seems similar to what was first received in your dream or mind. Now it is time to deepen your knowledge about something that is obviously significant. Allow the importance, ramifications, or future implications of what has been seen to sink in. Finally, as life experiences line up behind your vision, acknowledge the insight, and remember that it first came in your dream or mind. In other words, *you* created the event.

Another client, Alicia, told me a strange and wonderful story three years ago that illustrates this process. She dreamed of a very handsome man wearing a white robe who walked over a hill and into her arms. Since she was unmarried at the time and searching for a husband, the dream had a powerful effect on her. She was convinced there was someone out there looking for her. A week later, a poster of a town in New England—Putney, Vermont—caught her eye in a store because the hills around the town reminded her of her dreamscape. She was ready to leave and pay no attention, but she overheard a couple talking about a magical meeting between themselves that gave her chills. She looked again at the poster of Putney, this time more carefully, and then she walked out into a crowd watching two dogs mating!

During the next year, Alicia often thought of her dream, and her ordinary life seemed to lose more and more meaning. She didn't put as much energy into her job as before, and she made no significant friends. In June, she decided to get into her car and *move* to Putney, which she did. For a year, she had no idea why she was there. Then she went to a party and saw a man. She got dizzy when she looked at him; he seemed larger than life and then seemed to recede into the background. She felt crazy and followed the man around the party, but he didn't notice her.

She found herself doing something totally out of character: she told a friend she wanted to meet this man. A little later, she realized that he was sitting behind her while she was in a conversation, and she dared to turn around and look at him. They began to talk, and she was swept into the same tunnel effect she had felt when she first saw him. A half hour after, he said, "Do you realize we will know each other for the rest of our lives?"

Alicia was amazed to find out that just a week before, this man had also been drawn to Putney without knowing why. For years he had seen constant flashes of a dark-haired woman, whom he knew would be his true mate. At the same time two years earlier as Alicia had had her dream, he had ended a serious relationship, and since then he had been searching for "his wife" everywhere. He could actually sense her calling. Now he had met Alicia, who looked like the woman of his vision.

These two people's energies had somehow connected in the non-solid realm, and who knows how it works? The "other side" seems to have no time, place, or distance limitations, and meaningful connections can be made in the nonphysical faster and with less blockage than in our normal third-dimensional world. Alicia and her friend were richly rewarded for not shutting off the knowledge of the third eye. They got married, and as of this time they continue to have a wonderful relationship.

CROWN CHAKRA

Once the third eye is open, powerful light energy opens the crown chakra above the head. With this opening, electromagnetic energy that has risen in the body shoots out above the body and communes with spiritual forces and other dimensions that are not verifiable or visible in the ordinary sense in this physical realm. Although many people concur that there is some reality to nonphysical realms, centuries of "holy wars" right down to those in the present-day Middle East remind us that there is often disagreement to the point of death about exactly what the spiritual world is and how we should relate to it. Meanwhile, history shows us that questions about God, spirits, other dimensions, or other worlds are timeless and ceaseless. But what causes such intense spiritual seeking among people? The answer is, *they need to get high.*

What I mean by "getting high" is when, scientifically, an experience occurs that triggers brain receptors that cause a person to feel pleasure. Like responses in the root and heart chakras, those in the brain are very electrical. The human experiences that cause us both the most pain and the greatest ecstasy are sex, love, and religion. From this perspective, getting high is the result of kundalini energy flowing into the brain and causing a *brain orgasm.* After millions of years of human evolution, we know that the human will incessantly seek these peak experiences, so why not get smart about this basic drive?

Given the intensity of getting high, it's not surprising that our search for this intensity is often seen as addictive and completely irrational. But why do humans get hooked on destructive behavioral patterns that they would rather die with than give up? *Because we become addicted to the first experience we have of real orgasm, profound love, or ecstatic spirit, whether triggered naturally and spontaneously or by a substance that can enslave us instead of free us.* The ghetto kid first gets high on cocaine instead of on Beethoven or a great book. The yuppie Wall Street commodities trader disciplines him or herself all the way through prep school and Yale or Harvard, only searches for a good time when the optimal job has finally been secured, and then gets hooked on cocaine because it is the first big pleasure rush in the brain. In both cases, such individuals would be less prone to substance addiction if they had first gotten "high" from art, intense feelings of love, or a mystical experience.

The most important concern with opening the crown chakra is to become conscious of how we want to first imprint such powerful energies. The ghetto kid or Wall Street yuppie who gets addicted to coke is, like every other person walking the planet, a human being who is seeking spirit and ecstasy. We are living in an age of profound disconnection from spirit, and it is my contention that this split is what creates billions of abused and substance-addicted people. *Only full recognition of spiritual need will generate ways to provide brain orgasms that*

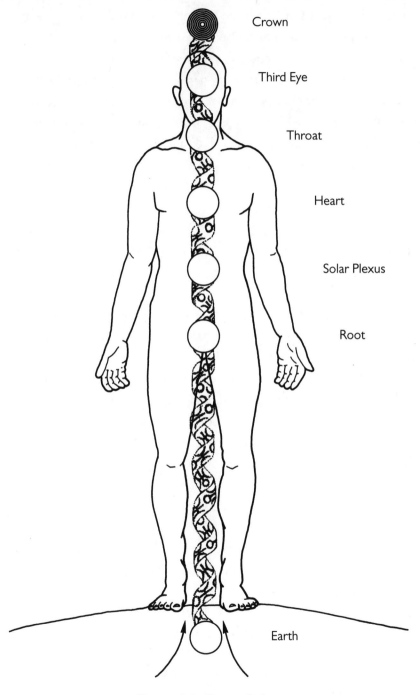

Figure 6.4. Crown chakra

are nondestructive. We must feed the spirit as well as the hungry. We must create a world in which the first experiences of opening the brain receptors are experiences of fusion with other realms that do not involve violence, abuse, and addiction to substances.

During your Uranus Opposition, you need only to clarify the first level of crown chakra opening—recognizing the universal search for spirit—to connect with the center of all realities. The more constant and intense work with the crown chakra will come later, around age 50, and is discussed later in the book.

TWO BY TWO

Couples who are two years or less apart in age experience major life transits together. This pattern is exceedingly stressful and is greatly helped by good counseling. However, such couples also have potential for an extraordinary level of closeness if they can stay together during the key life passages. Like schoolmates who had the same teachers and shared the same life experiences, they have a living knowingness of each other.

So what happens in a sexual relationship at midlife crisis as the male with a blocked heart chakra has alternating phases of sexual dysfunction mixed with intense needs for lots of sex, while the female with blockage in the throat needs lots of alone time while also needing to break through sexual inhibitions? The solution is to only have sex when both are deeply drawn to each other. This is a very hard goal to attain unless there is extremely sensitive and constant communication. Frequency of sexual intercourse may lessen considerably, or the patterns may become erratic. There may be great anxiety in the relationship since the man is quietly afraid of his woman's need for time alone, and the woman is afraid her man will stray.

But armed with knowledge about the potential growth that awaits them as well as the natural course of action it may take, the couple can weather the strain of simultaneous midlife crisis. No matter how often they have sex, they must attempt to learn how to unite more meaningfully by attaining a new level of consciousness about the feelings of their partner. Couples sharing midlife crises can often see that they are in the midst of an exquisite sexual initiation, since sexuality and kundalini rising are vehicles for personal transformation.

As kundalini rising charges through all seven chakras at the first hit of Uranus Opposition, the crown chakra penetration means there is a new level of access to spiritual merging, although this knowing is usually unconscious. Some clients have told me that they sense they are in the midst of such a great mystery that verbalizing about this spiritual force is difficult.

This merging takes partners beyond the polarity struggle of the 1st and 7th houses—self and other—since contact with spirit breaks down egoistic separation. By means of opening their third eyes, the two can see the more subtle levels of their union, and their throat chakras open so they can begin to express how miraculous their life is together. Then their hearts become flooded with all the power of their many years of sharing life. In the solar plexus, they are empowered to be honest about all the ways they have tried to control and manipulate each other, creating personal limitations throughout the marriage. (Quite a few of my clients have expressed amazement at how, during midlife crisis, their mates are suddenly willing to try to change behavior when for years they had stubbornly refused to even acknowledge the need for anything different.) Then the sexual opening and purification of the root chakra offers them an extraordinarily deep sexual bonding, and as they both discover grounding and resonation with the Earth chakra, a marvelous peace overtakes them.

At midlife, we can become conscious of how relational limitations have caused the suppression of the *inner female* by the male and the *inner male* by the female. Couples have the chance to see that restrictions they put on each other are all a function of their personal inner fears. The possibility of really trusting one another now exists so that full sexual sharing can begin to manifest. One reason that sexual frequency diminishes at this time is because so much individual territory is being stripped away and opened to the partner that there must be more rest between such fusion—so many hidden inner fears are being acknowledged that no more can be seen for a little while. Couples face each other in raw honesty now, and the degree to which they can communicate about their mutual changing and growth determines how joyful or painful this process will be.

Most couples experiencing mutual midlife crises have not known that they were in the midst of transformational cycles. They have found themselves concluding in agony that all their worst fears about aging and being rejected have been true. Therefore, the prevailing behavioral responses to these stressful changes have been affairs, withdrawal, abuse, and judgment.

However, with my clients and in my own life, I have found that the more the process is understood, the more loving and open will be the eventual outcomes. Obviously, in some cases, the two partners go through a major transformation process and find that they need to separate because they no longer can grow together. The goal here is to attain total trust and shared life experience, and any type of common or separate therapy at this time will support the evolution of the relationship. Like cranes executing a complex mating dance, the male should observe the female with comprehension that she is his own most inner female desire, and the female should see the male as her own inner male. An intense and focused adoration of the opposite sexual polarity emerges, and the two rediscover their inner magnetic poles of pure desire.

In this state of fascinated initiatic awareness, the man can feel *in himself* the primal female crisis—fear of penetration—and he will intuit the woman's need to be alone for a while. And the woman can feel the incredible bravery of the male who has to reveal physically through erections the truth about his own inner urges every time he has intercourse. In such states of knowing, male tensions about performance and the female resistance about her body being taken by a man become truly revelatory teachers. The male is by nature *electric* and the female *magnetic,* and this electromagnetic field created in total sexual union is liquid and filled with light. In our partnerships we can access both sides of Earth/sky; we can end the battle, which is ultimately within, and we can find harmony in sexual merging.

In the next chapter, we'll explore midlife crisis as a gateway to health, creativity, sexual fulfillment, and potential enlightenment. I have worked with clients for the last ten years who have consciously activated their chakra openings and have found ways to facilitate kundalini rising, and these individuals are the source of this knowledge about how to consciously attain enlightenment, the birthright of every human who incarnates on planet Earth.

SEVEN

The Chiron Principle in the Cycles of Life

AT AGE 50, WE ARE physically and mentally prepared for fusion with the spirit, the mysterious nonphysical realm of all that is. Up to age 30, when our Saturn Return occurs, we are realizing the structural basis for life. At midlife—Uranus Opposition—we mature the emotions. Then, at age 50, Chiron Return heralds the time for our full spiritual awakening.

What's Chiron? A planet, although probably not one you heard about in high school astronomy. Chiron is a small body orbiting the Sun, with an extremely elliptical orbit. As illustrated in figure 7.1, Chiron usually travels between Saturn and Uranus, but sometimes it passes inside the orbit of Saturn.

Chiron was sighted by astronomer Charles Kowal at Mount Palomar Observatory in Pasadena, California, on November 1, 1977. Astronomers have alternately termed it a small planet or planetoid, an asteroid, or a comet. Astrologers call it a planet, giving it a name that meant "wanderer" in the ancient days because planets wandered the sky among the visually fixed stars, and we will continue to call it a planet until modern science has been able to define Chiron with more consistency.

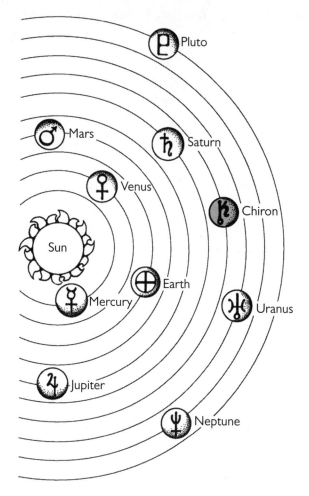

*Figure 7.1. Position of Chiron in
the solar system (Chiron is shaded)*

NEW KID ON THE BLOCK

The sighting of a planet is an event of great importance. A new facet
of the collective psyche, in relation to the numinous realm of archetypes, emerges from the unconscious simultaneously with this kind of
discovery. A new avenue of human experience on Earth opens up as
a voyager among the fixed stars is seen. The very sighting alone alters
Earth potentiality. The Berkeley-Hume debate—about whether the tree

actually falls in the forest if no one is there to witness it—explains how the archetypal knowledge of a planet is hidden from us until we can view the planet and study its path through the stars. Like a tree falling unobserved in the forest, the planet is out there whether we have seen it or not, but everything shifts once it is seen.

Astrologically, observable and significant changes in culture occur around the time of the initial sighting of a planet, and astrologers watch human affairs carefully during the planet's first orbital cycle around the Sun—fifty years for Chiron—to determine the planet's influence. For example, Ben Franklin and various other scientists were conducting experiments with electricity during the latter half of the eighteenth century, and Uranus was sighted by Sir William Herschel in 1781. Pluto was sighted by astronomers in 1930, and since that time the world has been involved in a contemplation of the underworld, Pluto's domain. At first, we acted out the most atrocious levels of the dark during World War II, which we triumphantly "ended" with the atomic bomb—releaser of Pluto/plutonium. So what was happening when Chiron was sighted?

In 1986, as part of my research while writing *Chiron: Rainbow Bridge between the Inner and Outer Planets,* I began investigating Chiron's influence on human affairs during 1977 and 1978, just after its initial sighting. The first area I examined was the *healing professions,* since the centaur Chiron was known as the "wounded healer" in mythology. I noticed that until the mid-1970s, the psychological community approached therapy with a radical division between body and mind. Outside of a few pioneers such as Wilhelm Reich, therapists tended to work on one or the other, but not both at once. If the head was processed, no attention was paid to how the body responded, or if the body was worked on, the possibility was not considered that this could trigger memories and new self-awarenesses, let alone feelings! The ultimate extension of this duality was electroshock "therapy" and prefrontal lobotomies in the 1950s and 1960s.

Suddenly in 1977, however, therapists, many of whom are recognized teachers today, found ways to integrate the body and mind as healing was taking place. In other words, as soon as this little planet orbiting between Saturn (ruling the body) and Uranus (ruling the spirit) was sighted, *the human being stopped being viewed as split.* And like the mythological Hydra, who suddenly looks into the eyes of her other head and knows her other side, we now have a chance to heal our profound dualities. One of Chiron's important lessons, therefore, is healing the duality of body and mind.

Additionally, I found that around 1977 strange breakthroughs in the human connection to the spirit world began to occur. As I said in the introduction to my Chiron book:

In the late 1970s, the general cultural phenomena of ESP, vision-ary breakthrough, and spontaneous channeling surfaced around the world. Historically, there have always been "visionaries," people who had paranormal experiences, or received communications from other dimensions. But this planetary eruption of communications from other realms appears to be a worldwide event which is only now in the beginning stages.[1]

This impact of intense spiritual light—I like to call it "spirit"—flooding into our lives is something many are experiencing. Another of Chiron's lessons, then, is about how to make our connection to spirit.

In addition to noticing what events were occurring at the time of an initial planetary sighting, astrologers also assume that the mythological name given to the body by the astronomer will reveal the archetype that the "new" celestial body rules. This has always turned out to be true! For example, in mythology the god Pluto ruled the underworld, and Uranus ruled creation, a process that is triggered by electrical energy. Neptune was the god of the sea, and the sea is a powerful symbol for the dreamtime and the subconscious mind, since it is deep, dark, and largely unexplored. Since all planets sighted in modern times have been named by astronomers—left-brained male scientists—these names are a gold mine of the collective unconscious of humanity, since mythology comes from the same energetic archetypal field as astrology.

According to Greek mythology, Chiron was a famed seer and astrologer who initiated healers, warriors, and magicians in the Minoan culture before 1500 BCE. Having been struck by Hercules with a poisoned arrow, he was known thereafter as the "wounded healer," who was able to source special knowledge from his own healing crisis. Chiron's wound was in his left foot, and since the left side of the body is traditionally associated with the female, he needed to heal his feminine nature.

Chiron was born a centaur—half horse, half man—of an illicit union between Saturn, who took the form of a horse, and Philyra, a sea nymph. In his parentage, we can see that Chiron's male side is carried by his horse part and sourced on the Earth, and his female side is carried by his human half and is sourced in the sea. Again, we see Chiron's emphasis on uniting duality right in our bodies, particularly around the themes of male and female as well as animal and human.

Following in the path of his father, Chiron mated with a water goddess, who gave him a daughter, Thea. Chiron initiated Thea into his healing and prophetic arts, and she became a renowned astrologer and seer herself.[2] Chiron's healthy relationship with his daughter offers wisdom about overcoming abuse patterns passed down through the generations, a major theme in culture and healing circles since the late 1970s.

Chiron did not indulge in the behavior of the other centaurs, who were rapists, plunderers, and sodomizers. Instead, he transmuted his centauric behavioral inheritance into a new form—an evolved animal/man—and founded the first healing temple, the Chironium, at least a thousand years before the Asclepium, the temple of Asclepius, who is purported to be the founder of Western medicine.[3] With all these themes around healing, Chiron speaks to the healer in each of us, and he is actually the founder of medicine in the West!

As a centaur, Chiron shines light into the mysteries of the ancient mythological creatures who were composites of various animal and human parts. These peculiar, mixed creatures have haunted the deepest parts of the human psyche through time. I have yet to study a major ancient temple, including Christian ones, that does not have frescoes, reliefs, or sculptures depicting composite creatures. According to some

myths, the centaurs were created in a union between Poseidon, god
of the sea, and Demeter, Mother/Goddess of grain. In certain ancient
sources, Demeter had the head of a mare, so this goddess of plant fertility has *horse* as her upper chakras! A major goddess of Egypt, Sekhmet,
has the head of a lion. Many Mayan goddesses and gods have human
bodies and animal heads.

As we contemplate Chiron, we begin to respond to an image of ourselves as *both* animal and human instead of as human only, with the
peculiar sense of being separate and superior over the biology of the
planet. This realization evokes an intensely sensual and beautifully integrated image of being an earthling. By uniting ourselves with animal
powers—a basic tenet of shamanic wisdom—we heal the separation we
feel from other beings on the planet.

Finally, Chiron is the mythological teacher who by his example
instructs us to follow our quest and then go to death peacefully when
the time comes. He was wounded by a poisoned arrow but could not die
because he was immortal. Concurrently, Zeus had fettered Prometheus
on Mount Caucasus for giving fire to humankind. Chiron set
Prometheus free in exchange for Zeus allowing him to die and descend
into the underworld.[4] That is, Chiron gave himself willingly so that
fire could be released and the human race could be trusted with power
again. The reemergence of the Chiron archetype means that we can
consciously awaken our power—that is, move kundalini energy through
our chakras to develop healed, bioelectric bodies. And this release of
power by the wounded healer to the fettered and tortured male hints
that Chiron's appearance in the sky heralds a solution to the horrible
bondage of nuclear weaponry; that is, this dilemma will be resolved
only through a healing of the tortured male side.

Chiron's lessons then, astrologically, have to do with healing and
with healing duality in particular. It teaches how to synthesize male
and female, human and animal, mind and body, life and death. Chiron
heals our connection to spirit, which is graphically demonstrated by the
peculiar course it takes between the inner and outer planets.

CHIRON: THE RAINBOW BRIDGE

Saturn is the *outermost* of what are termed the inner planets: Saturn, Jupiter, Mars, Earth/Moon, Venus, and Mercury. Therefore, when Saturn returns to its starting point in our birth charts after a full solar cycle of twenty-nine years, we feel a *completed structuring of the issues of the inner planets*. Saturn rules formation, Jupiter rules expansion, Mars rules force, Earth rules grounding, Moon rules emotions, Venus rules attraction, and Mercury rules mental activity, so with this *conjunction* of Saturn, the structure of our *self* is complete. It is as if the original magnetic field imprint at birth is reimprinted and solidified.

Meanwhile, as Uranus moves to the point where it opposes its birth position in our charts after Saturn Return, we feel a buildup of kundalini energy in our bodies that triggers emotional purification and maturation. Uranus is the first of the "outer planets," which include, respectively, Uranus, ruling activation of the healing mind; Neptune, ruling infusion of the spirit; and Pluto, ruling purification of all levels of awareness. As we've already seen, emotional and physical stress peaks during midlife at Uranus Opposition.

I call Chiron the "Rainbow Bridge" because it links the inner planets, which represent personal issues, and the outer planets, which represent transpersonal issues. Once the structuring of the energies of the inner planets is completed at Saturn Return, the linking to the outer planets begins. Before Chiron was sighted in 1977, when we sought the transpersonal we had no archetypal bridge. It is interesting that the concept "higher self" emerged in the late 1970s, since many body/mind healers use it as a bridge between personal and transpersonal perceptions; it may be that Chiron is the ruler of the higher self. In my own practice, I had been using Chiron since 1985 to shed light on the third major life passage at age 50, although why this concept worked so well for clients mystified even me.

With the publication of Percy Seymour's work on solar magnetic fields and the influence they exert during planetary conjunctions, squares, and oppositions, I began to see why my own emphasis on those angles was correct. Also, by integrating Seymour's causal theory into my therapeutic practice, a whole new awareness about the importance of the key life passages came forth.

Throughout the whole maturation of self, Chiron is moving into square and opposition to its birth position in an erratic way, since its orbit is so elliptical. The time it takes to reach its first square, for example, can be as little as six years or as many as twenty-four years. With each one of these squares and oppositions (the timings of which are listed at the back of the book) we experience spiritual breakthroughs. Thus up to age 50—that is, up until Chiron Return—the spiritual process is *totally unique to the individual*. I refer to these spiritual processes as "chirotic," from a combination of *chir*, for "timelessness," and *otic*, for "erotic." Also, because of its elliptical orbit, Chiron travels in some signs of the zodiac, such as Taurus and Gemini, for nine years, and in others, such as Leo and Virgo, for only two years—another erratic pattern.

Fortunately, in spite of these long visits in some signs and shorter visits in others, there is one overall trend of major importance that is easy to understand. Since Chiron's orbit around the Sun takes fifty years, children and their grandparents, who tend to be 50 years older on the average, tend to have similar *chirotic processes*. On the other hand, the chirotic processes of parents tend to differ radically from those of their own children, since their Chirons are located in opposing or squaring positions to each other. Chiron brings spirit into matter, and Chiron cycles rule the timing of spiritual enlightenment. The enlightenment process, therefore, is quite different from parent to child, but tends to be very similar from grandparent to grandchild, which would account for why grandparents are often spiritual teachers for their grandchildren, but parents often feel a wide philosophical separation from their children. Thus, in order to create a spiritualized culture, we need to have grandparents teaching the children.

The orbit of Chiron is exceedingly elliptical, but there are some general patterns that may trigger fairly specific memories of events for many of you. Check the simple tables at the back of the book for an approximation of Chiron's position when you were born. Then see at what ages you had your first square, your first opposition, and, finally, your first upper square, or the last square after the opposition. The return itself is always about fifty years after your birth date, and those dates are listed in the first set of tables.

These transits are the key growth points of what I call the "chirotic cycle." At the first square, we experience the initial shock of our link to the *numinous*—the all-inspiring qualities that we associate with deity. At opposition, we have maximum contact with *spirit*—personal development of our relationship with the numinous. At the upper square, we tend to become *hermetic*—develop a spiritual access plan. At Chiron Return at age 50, we are blasted with the *full light of the numinous realm*—bliss and ecstasy. How we cope with this conjunction can be compared to how we handle Uranus Opposition: in both cases, these powerful energies are *real* and our only choice is to aid and abet their flow through ourselves.

Information about these times in our lives is of great importance because most of us are prone to either spiritual emergency or spiritual illumination during Chiron squares and oppositions. During Chiron transits, psychological insights occur in the area of wounding or being wounded, and there may be identifiable traumas associated with these points. For example, there may be illnesses, deaths, near-death experiences, or other radical shifts in consciousness. These events are the contents of our personal workbook of lessons from which we can develop healing skills. Since this area of our learning is so unconscious and involves wounding and being wounded, this is the part of our lives that was inaccessible until 1977.

Notice how the orbit of Chiron sets up a phase early or late in its orbit with a square and opposition fairly close together, causing much chirotic progress, and then notice how a long period will pass with no aspect, that is, no square or opposition. For example, those born in the early 1940s have the square and opposition by age 20, with the last square at age 35 and the return at 50. On the other hand, those who have their first square at age 24 have the opposition, square, and Return in the twenty-six years that follow. Their spiritual growth speeds up later in life, while the group with early Chiron square and opposition experience contact with the numinous while very young.

As an illustration of these patterns, I have noticed that people born in the 1940s report astonishing mystical experiences at a very early age, and they have tended to assume that their own children would be having such early experiences with illumination. But their children often have no idea of what their parents are talking about regarding spiritual events, and this creates a strange rift. And the parents of the hippies and beatniks of the 1960s and 1970s mostly discovered spiritual awakening after their children had grown up, but while their children were at home and growing up, the parents felt like they were from another planet. At the time, they were worlds apart.

Chiron is a wild card because of its erratic orbit, and knowing how its timing influences two of the key life passages before it makes its return offers much knowledge about the chirotic awakening process, which invariably takes most people by surprise. For example, people born between 1948 and 1952 had their Chiron opposition right during midlife crisis! I observed and counseled many of them; they were very stressed by this double transit, but they are a very highly developed group of people who are also prone to instability. This group has the ability to hold memory of chirotic breakthroughs in form, and they are able teachers on how to infuse their bodies with light, or become "light bodies," physical vehicles that contain the numinous. As long as these experiences have been so poorly valued and understood, they have tended to get dumped into the subconscious mind, thereby becoming inaccessible to the conscious mind. However, the group born from 1948 to 1952 has developed a *conscious process of infusion of the light body.*

THE FIRST SQUARE

The most intense experience with Chiron takes place during the first square. For one group of young people, the first Chiron square occurs when they are only 5, with another during adolescence and another by their mid-twenties. For each grouping, the experience is radically unique; this is why classmates share such deep spiritual bonding and why peers become potent competition for parents.

A very young person's depressions during times of Chiron squares need to be taken seriously. At the first square, the piercing energy reminds us that we are not omnipotent, that we are chained on Earth, physically separate from the spiritual realms. A vertical axis of consciousness pierces us, shocking us into awareness of the other dimensions. We realize we are caught in a physical form and are not merged totally with spirit while we are in our bodies. This is a reality of which we are absolutely unaware until the first Chiron square, and it is the ultimate shock for all humans. Children do not comprehend their separation until this time, and reconnection with the inner or divine child is the way back to merging since it is the repository of nonseparative experience. We all share this existential dilemma, but imagine how different it is to experience this "piercing" when one is 5 years old versus 24!

Individuals who experience their first Chiron square before age 12 are systemically mystical, and they are so in touch with the other realms that they have severe boundary problems—difficulty knowing what is "self" and what is "other." They often tend to be negative toward their bodies, which they think of as prisons. They often live in their heads, but sooner or later their bodies will create disease from the emotional pain locked inside. Those living in their minds will heal their bodies only when they are forced to pay attention to them. This is the classic definition of how psychosomatic disease is created. The disease forces people to pay attention to the signals of their bodies, and often their unconscious brings forth each negative judgment festering inside that separated their bodies from their minds in the first place.

Those who experience their first Chiron square during adolescence tend to have very strong emotions. They suffer the shock of separation from spirit when their emotional bodies are in a state of heightened awareness. They probably act out their separation pain through emotional dramas. They wound easily and are frequently wounded by their fellows; this causes imprisonment in a labyrinthine emotional body, and they benefit exceedingly from counseling, which helps them see their crisis as *spiritual* and not *emotional*. Note that people born in the early 1940s had their first square before age 7 and experienced the opposition by late teens, and they will exhibit both the patterns described. These are the children of the 1960s, and many of them captured the spiritual imagination of the world in the early 1990s, as Chiron attained its first natal square position in August 1991.

Those who have their first Chiron square when they are near or into their twenties tend to have difficulties with belief and verification of spiritual realms and/or the embodiment process. Being so long in their nonspiritualized bodies, they often feel the force of this late Chiron square like a near-death experience. In fact, all Chiron aspects function very much like near-death experiences, and the literature in the near-death field is a fantastic source for better understanding Chiron, since Chiron rules this experience.

Those in this group are very prone to suicide, and they also may not feel that they are really alive until the first square. They have had so little experience with embodiment of cosmic consciousness that they think of spirit as a separate realm high above. They haven't figured out that their spirit can infuse their body. When the first infusion occurs at Chiron square, the intense light of the spiritual realm may cause them to disassociate from their bodies and reality, as though suddenly everything they had thought of as solid seems to be a dream. Regardless of how this process goes, what is important to see is that this experience is so bizarre and misunderstood that unless they have a grandparent nearby as well as peers with a similar chirotic process experience, most people feel like they've succumbed to madness. This is why children and young adults often view their peers as lifesavers—they are!

Our present culture has so few words for this "chirotic" experience and it is so shocking that most people forget, regardless of when it occurs, what happened when the light first penetrated. Consequently, there exists in their minds a peculiar denial about the *reality* of such transcendental experiences. The shock of spiritual light seems to create perceptual separations that make it hard to even verbalize or image such experiences. And much of the way we remember our experiences is by talking about them, as can be seen by our lack of memory about our lives before age 3.

In fact, the experiences triggered by Chiron are so radical and swift that most of us have no conscious awareness about this process until our late forties. Like with near-death experiences, we actually forget what happened, and these separation experiences are often disassociated until the *upper* square hits, which is the time to develop a spiritual access plan.

Therapies to contact the inner, or divine, child are exceedingly effective when a person has chirotic disassociation, because contact with the divine child is lost when we become extremely embodied. This child part of us is the place that remembers spiritual realms. Rick Phillips, author of *Emergence of the Divine Child,* comments, "The Child remembers the 'other side,' where experience is holographic, not linear. . . . Therefore, the Divine Child or Higher Self quality is infused with this unbounded awareness, which can act as a complement for the body's needs to live in relative time and space."[5]

TRANSMUTE NOW AND AVOID THE RUSH

From midlife until age 50, increasingly subtle energies functioning in the upper chakras are working in synchronicity with Chiron as this small planet approaches its return. Just as Saturn Return creates a crisis about the completion of *physical structures,* Chiron Return will create a crisis about the completion of *subtle structures.* At age 50, Chiron returns to its original position in the birth chart, and like the return of Saturn, this conjunction initiates a huge alteration of one's life course. Chiron is the archetype that makes it possible for us to feel like *energy* instead of only like solid matter. Its return sets off a period of maximal ability to consciously transmute subtle states of consciousness.

What do I mean by "transmute"? Transmutation is a biological term meaning *the changing of one species into another.* Thomas Berry was responding to the emergence of the Chiron archetype when he said in one of my graduate courses in the early 1980s, "The mission of our times is to reinvent the human at the species level reflexively within the community of life systems in a time-developmental universe by means of story and shared dream experience."

Only a small remnant of indigenous people had saved knowledge of ancient healing ways by the time Chiron was sighted in 1977. The modern world had forgotten how to heal by means of activating the inner survival skills of our bodies. After four hundred years of fascination with science and logic, we Westerners had almost lost the ability to heal ourselves without doctors and hospitals. The planet's sighting has reawakened ancient shamanic and healing knowledge, since Chiron is the bridge to the outer planets, which access the "dreamtime" and wellness.

The dreamtime is a realm in which we have access to intuitive knowledge about ourselves and all energies in our reality. For example, we have all had the experience of having a dream that warned us about something or someone dangerous. When we have access to the dreamtime and then try to remember our dreams and embody the memory, we can *transmute matter by means of spirit* instead of feeling like we *have to escape matter to find spirit*. That way, we are working with spirit while very grounded in our bodies, and the spiritual energy is felt and remembered. This is why writing down our dreams is such a great vehicle for raising consciousness.

Chiron is the bridge between the personal and transpersonal, between the known physical world and the world of images that emerges from archetypes. In a sense, this little erratic body flying around the Sun enables us to travel in the strange worlds of the imagination with Uranus, dreams with Neptune, and the underworld with Pluto, while carrying with us all our senses of structure via Saturn, safety via Jupiter, power via Mars, groundedness via Earth, feelings via the Moon, attraction via Venus, knowledge via Mercury, and self via the Sun.

The easiest way to grasp the archetype of Chiron is to think about how flower essences and homeopathy work. Flower essences are microscopic amounts of substances that have uncanny and potent healing effects on the emotions. Homeopathic medicine is the administration of a tiny amount of a substance that produces physical symptoms matching one's illness, which in turn stimulates the body's own immune system to heal itself. As Dr. Richard Gerber notes in *Vibrational Medicine,* "Homeopaths believe that microdoses interact with the human subtle energetic system, which is so integrally related to the physical cellular structure."[6]

Just as scientists are amazed by the effect of these minute substances on the physical and emotional bodies, astrologers are amazed to find that Chiron has a similar potent effect on the mental and spiritual bodies, even though it is tiny, erratic, and at a great distance from Earth. And I think it's no "coincidence" that flower essences and homeopathic medicine suddenly became very prominent worldwide after 1977 and continue to gain increasing respect in medical practice.

Chiron Return at age 50 sparks the spiritual transmutation of self that completes all the transformation work of midlife crisis. During midlife crisis, the chakra-opening work is very physical, while during the midforties and later this process becomes increasingly subtle and refined; it's like making a beautiful garden out of your inner being once you've tilled and fertilized the soil. Conscious work with the processes of Chiron Return also has the potential to radically accelerate your spiritual development. As your Chiron Return draws near, energy intensely reorganizes in your body. Your lower chakras now receive powerful spiritual force, straight from the cosmic realms, as energy flows right down through your crown, third eye, throat, and heart chakras into your lower chakras. Like a foaming wild river blasting downstream when a dam is removed, the light rushes through the opened lower chakras, creating the possibility of a tremendous physical, emotional, and mental breakthrough.

The structural growth process of Saturn and the energy reorganization process of Uranus go through a new phase of crystallization in a person's late forties as Chiron approaches its return, since Chiron links these two forces. Chiron Return, following the squares and opposition of this planet, offers a fourth opportunity to be spiritually reborn or to die, and this fourth stage involves integration and acceptance of death, which is our way of merging back into the cosmic.

Matter is never destroyed; it just changes form. This merging back into the cosmic realms at actual death can be a completely unaware end of life, a "death at death," or it can be a conscious return into the *cosmic life* by the person who dies with his or her light body completely infused. How we actually die is all a matter of choice. Death is the gateway into the spirit world whether one knows it or not, and Chiron Return is meant to be a time when greater knowledge about the spirit realm is attained while we are still in our bodies. Our souls can clear negative emotional-body imprints at this time, and we can die and travel into the realm of spirit free of all that baggage. Who wants to be angry when they die?

THE HEALING SHADOW

Astrologically, Chiron travels around the birth chart conjuncting every planet in the chart by age 50, and as it does so, a crisis over the issue of that planet always is very evident. Thus, during this time, Chiron has created a crisis about each significant planetary archetype, such as using power with Mars or expanding ourselves with Jupiter. Those archetypal processes have been successively transmuted, causing a much more spiritual outlook on life to gradually emerge.

Meanwhile, Chiron teaches us its own process through its movement around our birth charts in relationship to its natal position. Every time Chiron squares or opposes itself, we experience a major event that is a wounding, a healing, or a wounding of another. This pattern results in the emergence of the personal wounded healer, and the experience of that part of ourselves is how we all deepen spiritually by embracing pain. Pain cannot be avoided, and experience with pain is the greatest source of self-knowledge we have.

This can be most readily seen through the phenomenon of suicide, an action that Chiron greatly influences. We wound ourselves through suicide, yet the pain can be worse for those around us unless we have communicated our reasons and intentions for it to them. We may commit suicide to heal the split between this realm and the other side, and this pattern is a response to Chiron's desire for release from immortality. Or some opt for the ultimate wound to people around them by killing themselves as a "Now you'll be sorry . . ." This conflict is the nexus of the eros/thanatos—life/death—struggle that characterizes all human life, which is perhaps the ultimate duality to be healed during Chiron Return.

This key life passage is especially difficult because the emotional-body wounding patterns from all the other Chiron transits during our lives are reactivated all at once during Chiron Return so we can finally clear issues such as the pain we have felt ourselves or the pain we have inflicted on others. With each transit of Chiron, we are catapulted into experiences of being wounded, wounding others, and/or activation of healing skills. This is why many people become compassionate after they experience a tragedy. We cannot learn to heal others until we have healed ourselves, and so first we must be wounded, just as Chiron was poisoned in his left heel by an arrow. Notice that when we have been wounded, many of us wound others in return. We are so blinded by our own wounds that we often do not see what we are doing to others. And, of course, somebody has to wound somebody first so the teaching can occur at all!

At our Chiron Return, it is important to review our lives and examine the times when we did something terrible to someone else, even if we think it was necessary and/or justified. We must also look at the times when we were extremely wounded by death or emotional trauma, even if it could not be avoided. Regarding each one of these major life events, ask yourself, did you *feel* the wound intensely? How did the one you wounded feel while you were goring him or her? Can you *feel* the pain of that person? What were you doing to heal yourself or others during this time of pain? Things will show up in your life now that will make you feel very intense emotions, and you may find yourself dreaming about earlier painful events that were similar. With each event, examine it carefully for all three parts: the wounding, the being wounded, and the healing.

As you begin to look into those hidden and scarred places from various experiences in your life, you will notice that during the painful event *two of the three functions were activated*—being the one who wounds, being the wounded one, being the wounded one who heals—while the *nonactivated function worked like a shadow.* For example, possibly there was a time when you wanted all the power and you wounded people and got wounded back in the struggle, but you were healing no one. The wounded healer is your shadow—that which you most desire. Healing anyone at that time would have been seen as weakness by your conscious mind, and so you fed your voracious power needs by being obsessively involved in the painful dramas of yourself and others. Those people that you wounded will return to haunt you when you try to heal yourself.

Maybe you were a wounded child and always healed everybody else, while you could never consciously imagine striking out at another? Your shadow desire is to wound another hugely for all the pain you've suffered. You were so busy healing as a way to keep from feeling your own wounding that you were blind to how you were wounding others as you thought you were healing them! Remember how you thought those who needed you had better take what you offered because *you* knew better than they did? The people you "healed" will return to ask you to see your own inner anger from *your own* unresolved pain. A true healer sees and feels all the power and hot energy of the healing process itself and owns the joy he or she feels in this exquisite piercing.

Or perhaps you were the one who was always wounded by everyone else; you were the archetypal victim. Did you feel obsessive pleasure as you wallowed in your pain? The only problem was that you noticed one day that you were not healing. You were like a dog chasing its own tail and biting it hard as someone holding a whip laughed at you! Your shadow desire is to heal yourself and others. You begin to notice all the wasted energy of allowing people to wound you while you never heal. As soon as you really see that the drama you are in the midst of can just go on forever and accomplish nothing, you might be able to find a way to be honest.

This masochistic pattern is very hard to break, and often the only one who can break it is a wounded healer, who has matured to the piercing level and is able to hurt you and make it clear that he or she has no concern for you whatsoever. Since you cannot wallow in your masochism without believing that the sadist needs to hurt you for his or her own pleasure, this seeming cruelty might wake you up. If someone is willing to show you that your whole life has been a game of being hurt while allowing the other to wallow in the pain they inflict, *listen*. If somebody shows you that all your emotional games are actually vicious and masturbatory, then a desire to really heal might come forth within yourself.

The only way to see better the side you are blinded to is to examine the hot trauma events of your life. Notice which two functions were active at the time, and then you can identify the shadow, the real truth that lies buried. Generally, those with an early Chiron square tend to be wounded healers who are blind to how they actually wound others. Those with an adolescent Chiron square tend to be very sadomasochistic and live a circular life of wounding and being wounding with no effective healing taking place. And those with a late Chiron square tend to be wounded constantly by others and do not process how unhealed they are. They also revel in healing anything but themselves, including wounds they have inflicted that they then feel they have to heal. The Greek myths, which have had a tremendous impact on the Western psyche, are a repository of such healing/pain dramas.

Pain can be released only by acknowledging its presence and agreeing to discover its source and then release it. The pre-Greek sources on Prometheus recite the story of a trickster, since Prometheus played a trick on Zeus.[7] This caused Zeus to take fire from humanity, which Prometheus had created out of clay. Prometheus felt he had to retrieve the fire—the human possibility for warmth and connection to spirit—and so he stole it back. For that deed, he was chained to a mountain with vultures chewing out his liver every day, which was then restored each succeeding night.

This dilemma of Prometheus represents the cross of our mortality. The horrific image of liver-eating vultures represents our most secret judgment about our time on Earth: quietly inside, until we have trans-muted, every day feels like the diminution of our angry livers holding all our pain. These monster-birds are the angry male side inside of us eating away trust and hope in the future as our bodies disintegrate. Like Prometheus, our tired old people are imprisoned in pained bodies with Zeus as their medical doctor. The resolution of this dilemma lies in each person's own growth as a healer, beyond being wounded or wound-ing others—going beyond the body's life as a limit on the essential self.

Promethean mythology indicates we have to give up trying to be God, eternal and omnipotent. The fact is that we all will die: this is one of the few things we know for sure! The mythical Chiron gives the simple and illuminating response to this eventuality when he escapes his immortality—a supposed gift from the gods and a reprieve that men have sought since they first contemplated death—and chooses to go to the underworld. Chiron Return is not about choosing death; rather, the dilemma faced by the inner male of both men and women as they reach 50 is a resolution of the *fear* of death. And since our most intense and significant healing crisis is triggered when we take on our power—the Promethean dilemma—we need to face the fear that taking on our power will ultimately result in the punishment of death.

At Chiron Return, we are prone to illness and bitterness if at Uranus Opposition we have not cleared our emotional bodies of anger and frustration over early wounding. But if we have had a successful resolution of midlife crisis, our bodies will have sufficient transforma-tive kundalini energy to help us face the greater and deeper challenges of emotional clearing during our forties.

By becoming more transpersonal—in touch with the outer planets—with more functional heart and upper chakras, we realize how the solar plexus and root chakras still need more clearing. Our issues about the root chakra become more ethical as we are less the prisoner of our desires; and as the throat chakra opens, we are no longer willing to stomach the pain in the solar plexus.

Assuming that substance abuse, which would damage the solar plexus organs, is absent, it is possible to actually be aware of the functioning of our livers, intestines, spleens, and other internal organs, and this sensitivity in our bodies makes possible the incisive skill of *feeling* the wounding process by means of pains and contractions in the abdominal area. Several of my clients in their late forties have told me that angry people make their stomachs ache, and so they avoid them. They begin to feel so intensely the angry barbs from those people attempting to wound that they reevaluate what they are willing to put up with from others. They tend to withdraw when energy is bad and do something better with their time.

CHIRON RETURN

For about a year and a half around age 50, the opportunity to break the Promethean chains and choose Chiron's solution is present, even for those who did not resolve their midlife crisis. But opting for healing means being *brutally honest* with ourselves. We must journey into the underworld and face the inner demons of fear if we are to break the chains and face eventual death. The longing for personal immortality must be released. Ask yourself in the brutal face of aging, are you really resolved, totally at peace, complete with your work, and not afraid to die and leave your loved ones behind?

Which will it be? The *Promethean dilemma*—being chained eternally to a mountain with monster-birds eating your liver—or *entering the Chironium*—assiduously transmuting all inner anger and pain by going into the ancient healing temple founded by Chiron. Chiron Return is the passage into contemplation. All that is asked of you now is total honesty. The Latin root for contemplation, *con-temple,* means "within the temple." After 50, Earth can be your temple—you can return to the Garden—but *it is tricky to regain lost innocence.* You can be free to avoid bad energy, live your life exactly as you want it, and reenter the healthy web, however, if you can just *face yourself.*

As already stated, some people just stop growing at Saturn Return at age 30, many more stop growing at midlife, and the same fork in the road of physiologically, psychologically, or spiritually living or dying exists as we approach 50. At this time, we can look *toward* death, and the emergence of the chirotic archetype is forcing us to look at the "state" of our consciousness as we approach death. In the past, few people have managed to actually transmute themselves—become a new species with the light infused in their bodies—at age 50, since most "educated" cultures have been obsessed with the fear of death, which prevents transmutation. But now that we can consciously utilize Chiron's archetypal force (since the sighting of the planet in 1977), many more of us can create successful Chiron Returns. We can choose to be gloriously alive while we are in our bodies past the age of 50, and we can die later on as lighter and freer people.

There are two ways to handle this last key life passage: consciously or as if asleep. Many people in their late forties avoided growth in their earlier years, which would have forced them to transmute the angry inner-male monster-bird. As a result, they are excessively abusive wounders who are often very rich, seductive, and/or controlling. One way or another they were able to avoid facing their inner pain while they managed to gain power. But they continued with wily-coyote medicine too long and avoided clearing blocks during midlife crisis by manipulating others and not being honest with themselves. Anger and fear now possess their solar plexus areas, as they control others around them by means of the tyrannical, angry inner male. Like a vulture swooping down for the kill, the fear of death paralyzes the uncleared one who has taken on so much unconscious power.

These types of people blame friends, colleagues, family, or lovers for their difficulties. But aging has a way of stripping away facades. Over time, many people will not put up with this negative energy field, as the uncleared powerful person makes more and more angry and infantile demands. Addictions intensify, the solar plexus organs deteriorate, and when the shock of Chiron Return hits, its force can be astonishing. Hooked on the emotional-body addiction to wounded/wounder, victim/victimizer, they play games that become more apparent to others. Often at this stage, many of the people who once altruistically supported these uncleared but powerful persons leave the scene, for the game of wounding isn't worth it to those who have learned from the game. The lead game-player then ends up surrounded by a pack of sycophants who are willing to keep playing the game just so they can bask in the limelight.

I have had a number of very powerful clients who are leaders in various fields, but they have not done their inner work and stubbornly refuse to do so. Often these are the people who become the most incensed with the New Age teaching that suggests that we actually create our own personal realities. How could they need to process themselves, since in their minds they are above everyone else? At their Chiron Returns, it is painful to watch the carnage in their lives, which is such a clear mirror of what they contain within; often there is a lot of death around them. It is like the experience of someone walking barefoot on the up-ended edge of a razor blade: eventually the razor hits bone.

The alternative approach to Chiron Return, undergoing it *consciously,* occurs after we experience a transformative midlife transition, following positive growth at Saturn Return. This is the pattern of a consciously evolving human. I have worked with a number of clients and students who fit this description.

When Chiron reached its first square in their charts, these people watched the spirit merging into themselves as if they were separate observers. They became spiritually aware and yet remained in their bodies. With their Saturn Returns, they took on a new form that enabled them to focus on emotional maturation. In their thirties, they deepened their relationships, so that the electrical force of Uranus was able to transform their bodies into resonance with the spirit at midlife. Following their midlife crises, they lived in bodies that were relatively unblocked so that kundalini could flow within, transmuting the pain of life experience within their bodies, thus allowing the total infusion of the spirit at Chiron Return.

Often those who have learned to transform the most consciously are people who had ceased to *feel* the power of the Earth and were in a state of separation from the Source caused by the shock of the moving into form at birth; their hearts had closed in varying degrees due to loneliness for spirit while they got used to their bodies. But as the kundalini energy flowed through them and out to others at Chiron Return, they began to feel from the heart the wounds in other people. There came a day when their hearts were fully open, and they had the power to feel true compassion. They could feel the spirit in other people, since the true access to spirit is by feelings.

Next, they saw with illuminated eyes their own blind places, and they understood that those were the sources of wounds inflicted on others. They went into those blind spaces and found that the separation they had *thought* was there really existed only in their minds! At this point, light illuminated their brains, for the original separation is right in the head, between the left and right sides of the brain. They'd been walking around for fifty years with one side or the other of the brain dominant, and at Chiron Return, their brains—no longer blocked by solar plexus trauma—began to synchronize the two sides. At this point, they ceased to be divided against themselves.

If we do our work honestly—even if for the first time in our whole lives—there is nothing to block the awareness of merging that flows through our bodies as the result of having synchronized our brains. Like children suddenly dropped into a new world without any sense of separateness, we look around through the multicolored, flowing dimensionality, and our numinous inner selves pulse like waves that are living and resonant. We are in bodies filled with spirit, which are merging with the web of life, and we wake up and look around to see that we have always been in the Garden. We just haven't been able to see where we were because we have been asleep.

EIGHT

More Complex
Key Life Passages

THERE ARE MANY PEOPLE who now understand how the key life passages—Saturn Return, Uranus Opposition, and Chiron Return—trigger human growth processes influenced by kundalini energy rising in their bodies. By learning to intelligently deal with the intense physiological and emotional patterns that occur during key life passages, many avoid being catapulted into crisis, particularly during midlife. So now it is time to discuss a few more advanced influential astrological transits that affect our growth—the second Saturn Opposition and Pluto-Square-Pluto.

Saturn Opposition, which first occurs around ages 14 to 15, is our first experience with *polarity and paradox*. How comfortable we are with paradox during our adult lives is determined by how we handle our adolescent crisis, as explored in detail in chapter 3. What was *not* stressed there is that our ability to be comfortable with paradox and complexity greatly influences how we handle the typical dilemmas that surface during midlife crisis in our forties. These personal dilemmas—emotional blocks that can retard spiritual maturation—must be dissolved at midlife so that we can age gracefully.

Now that you've become more familiar with the basic key life passages and the principles of astrology, it's time for some in-depth material on the second Saturn Opposition that comes around age 44 to 45, and

Pluto's first square to its birth position, which occurs between ages 36 and 65. Second Saturn Opposition tends to dredge up all our unresolved emotional issues, usually right after Uranus Opposition, which has triggered kundalini rising. To top this off, those born in 1960 to 2010 get an added kick from Pluto squaring their natal Pluto while they are also handling Uranus Opposition and the second Saturn Opposition! Pluto-Square-Pluto alchemizes—burns up the old emotional-body dross and purifies the chakras—while the second Saturn Opposition is resurrecting unresolved adolescent dilemmas. This second Saturn Opposition—"second adolescence"—is usually as critical and treacherous as primary adolescence was. Think of all the seemingly solid marriages you've seen break up when people are in their forties!

PLUTO-SQUARE-PLUTO

To consider Pluto's square to its natal position, we need to know some things about Pluto's orbit around the Sun, which is around 240 years in a slightly elliptical orbit. During most of this lengthy cycle, people experience Pluto square—the only truly stressful Pluto-to-Pluto aspect in a lifetime—when they are in their fifties or sixties. However, due to its orbital ellipse, during fifty years of Pluto's orbit people experience Pluto-Square-Pluto much sooner in life. For those born from 1960 through 2010 this square is occurring when they are in their early forties. Many born in the 1960s experience this alchemical upheaval when they are as young as 36—*before* Uranus Opposition! Pluto-Square-Pluto is very intense, so the basic information in this book is greatly enhanced for anyone born from 1960 through 2010 by knowing about this early square.

Eventually, Pluto causes us all to process the deepest emotional shadow issues—the "unspeakables"—but the younger we are, the harder it is! By having Pluto-Square-Pluto sooner, this group experiences deep emotional alchemy before, or close to, kundalini rising during Uranus Opposition. They process the deepest levels in their emotional bodies *before* they get activated by kundalini rising. They burn off the "dross"—residue of junk in their chakric systems left over from negative experiences—before kundalini rising purifies them. This group has learned how to use energy very consciously because they have faced such deep issues. For instance, this group is playing a big role in the exposure of rampant sexual abuse of innocent children. Attuned young to deep Plutonic forces, they see and report things that have flourished in secrecy. Maybe this is why this primal group loves symbols and tattoos? They instinctually know how to be catalysts for Earth, to be midwives for the critical leap to global shamanism described in chapter 10. Years ago I was reminded that many people were changing in this way when I saw the popular bumper sticker, "Transmute or Die." Knowing about these patterns and navigating the key life passages with more awareness can empower anyone, but this is especially true for this group. Remember, *Pluto rules truth and the will.*

OH NO! NOT ADOLESCENCE AGAIN!

Next let's explore another subtle mechanism that influences the kundalini activation phase (ages 40 to 46)—second Saturn Opposition. We return to Bob, who opened this book staring at nubile California girls on the beach during his Uranus Opposition. Let's see how he fared a few years later, when his Saturn transited opposite its birth position for the second time. Recalling the general pattern of Saturn described in chapter 3, Saturn would have first reached opposition to his natal Saturn when he was 14 or 15, setting off his first experience with paradox. (You may want to quickly scan chapter 3 to review the adolescent crisis, since it is the pattern that sets up the dilemmas that surface again during our forties.) Bob's Saturn is located in his 7th house, and Saturn transited opposite in his 1st house for the second time when he was about 45. This meant he needed to focus on his own self-development and let go of being totally focused on his relationships. Right on target during midlife crisis, obsessive girl watching took over Bob, regardless of his wife and two children! He got more mixed up when he simply lost interest in all the things he felt responsible for; he carried on, but he only wanted to know himself.

Bob had already done a lot of work on himself, as described in chapter 1, but now the inner time bomb—unresolved adolescence—was set to go off during his second Saturn Opposition. Like dynamite ready to explode, midlife crisis was only the beginning of the eruption. Due to the relational agendas of Saturn in the 7th house, Bob was Mr. Responsibility until he was 15. He paid attention to what everybody else expected of him and never considered putting himself first. However, *that time must come for all of us.* Luckily, as an adult his family encouraged his "inborn" (a word often used about qualities that are actually the strong aspects of one's natal chart) turn, they were aware of how much attention they were always receiving. Back when he was a teenager, Bob's mother thought his minimal potential was to become Senator of his home state and his maximal potential was to be President of the United States. He was directed and educated accordingly, but these opinions did not match his astrological qualities and timing. Thus when he was 15 he turned inward to discover who he was because he felt vacant. How could he carry all that weight if he had no idea who he was? For the next few years, like so many adolescents, he suddenly became a disappointment to that proud mother who was making bets on his big future. All he could do was struggle with this outer rejection of his nascent self, which complicated his inner turmoil. Bob became confused—further proof for him that the painful outside devaluation was valid. I've noticed that people are usually so surprised by the onset of teenage confusion that they respond very poorly to what adolescents need. It's amazing that anybody survives this critical passage!

Luckily time goes forward and we heal and grow. When Bob was in his mid-twenties he felt inner urgency building again as Saturn edged closer to its natal position. He married, an excellent move since Saturn in the 7th house meant he could eventually become an adept in relationships. But this would not have been possible without his turn inward during his adolescence; how could he ever become an adept in relationships if he didn't know himself? Saturn always gets his due, so during Bob's Saturn Return he had two children, again giving himself totally to others, his preadolescent pattern. This was an appropriate response to help him build foundations for being an adept in relationships, but his inner emptiness gnawed at him like the empty stomach of a hibernating bear. Ironically, during his Saturn Return, his mother thought he'd finally come to his senses! She credited his wife with this improvement. However Bob was preparing to wake up again. He sensed that his inner dream of discovering who he really was would commence again, which it did fourteen years later during his second Saturn Opposition.

When midlife crisis began at 38, Bob did not deal with the pressures of Uranus Opposition by actually having an affair because, with Saturn in the 7th house, he realized how important his partner was to him. He also did not give up being in business, which is an excellent field for anyone with Saturn in the 7th house. Yet when Saturn attained second opposition at 44, he felt like the nightmare was recurring— the Grim Reaper had come knocking again! Oh no! That yucky nightmare—adolescent confusion! Unlike the wild unfulfilled temptations of Uranus Opposition, this force was more primal and unavoidable. He was feeling he needed to explore a basic survival mechanism that was so potent he might even need to leave his family and responsibilities. He felt like he would die if he didn't seek himself no matter who needed him, the classic self/other dilemma.

Second Saturn Opposition is usually a landmine in the path for anyone who was severely blocked during adolescence. It makes people feel like throwing out everything they've done since Saturn Return at ages 29 to 30. The psyche literally cannot mature unless one finally explores the side of self that was denied at age 15. This is a major life crisis since such *extreme personal needs are easier to facilitate during the teenage years,* when people are still under the guidance of parents. It's usually not okay to dump your life in the trash at age 45 to try something new. Luckily by then many people have learned a lot about polarity, so they sense developing both sides of their personality will work. *The more repressed a person was during first adolescence, the more they will need to take radical action during second adolescence.*

Bob needed to pay unusual attention to just himself for a while. His wife and children had always been amazed by his beautiful devotion and attention, so they were relieved when he began doing things just for himself. Cautiously, his wife encouraged him to just take some real time alone. He did that, and at first he was terrified! He realized he didn't even know how to be alone! Once he got through the fear, he began discovering the exquisite delight of being totally alone just with himself. He began to find his own rhythm. He was amazed to realize that he really liked himself, and then he began to learn how to stop being reactive to everyone else. As mentioned in chapter 3, he was discovering his inner pool of knowledge, his own source of personal creativity.

SECOND SATURN OPPOSITION

As we can see with Bob's story, the second Saturn Opposition can be a great crisis, and just like Uranus Opposition, knowing how to navigate it is the key to allowing this exquisite breakthrough of the primary self. While teaching this material, I've been profoundly moved by students in their forties who share their pain from adolescent repression. Primary adolescence is the ideal time for any child to awaken his or her deep potential while still guided by parents. For indigenous people this is the time of initiation and vision quests when maturing children name themselves and identify their clans. Adolescence does not have to be a time of confusion and deep pain that limits adulthood. Healthy cultures carefully guide teenagers.

The fact is most people in Western cultures were repressed as teenagers, most of the readers of this book. One or both of your parents inexplicably turned on you just when you haltingly began awakening your inner dream. You felt they were rejecting the part of you that was truly you, and so you rebelled and tried to be yourself, no matter what the consequences. But parents and society usually overwhelm teenagers. *This imprints the belief that the most unacceptable mode of behavior is to be oneself!* Because of this early repression the second Saturn Opposition at ages 43 to 45 is one of the greatest opportunities of your life. To maximize it, getting the exact dates from an astrologer would be good, and it would be best if you knew which house Saturn is in. Even if you don't do that you can identify your Saturn house position just by remembering what your key issue was during your Saturn Return and referring to the material in chapters 2 and 3 of this book. What was your big goal in life when you turned 30?

Second Saturn Opposition forces you to access your own inner pool of knowledge, your "ground of being" as the Jungians call it. This awakening is the key to developing a spiritual basis for life, which becomes more important as you age, even for people who seem to be very shallow. Now that we are all living longer, a shallow root system and depleted soil will not carry us forth. You'd be surprised at what goes on in the minds of supposedly shallow people after 40, the kinds of things astrologers and counselors hear about confidentially. After age 40 many people are terrified inside—deeply anxious because they've avoided maturing their deepest elements. If they avoid exploring their depth, they may become violent and abusive. This is why drugging people to calm them when they are wrestling with personal growth is dangerous. Anyone or anything that reminds them of their repressed inner shadow can become a target for that unresolved anger, even themselves. Watch for this pattern when you see people inexplicably destroy their lives and families during their forties. The outcome of second adolescence directly determines whether we enjoy our maturation or fear aging. We need peace, joy, and a rich inner life as we age.

Next, around ages 58 to 60, comes the second Saturn Return when we begin a *third* thirty-year cycle of exploration. One thing about Saturn . . . it never goes away! None of us can help it much that our parents repressed us when we were teenagers, but (1) we can choose to break out of that repression in our mid-forties; (2) we can refuse to repress our teenage children; and (3) we must really commit to this inner awakening to avoid being half-dead until our seventies, when a *third* Saturn Opposition occurs. That's when we get a third chance to release the repression.

Those who were repressed as adolescents and then repress themselves at ages 44 to 45 are often plagued with a depleted sense of deep self and struggle to avoid aging. They seem to toy with the idea that their lives are cruel jokes of fate. Life becomes a nightmarish bore, and then they become boring. Sometimes people in their forties have to care for aging parents, which can distract them from accessing their ground of being because the parents are still repressing them! People who do not deepen, especially while in their forties, are often not pleasant to be with in their fifties and sixties. Then, miraculously, sometimes these aging nonentities deepen and become wonderful individuals around ages 72 to 73! This is because they've finally broken the repression down and accessed their inner wealth.

In chapter 3, the six polarities are described to help you reflect on the major life changes you made when you were 29 to 30, and to encourage you to think about your first polarity crisis when you were 14 to 15. Why? *The inner discoveries you aborted when you were a teenager must be brought forth into light when you are in your mid-forties.* Now it is time to consider this issue much more deeply, since polarity mastery is the way to activate twelve-strand DNA, the DNA of our emotional bodies. Ideally, a totally unrepressed adolescent who was encouraged to dive deeply into his or her ground of being at age 15 would fully experience all six polarity paradoxes by age 29. Then, at Saturn Return he/she would begin to awaken twelve-strand DNA, the emotional patterns that link us to nonphysical realities. What would this person be like? This person is fully operational in all twelve life paths because he or she has mastered feelings.

OUT OF DUALITY AND INTO TWELVE-STRAND DNA!

Working with polarity is the key to human evolution in linear space and time. Once polarity is mastered, then a whole new level of personal emotional power emerges. This *expressive twelve-sided response pattern,* which is structured into six polarities, is accessible *only* by means of our feelings, which then direct our actions in linear space and time. This alignment tremendously enhances our ability to create realities in the physical plane by means of intentional thought in our hearts.

Seemingly we are cut off from nonphysical realities, yet through our feelings and clear intentions, suddenly magic does happen. Very few individuals learn how to take action based on *intention/feeling alignment,* the real source of harmony and happiness. Unless we develop this *action/feeling potential,* we are always stuck on one side or the other of a duality. Cut off from the full range of our feelings—the source of the next order of complexity beyond physical existence—we can't find the doorways into nonphysical dimensions. Yet this is where pure energy exists that takes us beyond limitation.

Knowing how this pure energy *feels* teaches us ways to avoid being stuck on one side or the other of a dilemma—false perspectives that first got created when we were first repressed. But repression is not real; it's just a pool of limiting judgments that we unconsciously adopted. When we can release limited thoughts that got stuck when we were repressed, dormant energy releases and the full range of a polarity, such as self/other or inner knowing/outside power, becomes ours. We see clearly what is going on around us by knowing both sides of the dynamic. Our consciousness becomes a laser beam that penetrates linear space and time.

Once you break through your primal repression—the blocked side of the polarity that is opposite the house where Saturn is located in your natal chart—then you will be balanced enough to begin to work on the other five polarities. This is not too difficult: Once you experience the difference between being eternally caught in one dilemma after another versus expressing the full feeling range of any polarity potential, you automatically rebalance yourself whenever you are pushed too far to one side or the other. By learning how to hold this "structural tension"—staying totally balanced in six polarities simultaneously as events continually trigger you—you become a master of energy. Your field has evolved from potential activity into twelve totally activated fields! This—the twelve-strand DNA of the emotional body—becomes your action guide in physical reality. You are no longer a rat in a maze being pulled this way or that way, you feel when you are being repressed and manipulated. You have moved beyond duality into the circular field.

Once you overcome the control program that repressed you when you were a teenager, that aborted your evolution temporarily, you will find you get extremely sensitive when anybody tries to jerk you around. Please notice when any person or situation unbalances you! You may see what people are trying to accomplish just by looking into their eyes. *The reclaiming of your primary self is the source of all human freedom and multidimensional access.* This requires constant attention! Your parents may be gone, but your siblings may still be jerking you around when you fully express yourself. Why? They aligned with your parents when you were repressed around ages 14 to 15! You must not allow yourself to regress, even if this means finally cutting a sibling off who may try to come back to repress you when you are very old, interfering with your third Saturn Opposition at ages 71 to 72!

To help you imagine the potential of full emotional maturity, I describe below how the six polarities function in fully activated individuals. You may want to review the less cosmic description of the polarities on pages 62–64 to recall the more elementary and grounded function before contemplating multidimensional levels.

THE POLARITIES AS TOOLS
FOR ACTIVATING TWELVE-STRAND DNA

Polarity One: 1st and 7th Houses

Mastery of the *exploration of self/other* happens when you are not separate in your relationships; your boundaries are secure. Merging without being swallowed by the other is natural to you. The rich fabric of your primary relationships is why you are such a developed person. You are more in a relationship than you could ever be on your own, and the qualities you acknowledge in yourself are not prideful. *You see your own beauty by observing yourself in another.* You see the magic in your other side, which frees you from the gripping expectations you've secretly had of yourself ever since you can remember. You're bored with all those unattainable ideals that somebody projected onto you long ago. All that is left is fascination with the awesome energy you find in others. You are waves of love and light in the universe! As this multidimensional sense of self awakens, new levels quicken in your relationships. Your partner simultaneously sees your vibrancy and basks in wonder.

Polarity Two: 2nd and 8th Houses

Mastery of the *experience of grounding and emptying* occurs once you've made home on Earth. Whether you move about with just a knapsack on your back or dwell in one home and never leave it, wherever you are, you are grounded and vibrate with the center of Earth. As you exist profoundly intermeshed in the planetary fields, you do not allow things into your space that distract you from the planetary pulse. This focus links you into the Galactic Mind, an empty space holding Earth in form—Gaia. Once you attain this linkage—which is based on grounding and letting go of anything that is not needed in order to stay in form—you discover how to circulate this field by using thought to manifest things. Since you are clear about what you really need, you keep it just by paying attention to it. You eliminate things that are extraneous or intrusive. With no junk in your space, you visualize what you need, and it appears within a matter of time assuming you still want it. This is co-creation with the divine.

Polarity Three: 3rd and 9th Houses

Mastery of *self-integration in ordinary reality and connection with spiritual realms* occurs when you can feel the spiritual flame that exists in the most ordinary and mundane things in life. For years you've learned the tricks of *how* and *when* to be totally in touch with your primary contacts. You know how to respond quickly and effectively when you are really needed; otherwise, you are free from physical linkages. You travel freely in many nonphysical zones by means of clairvoyant, clairaudient, and clairsentient skills. When intelligences that can assist you are nearby, you see, hear, and feel them. You live in ordinary reality in total contact with unseen worlds that are the source of higher guidance. In ordinary reality, rare breakthroughs—such as a deep conversation with an ancient, wise relative or a chance encounter with a long-lost friend—link you with awesome spiritual forces crossing chasms of time and space. With this penetrating awareness, you hear exactly what someone is saying to you when they are speaking to you.

Polarity Four: 4th and 10th Houses

Mastery of *inner knowing and outer power* exists when you can read someone else's reality just by going into yourself and observing your own responses. You don't have to examine outer forces to know about anything; you feel the vibrations of others within your body. When you are in a power role, you can read any situation by observing energy coalescing around desires: you see things moving in and out of form to know what to align yourself with. As for your powers, they activate when situations offer new insights that ignite your passion. You immediately drop any pursuit that drains your energy. Moving through scenes without being noticed, realities shift when you pass through.

Polarity Five: 5th and 11th Houses

Mastery of *your desires and giving away your gifts* enables you to consciously participate in the creative flow of the universe. You manifest realities with pure intention because nonphysical beings participate in your creations. You open the world to these energies and invite them in to play with you. By making pillars of light in Earth, you open the vertical axis that circulates energy from one reality to another, thus new intelligence arrives. You see creation as it occurs and shape it into tangible things. As you create visuals of things in your mind, they take form, just like a painter creates images on canvases. Creating with thought is palpable.

Polarity Six: 6th and 12th Houses

Mastery of *being in the moment while merging into the divine fusion* occurs when you are totally aware in ordinary reality and blissed out. This state opens extraordinary perceptual skill; while you're in this state, things are timeless and you notice minute shifts or change in your reality. Things and people are always changing, but you actually notice these changes right when they happen. Your own body has always been your best teacher, and you can actually feel viral or microbial invaders. You work with them and rarely get sick except when they have something to teach you. As you watch things manifest, you see the actions of the Divine Mind.

RELATIONSHIPS AND COMMUNITY

Over time I've become much more aware of the need for long-term marriages and partnerships in order for us to attain the next evolutionary leap. The breakdown of community and significant relationships is at crisis level in most parts of the word. Everybody knows the people in power accomplish their end by using the method "divide and conquer," which destroys bonds we require for protecting the collective. Woven relationships are the basis of creative power that can then move out into community. Taking our world back may not be an option if the precious thread of human connection is totally lost. *My admonitions in earlier chapters to hold together partnerships during the most difficult time—our forties—are of greater urgency than ever.* For those who have been able to do it, a sense of freedom and power is growing that is beyond anything ever imagined before.

WILL PLUTO USE YOU, OR WILL YOU USE PLUTO?

The insidious divisions used to break down our freedom are *plutonic forces*. Pluto is the driver of the evolutionary force as it alchemizes our emotional bodies, making paths for new energy amidst cataclysmic changes. I love Pluto because it opens us to the actual forces of creation. Nothing could be more ridiculous than Pluto's status reduction by astronomers, who seem to have forgotten about 5,000 years of mythology. Pluto strips out our beliefs and judgments; he teaches us to not resist change. When Pluto tells us it is time to grow, we do it! One of his favorite tools is death, since death always gets our attention. With

Pluto, one way or another, limitations go, new paradigms come, and dormant potential is revealed.

The short phase of Pluto's orbit from 1960 to 2010, is inspiring deep levels of change that most people resist. As Pluto speeds up into the inner curve, the tightest arc of its 240-year elliptical orbit, evolution speeds up. The last time Pluto passed over the inner curve was 1720 to 1770, the period when revolution flowered at the grass-roots level in the North American colonies and the industrial age was born in Europe. Pluto's speedup and earlier squaring for individuals from 1960 to 2010 is a period that will eventually be seen as extremely formative in history. Here's how it works: Pluto stays in one sign for an *average* of twenty-two years; however, during the *inner curve* (2008–2024) the time is shorter—Leo, about nineteen years; Virgo, about fifteen years; Libra, about twelve years; Scorpio, about eleven years; Sagittarius, about twelve years; Capricorn, about sixteen years. Then the time in each sign lengthens out again. The result is that people born in the 1960s through 2010 experience their first Pluto-Square-Pluto early. This causes them to be seekers of truth who expose the hidden agendas of "the dark side." For any planet, the first square of that planet to its natal position activates its full potential. Pluto governs the shadow, the parts of our consciousness that we resist seeing. This personal shadow does not tend to become visible until Pluto-Square-Pluto, unless there are unusual personal aspects in the natal chart. Of course exposure of personal shadows influences the collective patterns.

During most of Pluto's cycle, people experience Pluto-Square-Pluto when they are around age 60. For example, people born in 1900 did not get a Pluto square until they were 64. Their children born in the 1920s had Pluto square when they were in their fifties; their grandchildren born in the 1930s and 1940s had it when they were in their forties; and their great-grandchildren born in the 1960s, 1970s, and 1980s had or will have Pluto-Square-Pluto at ages 36 to 38! *This differential causes painful generational stress;* the intensity of the younger generation threatens the older one. People born in the 1960s through 1980s experience Pluto-Square-Pluto even before Uranus Opposition, which causes them to process the shadow side before they begin to individuate. For example, a person born in 1960 experienced Pluto-Square-Pluto in 1997 when this highly transformative influence intensified.

Before I describe the dynamics of early Pluto square, let's examine the more common pattern. As a result of late Pluto-Square-Pluto, for those born before 1930, there was a general cultural tendency to always look on the bright side and scorn complexity and darkness as long as possible. Some individuals deviated from this pattern because of individual natal dynamics, but the culture debunked the serious pursuit of difficult questions. It was just not chic, and most everybody buried their feelings. About the most liberal thing you could do was be a cynic. You were expected to buck up and smile and look the other way when something nasty was going on. Then when this generation experienced Pluto-Square-Pluto in their fifties, the square brought forth new emotional depth. Suddenly it was acceptable to be thoughtful and philosophical. But this generation has not tended to share their newfound wisdom with younger people.

Pluto-Square-Pluto for those born after 1940 added a very dynamic evolutionary push to the midlife crisis phase. They were more comfortable with feelings, and some attained a tribal identity. For those born in the 1950s, Pluto-Square-Pluto occurred close to or during Uranus Opposition and before their second Saturn Opposition. This maximized emotional cleansing during kundalini rising; the common word for this group is "intense." Their focus on emotional issues is very heavy; they demanded what they need during second Saturn Opposition. Many in this group also had multiple transits because Saturn, Uranus, and Neptune were traveling close together in Capricorn in the 1980s and early 1990s. Second Saturn Opposition was easy by comparison, and a second crack at resolving adolescent repression was a focusing device.

For people born from 1960 to 1980, cataclysmic change and deep emotional exploration is the way of life. They will have Pluto-Square-Pluto a few years before Uranus Opposition, and they are going to be a powerful force for social change, much like the new generation that catalyzed the American Revolution. They will face their shadows and deeply question everything about themselves before they even experience kundalini rising during midlife crisis! They will be fiercely honest, uncompromising, and volcanic. As their deep plutonic urges rise to the surface in the collective, they will resist the imposition of the New World Order as it attempts to establish global control during the time this group is experiencing Pluto-Square-Pluto, from 1996 through 2015. The only way to stop them would be to kill them, but there are too many of them. The great god of the underworld, Pluto, will be leading this wave to destroy the control pyramid.

The more conscious you are of major transits, the better. This is especially true with Pluto, because Pluto will break down any old energy that is blocking a emerging creation. It's easier to allow the breakdown of old encrusted patterns than to resist change, so you might as well just let go of old stuff. Once you let go of old patterns and energies, new forms emerge. We have arrived at the critical leap when we will either transform ourselves or our species will be irrelevant in the future, just like the dinosaurs. It's time to work with these transit patterns that nudge us to grow and evolve. It's easier when we utilize the powers of the planets and stars, the outward expressions of our inner dreams, the creative matrix.

NINE

More about
Our Friend Saturn

....

"For Everything There Is a Season"

USING SATURN AS an ideal guide in life, now we will explore a great
tool for *intentional astrological planning*. Usually people who figure out
how to do this are between their first Saturn Return (ages 29 to 30)
and their second Saturn Return (age 58). Saturn takes twenty-nine to
thirty years to go around the Sun, thus it takes twenty-nine to thirty
years to traverse all the way around your natal chart. Saturn returns to
its natal placement two or even three times in a lifetime, since more and
more people are living beyond the third Saturn Return at age 88 to 91!
As you approach your second Saturn Return in your late fifties, it's an
ideal time to use Saturn transits to review what has happened in your
life so far. Then you can use this information to plan what you really
want during the rest of your life, or until your third Saturn Return.
Precocious readers sometimes start using this information intentionally
right after their first Saturn Return, or even before.

By age fifty or so many people realize they could have made better
personal and career choices. At this age, some see that their lives play
out in cycles that relate to larger cycles in the world. *Something repetitive is going on.* Most people will live way beyond the second Saturn

Return at 58 to 59, so why wouldn't we examine our lives up to that point to see if there actually is a cycle that modulates our chances and learn how we can use it in the future? As you will see, there *is* a cycle caused by Saturn transits to your rising sign, your Ascendant. The information in this chapter is mostly useful for readers who have a casting of their natal chart, and the Ascendant is the sign and degree that is at the cusp of your 1st house. Sources for having your natal chart cast are available at the end of this book on page 224. This more advanced information for planning your life *tremendously enhances your growth*. The techniques offered here can vastly improve your whole life because it enables you to identify Saturn's influence in your natal chart, even helps you plan for retirement. You can *live in concert with outside forces by planning for the normal ups and downs of life.* "For everything there is a season!"

If you are around 30 years old you can direct your life intentionally right after your first Saturn cycle. I began living my life by conscious Saturn timing when I was 32 years old, which greatly increased my potential. This technique *works,* and it is a great life review. Unlike the rest of this book, you need your natal chart in hand for this process; it will be worth the effort.

Many of you have already learned about aligning with the planets, something I believe most humans did until around four hundred years ago. A structure and plan for your life commenced with your birth, and its director is Saturn—good old Father Time. It's crazy to run a business without a good business plan or build without drawings by an architect, and it's crazy to run your life without consulting your natal chart!

THE CYCLES OF SATURN
TO THE RISING SIGN

You need a clean natal chart on which you can mark the dates when Saturn crossed—or will cross—your twelve house cusps (see figure 9.1). To identify these house transits exactly, you must use an ephemeris or an astrological program. Any astrologer can do this for you, but you

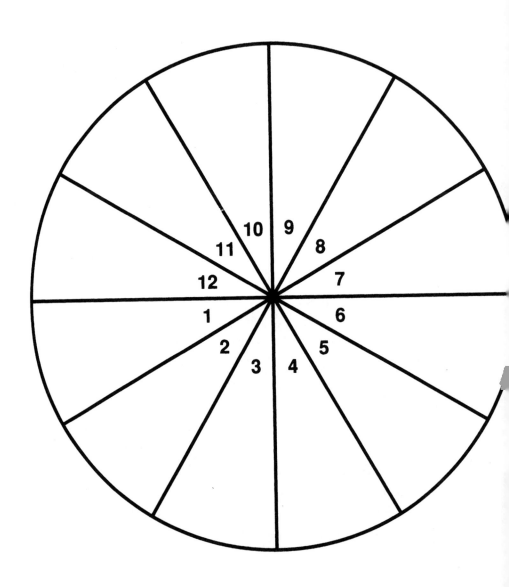

Figure 9.1. Blank natal chart

can also do it yourself. Begin with Saturn located in whatever house it is in when you were born, for example *Saturn in the 1st house,* and then mark it when it crosses into the next house, which in this case would be *Saturn transiting the 2nd house.* If you are 60 years old, you will draw two cycles. Put the Saturn transits during the first thirty years of your life close to the wheel by the house cusps. Then mark the next thirty years outside the first dates. If you are older you may have a third series of dates outside the first two. Trust me, it will be worth it when you see the *potency of this cycle.* Mark the dates on your natal chart for these Saturn transits over your house cusps from after your birth until now and even into the future (it may be useful to use two or three different colors). Then you are ready to start thinking about what happened in your life during previous Saturn transits, so that you can use this information to direct your life from now on. You may wish you'd known about it a long time ago.

For young readers who have already experienced their first Saturn Return (age 29) and are adept with astrology, you can direct your life beginning right now. Literally from the moment you are born *the transits of Saturn in relation to your rising sign exactly time your personal unfolding.* It is not that you lack free will—quite to the contrary—you will have *more* free will by accepting some temporary limitations or by attempting to reach high potential at the right time. Saturn merely structures our journeys in time. Saturn is not your soul, your individuality, or your essence. You can master the personality that developed during your first thirty years by utilizing your *personal unfolding cycle,* then you can use your potential wisely. It's amazing how our natal charts reveal the quality and timing of our lives in concert with the outer world! The growth structure is there, and we can use it. Saturn's cycle to the rising sign shows when it is time to focus inward and when it is time to engage with the outer world. Not using this information is like choosing to drive your car in a blizzard or tornado, or staying inside the house during an exquisite sunny day.

I began using the power of Saturn intentionally in 1975 shortly after my first Saturn Return when I found a pamphlet titled "The

Critical Ages in Adult Life: The Transit of Saturn," by Marc Robertson (no longer in print). Robertson delineates the cycle of Saturn in the quadrants, breaking them down by the first three houses, second three, and so on. By following this cycle carefully, anyone can easily understand his or her Saturn timing. I was so amazed by how this cycle had already influenced my life that I have used it for planning my life ever since. When I used this cycle in readings, I was amazed by how *Saturn to the Rising* was influencing the lives of my clients.

THE DOUBLE SATURN INFLUENCE
IN YOUR NATAL CHART

Chapter 3 describes how Saturn transits through the houses in the natal chart beginning with the birth position. Depending upon which house Saturn is located in at birth, during the first few years a basic personality structure forms. As Saturn moves through the next five houses, a basic identity forms. When Saturn opposes the birth position for the first time around ages 14 to 15, a series of polarity paradoxes reveal both ends of the spectrum in life, such as *Self—Others*. As Saturn moves along the next five opposing houses, it stimulates the opposite side of the original formation patterns that were developed by age 15; complexity and paradox become apparent. Please go back to chapters 2 and 3 to make sure you understand the six polarities in the twelve houses, our *basic operational field*. By age 30 Saturn has made you the person you are.

The transits of Saturn to the rising show when it's time to draw deep inside and nurture something new and original, regardless of what anybody else wants. Or is it time to go on stage, to get support and attention? As you will see below, there is a *lifelong double Saturn influence* that creates a wonderful interplay between the basic nature of the person and how the world supports him or her. Of course many already sense when to go out in the world and when to stay inside, so what's the point? Well, knowing about this cycle makes it possible for anyone to craft a *thirty-year life plan for career and family*. This really helps couples make plans for their personal and public needs together; it allows them to assist each other. As for those who hire and fire, know-ing when an employee needs to withdraw or get thrust into the spot-light is good information. If you have children, you will find it is much easier to raise them if you know about their Saturn timing cycle. We all have this waning and rising tide in our lives while the world rolls along.

SATURN TRANSITS BY QUADRANT IN YOUR BIRTH CHART

We begin with the quadrants because it is easier to understand our inner and outer flow that way (see figure 9.2). The transit of Saturn to your rising sign begins with Saturn's influence at birth according to which house Saturn is located in. For example, if Saturn was in your 4th house at birth, you were very creative as a young child, and you were very noticed and successful in school and community from around 8 through 21 years. Then mysteriously you just wanted to withdraw from the world. Nobody could figure this out, especially *you*. If Saturn is in your 10th house, you were an astonishing shining baby and bright small child. You probably did fairly well during grade school, but you were troubled by social difficulties because you were very deep. You became more introspective and deep through adolescence. When you were around 21 you became a very powerful person because you understood yourself very well, and you just got stronger during your Saturn Return at the top of your chart. No matter where Saturn begins, during our first 30 years we *all* experience how each house Saturn moves through matures us. We notice how the outside world responds to our growth processes, and we are all influenced by the expectations of others in varying degrees.

Figure 9.2 shows the four growth quadrants of the birth chart. When Saturn crosses the rising sign and enters the first quadrant, whatever age we are we fall into *inner contemplation;* we must empty ourselves to conceive a new creation. Like pregnant women with little awareness of the embryo during the first three months, we may not even realize a creation has begun. In a few years we seek to understand new

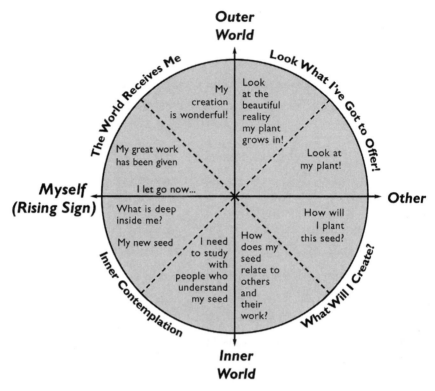

Figure 9.2. Saturn transits by quadrants of your birth chart

ideas, but we don't yet know what is incubating within. We want to go to workshops and to travel.

When Saturn moves into the second quadrant, we ask, *What will I create?* Intuitively, we look for ways to develop our new seed within. We may demand attention from teachers and leaders but barely know what we are asking for! Usually this phase feels urgent and unclear because we're building our own background and context for our new creation, and we don't yet realize why it matters to us. This is like pregnancy from the fourth month to birth, when the growth of the baby is evident but the baby remains invisible. A covert treasure hunt has been going on, and it's hard to form goals. This is how Saturn makes us feel the first time around the first six houses. However, many people manage to utilize this phase during the second cycle. How? When Saturn transits the first quadrant, you can intentionally empty yourself to explore new things. Then when it is in the second Quadrant, you can create madly and ask others to consider supporting you!

Everything changes when Saturn moves into the third quadrant, *Look what I've got to offer!* We are like flushed pheasants or woodcocks taking flight in the fields. We've created something that others might like to see! If this is your second time and you are around 40 to 50, stripping away the outside world fourteen years ago when Saturn went over your rising sign was very difficult. Second time around you explode with joy when the world wants you again; you aren't invisible! You develop your ideas joyfully with other people. You eliminate people and things from your life that aren't aligned with you because you're ready for big arenas.

When Saturn goes into the last quadrant—*The world receives me*—you are ready to share what you know in very big fields of related interests. You may be amazed to see that a creative idea you felt compelled to develop twenty years ago now bears fruit in the real world. Most people experience five to seven years, even nine, of riding high with success and getting rewarded for it while Saturn is moving through the third quadrant and fourth quadrants. Really successful people may experience as many as fourteen years of riding high. Then the world feels too busy and intense again as interest in the great work wanes. It is time to empty yourself again to make space for new creation, even if you are 70 years old! It's time to let the old go and empty a third time; new creation won't blossom for another fifteen years.

INDIVIDUALS AND PARTNER USING SATURN FOR LIFE TIMING

Figure 9.3 divides the Saturn influence into the twelve houses. Let's see how it feels when Saturn comes to the rising sign and transits through the houses. As Saturn enters the 12th house and approaches the rising sign, you feel like withdrawing from the world after achieving something big during the last ten years or more. Success just doesn't excite you anymore; you feel empty, lost, strangely cut off from old friends

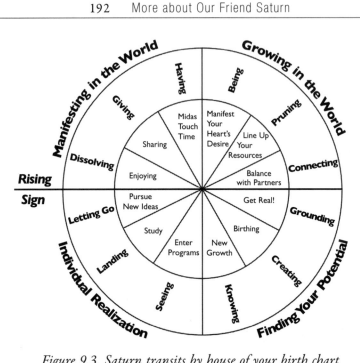

Figure 9.3. Saturn transits by house of your birth chart

and pursuits, and you may be bored by your own successes. It's time for *individual realization.* You want to be quiet, be left alone, and be free to pursue exactly what you want. If you are extremely involved in a job or business resulting from your success for the last fourteen years, you feel like dumping it to discover yourself. Be warned! Many need to milk the success gained when Saturn was at the top of their chart, so they are able to do things such as support their families. Also, what we have already created may be the ideal field for seeding the next new idea. Many find ways to pursue new interests while maintaining old support systems. This is a great time to learn to meditate, work on a hobby, attend workshops for personal exploration, or ask for new training on the job, but watch out for burning valuable bridges. If you do leave your work, you may find it *very* hard to succeed in a totally new career because you are in the idea phase, the seeding time. If you retain your current lifestyle, do not expect the notice and praise you've had for the last ten to fifteen years; coast on your laurels as long as you can. You are just not as enthusiastic as before. If you've been able to plan ahead to go within and can let the old ways go (retiring?), you can pursue new ideas easily. Trust what fascinates you now because that's what you will want to pursue for the next twenty-five years!

First Quadrant

When Saturn transits your *1st house,* the more you pursue your curiosities and live by serendipity the better. If you cannot, new things will nonetheless develop inside that fascinate you. When Saturn transits the *2nd house,* you feel like choosing a course of study based on your new interests. Do this regardless of the consequences, or your ability to maintain your lifestyle will dry up. If this comes when you are in your 40s or 50s, you sense that these new interests could propel you out of your current work. This is the time to widen your options, but you probably won't leave your current work until Saturn moves into your 4th house. You still have time to prepare yourself for a new avocation while maintaining your lifestyle.

When Saturn transits the *3rd house,* you may enter school or a training program, and your new discoveries may enhance what you already do. One thing is certain: a new path is opening, and you sense that you'll abandon old contexts that can't accommodate your new interests. Smart companies cull these new ideas from employees.

Second Quadrant

Saturn transits your *4th house* and the people around you notice your new interests. The 4th house is the *emotional taproot of your consciousness;* you can't breathe without developing this part of yourself. It's time to *find your potential.* The people around you will have to support your needs or you will grow beyond them. Job, family, and community feel stifling unless they can encompass your new needs. This can be a stressful time in marriages, yet marriages that are dedicated to growth for each partner are often invigorated by this new creativity. Long-term partners may have some freedom to open new vistas. By knowing about Saturn's relentless time demands, couples can save their marriages and careers by planning together. If you've been married a long time, your partner may see that you want to create something that you tried to create when you were younger but could not. Supportive partners will know you must pursue your lost dream. They may have been waiting a long time for you to do it!

When Saturn moves into the *5th house,* the journey starts to be fun and easier; the baby is ready to come! For most, Saturn transiting the first four houses is the difficult phase. You feel like you can identify this creative force and birth it. Looking back seven to nine years, now you know you've been pregnant! If your partner or boss doesn't want the baby, you've got some tough issues. Dumping the baby won't work, especially if you had to dump it thirty years ago. If you give up your dream, you'll just get old. Don't do it.

However, when Saturn transits the *6th house,* you sober up. Get real! If you're here for a second time, you're not a spring chicken anymore. You know how tough it is to do something new. How are you going to *use* this idea? Earn money from it? Fit it into your whole life? Get respect for it? This is the time to set yourself up to manifest your new creation.

Third Quadrant

When Saturn transits your *7th house,* it is time to balance and integrate your new creation with your relationships. It's time for *growing in the world.* Many marriages are very stressed now: new colleagues align with you, new jobs and opportunities come that can help you manifest your dream, but your partner might not have even noticed something was cooking, especially in these days of busy dual careers. You may need to move or change your job or social life, but how would that affect your partner? If you have a partner who was horrified when you started to change fourteen years ago—hated all your new ideas when Saturn was in the first quadrant and then hoped all this stupid stuff would go away when Saturn transited your second quadrant—you have a problem. *Your partner may seem to be somebody who just won't change and grow with you.* However, since long marriages are so rich and potentially supportive, why not use the cycle described here to study both your partner's and your own Saturn-to-the-rising cycles? If you both have Saturn in the same house, your partner may be just as ready for change! Or possibly while you're ready to go for it, your partner has Saturn about to go over his or her rising and may be afraid to tell you he/she wants to dump the past. In such a case you need to manifest your dream in the world, which also could enable your partner to dump the old to nurture something new. *Using this particular cycle for timing in marriage enables two people to support each other's dreams!* My partner Gerry Clow and I have been doing this for forty years. Saturn transiting the 7th house is about adjusting your relationships to meet each person's needs and desires, a good definition of marriage.

When Saturn transits the *8th house,* it's time to assess your resources and line them up for the next stage. You must get rid of things in your life that will stop your ascent to manifesting your creation. Your time in the Sun is coming, when you will be like King Midas with his piles of gold—Saturn transiting the 8th through 11th houses. This time can also be weird and intense because things and people you really like may be in your way. Even if you try to retain them, they will drop away, and this can be difficult. This is when a lot of marriages crack up. It will make sense later, but this is often a grievous time, which is not surprising since Scorpio rules this house. If you know you must let something go, even if it's your job, a relative, or an old friend, do it. But, considering it's Scorpio, try to be kind.

Then when Saturn transits the *9th house,* the real purpose and importance of your creation become very apparent to you and many others. Now you *value* it; it's your heart's desire. You deepen easily as you complete and improve things that are needed for supporting your gift. You naturally refine your potential. Spirit aligns with you and helps because you are manifesting your dream. If that was a real friend or loving relative you got rid of a few years ago, they may understand and reenter your life.

Fourth Quadrant

If you haven't done so already, now is the time to remember exactly what was happening in your life twenty-nine to thirty years ago when

Saturn *previously* transited your 10th house, your *Midas touch.* It's time for *manifesting in the world.* Can you remember what a joy it was when you had the Midas touch? We all love that time. You were the one who got the jobs, prizes, promotions, opportunities, fabulous dates and presents—the praise. If Saturn is *in* your 10th house you were a baby the first time around, maybe a lucky baby. If Saturn is in your 6th house, when you were in grade school, you were an honors student. If Saturn is in your 4th, you were popular when you were a teenager. If Saturn is in your 2nd or 3rd, when Saturn transited to the 10th house, you had the brilliant career in college or landed a fantastic early job. Of course, other aspects in your chart influence your success cycle, especially Jupiter transits. But recall what happened when Saturn was at the top of your chart, since the influence repeats again in a new form when Saturn transits your 10th house.

If you received extraordinary notice the first time around and have been nurturing your new seed well, you will be stimulated by an amazing wave of energy in the world that *wants you now.* You can manifest your dream in the outside world, which will furnish you with resources for your elder time. Now is the time to demand that high salary, get recognition for your ideas, for example, by retaining patents and rights. Ask for what you desire in the world! You will release this creation in some way when Saturn transits your 1st house in only seven years when everything strips away again.

This powerful wave continues and is even more fun when Saturn transits the *11th house* when your attention turns to sharing your gift. The 10th house transit is more about taking on attention; the 11th is more about *giving* your gifts to those who want and need them.

Then when Saturn transits the *12th house,* the real value and beauty of your gift is simply enjoyed because it is fully formed and beautiful. It is an ephemeral treasure that you sense will soon go away. Great joy is in your soul and heart! You feel grateful for so much appreciation and enjoy knowing you've helped others and the world. You've become a greater person and people admire you for it. With your newfound gratitude, space opens within for something even more sensitive and exquisite. You don't mind letting go of being the big cheese. When you exit, garner whatever you will need for seven to fourteen years. Saturn is going over your rising again, everything will tend to strip away so that a new seed can be planted. If you are depressed when Saturn approaches your rising, forget the drugs, open a savings account, and go meditate!

HOW TO USE SATURN'S PLACEMENT IN THE BIRTH CHART TO TIME YOUR LIFE

In considering Saturn's influence in your life, please be aware that I am not even factoring in the location-by-sign of Saturn, your Sun sign and house location, or the influence of the other planets. Even without all of these factors considered, Saturn really does trigger the timing of our inward journeys and our time to shine in the world. By first understanding the Saturn principle explained in chapter 3 and then knowing Saturn's house location in your natal chart, you are ready to review your own inner/outer timing in life as well as be able to anticipate your future. Since the time Saturn is in each house varies based on your natal charts, the years cited for transit times are only approximate. You *must* have the accurate dates for your transits over the house cusps, most importantly when Saturn goes over your rising sign, and your 4th, 7th, and 10th houses. Now I will offer a sense of the high order you can attain by intentionally using Saturn's timing cycle in your chart.

Saturn in the 1st House

With Saturn in the 1st house you want to be disciplined, in control at all costs, which requires mastering relationships with others. You were extremely serious and on track during childhood—a loner—and then at ages 14 to 17 when Saturn transited your 7th house, you dove into relationships with everybody in sight! Because you changed so radically, family, peers, and educators were aghast at your explorations. But this is what you needed to do in order to learn about how to handle relationships as an adult. However, you still feel most balanced when you are alone. You were very sociable from ages 18 to 26.

At Saturn Return (age 30) you go back to being very disciplined until around age 44, when Saturn attains opposition for the second time! Freer as an adult, you dive into relating to others with fervor; your midlife crisis may be the talk of the town! These deeper relationships balance and deepen your serious nature.

You make a big impression in the world from ages 46 to 56. Then your second Saturn Return comes right after Saturn goes over your rising. You can't wait to go deep inside again because you have a fascinating inner world. This is a great position for psychotherapists and analysts. For example, Carl Jung has Saturn in his 1st house. Ideally, you will have good self-discipline by age 40 so that you can avoid falling into wild relationship chaos during your mid-forties. Hold your family together if you can and enjoy collegial relationships. This is the best way to prepare for your time in the Sun, the Midas touch from ages 46 to 56. Then Saturn goes over your rising and you have the second Saturn Return.

Saturn in the 2nd House

With Saturn in your 2nd house, you want to be grounded, enjoy material things, and attain peace. You were a careful and balanced little child who got along well with people. But at ages 14 to 17, you plunged into dark and rebellious ideas and relationships. Your family, peers, and educators tried to curb this behavior, but you needed to explore these darker realms, the opposite polarity of the peace you desire. You also may have been repressed. If you were, people would have been shocked to know what was in your mind, the dark side of life.

You were probably wild in your twenties and manipulated others a lot. During Saturn Return, you returned to being totally reliable and sensible; people counted on you during your thirties. At age 44, the second time around you've got the dark side under control unless you ended up in prison! You are very deep, powerful, and in control of your life. Because of what you suffered when you were 14 to 17, you become a powerful being of awesome integrity from ages 44 to 54. Maybe you're an ecologist or an honest prosecuting attorney! When

Saturn goes over your rising sign a second time when you are around 56, you feel content.

Saturn in the 3rd House

With Saturn in the 3rd house, you want to express your unique ideas to others. You were a curious and friendly child who was always ready for the next adventure. When you were 14 to 17, you became fascinated with spirituality. People thought you'd gone loony! You got very serious and lost interest in simple fun. Were you ridiculed? If you were, you may have become defensive about the things you know.

Saturn opposes itself right during your Midas touch cycles—ages 12 to 22 and 42 to 52. Thus, you were drawn to pursue spiritual interests when you were only 12 years old, but you felt conflicted. However when this desire comes back again in your forties, mastering spiritual practices is part of your success in the world; it enhances your excellent communication skills. This Midas touch cycle makes you charismatic and alluring, and you may be a successful guru. Who says spirit doesn't belong in the world? This is a great position for an entertainer, so don't leave the limelight when you feel spiritual—share it! It's what everybody wants.

Saturn goes over your rising sign a second time when you are around 54 years old, four to five years before your second Saturn Return. So coast until Saturn Return when you may want to enter a new field, more for pleasure than money. By integrating the mundane and the spiritual, you can reach people's hearts. Scientists and inventors with this position see the unseen and find ways to demonstrate it in the real world. Your third Midas touch cycle is ages 72 to 83 when you may receive acclaim.

Saturn in the 4th House

With Saturn in the 4th house, you are fascinated with deep feelings. You were a very sensitive child, and your home environment was critically important to you. Were you happy and supported, or were you traumatized? Maybe you retreated into books, and deep inside you knew someday you'd show the world something they would never forget.

From ages 14 to 17 suddenly you wanted to have things your way; you became ambitious! But due to your acute sensitivity, you found it difficult to take power without feeling vulnerable, and people probably picked on you. This was extremely frustrating because it was the peak of your first Midas touch cycle, which started when you only 10 years old. Intelligently nurtured teenagers with this position often accomplish amazing things, such as entering the university when they are only 15 years old. Or, with Saturn in the 10th house around ages 14 to 17, you may be very defensive due to inadequate childhood nurturance. Since so many children are limited in this way, you may feel *great* power but not know how to use it yet.

You probably were a brilliant student and tested high for college. But Saturn went over your rising sign when you were about 21 years old, and the sense of loss may have overwhelmed you. If you married and had a family in your early twenties, therapy can really help you to be ready to take your power when Saturn comes to opposition in your mid-forties. Being emotionally powerful and successful requires the resolution of the early childhood complexes of Saturn in the 4th house. When you master your emotions, you will be powerful and confident.

Saturn goes over your rising a second time when you are over 50 years, your Chiron Return! At this time you will assess your relationships and let go of people who drag on your energy. It's time to end power games and to experience deep bonding with those who love you.

Saturn in the 5th House

With Saturn in the 5th house, you are destined to become a powerful creator. You were a very imaginative and self-centered child, who did very well in grade school because you were a charmer, since your first Midas touch cycle was from ages 8 to 18. Anything was possible, and you loved creating all kinds of things that everybody else wanted. Strangely, when you were 14 to 17, you probably gave away the stuff you were creating and hoarding! This amazed everybody, and you just kept on creating more stuff! If anybody inhibited you, the flow may have stopped causing you to hoard your stuff, which diminished your desire to create. You are a serious artist during your teenage years.

Saturn goes over your rising sign when you are around 19, so you didn't want to go to college or get a full-time job. You just wanted to create. This is the time to plant the seeds for what you will manifest when you are 38 to 48 years old, so go to Paris and paint! If you can't do that, then figure out how to get paid for all the wonderful things you make, your ticket to freedom. Saturn transits your lower houses around ages 19 to 33, so ideally you will work as a serious artist during this time. Then you can deliver a significant work around the time of your Saturn Return, allowing you to be an artist for the rest of your life.

When the second Saturn Opposition comes in your mid-forties, your Midas touch cycle is ending. You'd be wise to get paid well for your art, since Saturn goes over your rising again soon. What you do from ages 35 to 45 is critical for your financial security. Your second Saturn Return is about being a child again and being totally creative, so you need to milk the second Midas touch cycle to establish the basis for living as an artist while Saturn is in your lower houses again. Since 35 to 45 is a great time of life to be successful, why not do it? But avoid giving everything away when Saturn is in your 11th house again because it goes over your rising sign around age 47.

Saturn in the 6th House

When Saturn is in your 6th house, you want to be responsible. You were a very dedicated and friendly child, so bright and perfect! When you reached ages 14 to 15, you became intensely spiritual. After being perfect in school with your Midas touch cycle from ages 5 to 14, at around age 16 you didn't care anymore. Order always made you feel secure, so this was a gentle and invisible shift, but you were out of the world. If you kept after any details, it was to have time to meditate. You probably retained some orderly habits, but you weren't thinking about the future very much. You may have had some difficulty forming goals and following through on them. So many things seemed to be slipping out of your grasp at 16.

Your Saturn Return comes after Saturn transits your lower six houses, so you know yourself very well. Saturn Return awakens the orderliness you loved as a young child! Your second Midas touch cycle is around 35 to 44 years, when you are *ready* to succeed in the outside world. You are a master at being in the real world while flowing in spirit. You don't really care much about the material world, so it's best to milk this Midas touch cycle to secure what you need. Your third Midas touch cycle is from ages 63 to 73, potentially a very rich time.

Saturn in the 7th House

With Saturn in your 7th house, your big project is to master relationships. You cared about others when you were a small child. You are very responsive to the needs of others, so it's difficult to find yourself. You did very well in school; in fact you were the model student, since Saturn transited the top of your chart when you were around 7 years old. Your first Midas cycle was from ages 3 to 12.

When Saturn went over your rising sign when you were around 14 years old, relationships may have stripped away because you drew into yourself. You probably sought ways to communicate, possibly to write. In your early twenties relationships intensified with Saturn in the lower part of your chart, and you may have married young. Your second Midas touch cycle is ages 33 to 44, when mastering relationships on all levels becomes the central issue. This is a good pattern for success in business.

You develop yourself very aggressively from ages 33 to 44 because your own self-development feeds your relationships. Then, like a ghost coming back, Saturn goes over your rising again when you are around 44 and things strip away because you want to go on your own journey. Now you are certain that self-development is the key to relationships! You will tend to seek a new field that involves deep relating, maybe as a therapist. The next Midas touch cycle is from ages 62 to 72, when you are a mature and self-developed individual. What you have to say is very valuable to other people.

Saturn in the 8th House

With Saturn in your 8th house, you are destined to master the deep forces in life and to develop great character. Saturn is very important to you because you need will power. You were a brooding and determined child with very deep feelings. You did well in the early stages in school but had trouble succeeding after grade school, since your first Midas cycle is birth to 10 years. As a teenager you were so interested in truth and clarity that few people understood you, and traditional education had little to offer. You were an iconoclast. The psychoanalyst Sigmund Freud and the psychiatrist R. D. Laing both had Saturn in the 8th house. Saturn went over your rising sign when you were about 12 years old, and other people's agendas meant nothing to you.

When you were around 14 to 17, suddenly you changed! You realized you needed to figure out mundane life in order to understand chaos. You came alive and connected with people. Your parents and educators concluded you'd woken up—you actually had, but not to their values. You were merely trying to adopt something that other people valued to fit into a weird world. You also set serious goals when you were around 12. As a totally inner directed person, you took a practical stance in the world.

At Saturn Return, your goals have been achieved and you succeed in whatever you want until midlife. Few people realize the depths of your nature or the intensity of your self-discipline. Saturn goes over your rising again when you are about 40, when you must be careful to take care of your own needs. You will tend to have big things going on in your life, so you may need a place in the country with a garden and/or a dog. You need to be silent because you will always contemplate the deepest meaning of life.

Saturn in the 9th House

With Saturn in your 9th house, your desire is to live a spiritual life and share your wisdom. You were a sensitive and thoughtful child. Your first Midas touch is when you are an infant to age 7. If you did well in school much past the third grade, it was because you already had all the answers. Saturn went over your rising when you were about 10 years old, when you were very contemplative and not interested in ordinary reality. Suddenly when you were 14 to 15 and Saturn transited your 3rd house, you became a social butterfly! You loved people and couldn't wait to learn more about them, and you were a very popular teenager. Where did the serious child go? You became emotionally intense and creative, and you learned to get along with everybody.

But you became serious again when you were about 27 years old; you brooded again about the meaning of life. During Saturn Return you turn back to being a serious spiritual person, since it occurs in the beginning of your Midas touch cycle, ages 28 to 38. Maybe you go to divinity school, since all you care about is your spiritual quest. If you don't develop this aspect of yourself in your early thirties, when Saturn goes over your rising when you are around 38, you will find a spiritual discipline. You will teach spirituality in some form by the second Saturn Return around age 58, possibly as a wonderful grandparent.

Saturn in the 10th House

With Saturn in your 10th house, you want power! You were a very studious and intense child with deep and hidden feelings who was often misunderstood. You did well in your studies because you were so serious, but you tended to use rational analysis to avoid strong feelings. Saturn went over your rising when you were 6 to 7 years old, so you went inside. When you were 14 to 17, with Saturn in the bottom of your chart, you dove into emotional exploration. You read novels, loved drama, and analyzed your primary family. Little did anybody know you were mastering feelings because you wanted to understand people in order to gain power in the world.

You were very disciplined during your twenties, and achieved something noticeable at Saturn Return, since your second Midas cycles is ages 25 to 35. You made changes in your life to master your emotions in order to handle power. Your life was very exciting for five to seven years after Saturn Return, but you hated the loss of attention when Saturn went over your rising around age 37. So you went inside to find a new seed that could bear fruit around ages 55 to 65. You learn how to handle power when you are 25 to 35 years old, so during the second Saturn Return, you have emotional power. When Saturn goes over your rising a third time, it's easier to lose the world's attention. Now the power is in your heart, and it feels good to withdraw when you're around 65 years old.

Saturn in the 11th House

When Saturn is in your 11th house, you want to gift the world with your creations. You were a charming and curious small child who turned serious very young because Saturn went over your rising when you are about 3 years old. You didn't care much about school when young, yet eventually you have a long education as a student of life. Around ages 14 to 17 you created an original plan to focus on, and your uniqueness becomes visible in you during your Midas touch cycle ages 23 to 33. What matters to you then will probably guide your whole life. All you really care about is finding a way to deliver your gift, and you get really serious about it during Saturn Return. Your ability to create is like a flowing spring, so you easily attract support for yourself. This is the ideal Saturn pattern for a philanthropist. You may form a school or organization around your creation near the time of your second Saturn Return.

Many people with this position were emotionally crippled or limited in some way, so they can't realize their dreams, which require the support of others. However, many with Saturn in the 11th house build organizations for the world because they've learned how to create things at a young age and developed their will power. Of course Saturn goes over their rising sign a second time when they are around 32, so while Saturn is in the lower houses, they are building systems they will manifest in their forties. Sadly, a bum by the side of the road may be a gifted person who was repressed as a teenager and then didn't get any support in his thirties!

Saturn in the 12th House

If Saturn is in your 12th house, you are fascinated by the occult. As an infant you were in tune with the unseen, the multidimensional aspects of reality. You started out knowing the big secrets, and then you incubated your knowledge by going within when Saturn went over your rising before you could speak! This causes you to spend your life seeking evidence for the subtle realms in the world. At ages 14 to 17 you began creating an active method to access, file, and deliver what you know. You seemed to be genius in your early twenties, since your Midas touch cycle is ages 20 to 30. What you knew was so advanced it seemed impossible to go to school. You may have found a master teacher to guide you. Most with Saturn in the 12th house will get the credentials they need to deliver their knowledge to the world, and they will tend to be quite successful in their twenties. This is a typical position for diagnostic researchers, inventors, and leading-edge teachers.

You get your Saturn Return just before Saturn goes over your rising a second time when you are only about 30 years old. You probably will hatch your big idea in the world when you are about 48 to 58 years old. If you are still developing the great work you began in your early twenties, you may experience a rerun of the attention you got long ago. This time you know how to use it. Your amazing consciousness may not be visible out there, but your mystical powers penetrate the center of the universe. However you do it, master the mundane so that you can radiate the spiritual energy of creation.

TEN

Toward a Global Shamanic Paradigm

When God created the world He divided the waters which were under the firmament from the waters which were above the firmament. The human body is a recapitulation of this principle of order, for the body itself is the firmament which divides the waters of the brain from the waters of the genitals. Because of the sacred numinosity of the waters, all the fluids of the human body—saliva, sweat, semen, and blood—are sacred and mysterious substances.

WILLIAM IRWIN THOMPSON,
THE TIME FALLING BODIES TAKE TO LIGHT

NOW IT IS TIME to look at how my clients' experiences during key life passages may influence the collective world. How *would* our cultures change if people were more evolved? We humans differ from all other species because we have the ability to observe ourselves within a changing universe. We can think about what we've come from and where we may be going. We know that our cultural and historical records influence our lives. This book encourages us to become more *self-aware* by learning from our past experience and planning for our future ones. I also suggest that we are now becoming multidimensional.

207

In conjunction with gaining comprehension of quantum and string physics, many wonder if accessing multiple dimensions is expanding human consciousness.

Meanwhile patriarchal, technological society threatens our species and our planet, and so many wonder if we've lost our survival instincts as people float around in a mass hypnosis pushing keys connected to cyberspace in drugged and fat bodies. As I've observed my clients and readers passing consciously through the key life passages, allowing kundalini energy to move in healing ways through their bodies and souls, I notice they are not floating in the mass hypnosis. What *does* my planetary-growth hypothesis in this have to do with mass culture?

The answer is, *"Everything."* Activated kundalini energy is the *source* of the survival instinct! When we feel this exquisite life force rising in our bodies, we release eros into the web of life. I have demonstrated how the major life cycles can be used to enhance personal growth. We need conscious initiation into these more evolved states of mind, and we should use this knowledge to guide our children. Until recently human cultures initiated their children. We must return to helping our children realize themselves when they are young; then cultures and the planet will move back into balance.

Powerful sexual forces are often the cause of radical evolutionary shifts. The reason I'm such an optimist is because the sexual force seems to be greater than the death wish. Others have said this, however the hypothesis presented in this book offers a *how*—a doable method by which modern families and individuals can evolve and create change in the collective universe. We can break free of the current paralysis to activate our powers of life and creativity. We can choose to direct our evolution to the next step: conscious creation.

In counseling I've found that permanent change rarely occurs in people unless their minds have fully embraced an insight that leads them on new pathways. This book discusses how the physical sensations of kundalini energy flowing in the body alters the way we think. Basically *this book teaches how to think about what the body does.* The biological basis of kundalini has not yet been "found" in the body, but researchers think the trigger for kundalini rising is probably in the brain. Neuroscientists such as Erik Floor and Philip Lansky, for example, associate the pineal gland with the raising of kundalini.[1]

According to ancient Eastern wisdom, the serpent power—kundalini—is coiled in the root chakra and rises up the spine to the head. The latest research on brain biology, however, suggests that the biological release is *in* the brain. Then, as with all human sensations, what is transmitted from the brain is felt in the body. If the kundalini trigger is the brain, then our mental appraisal of our own evolution is the most liberating way to intelligently reflect on ourselves. That is, what we think is possible must be the next stage of human development.

POISED FOR THE DIVINE LEAP, ARE WE GOING TO FALL ON OUR FACES?

Poised at an omega point, many feel like we are at the end of some big cycle. We await either an apocalypse or the revelation of our true purpose on Earth. There are differing opinions as to what this end point might look like, such as the polarized views of the New Age seekers and fundamentalist religious groups.

New Agers await the new human who will live in the new "heaven" here on Earth, so they advise us to stop judging others based on our previous experience. Christian fundamentalists await the end of time based on their readings of ancient prophecy. They await a cataclysm and the return of Christ to verify their interpretation of patriarchal history, and they can't wait to be proven right. Meanwhile the New Age seekers of new consciousness await Earth's transformation to a planet that is not limited by past history. Either way our times are inherently revelatory; both groups believe that we are on the verge of finally understanding why we are here. So which is it? Let's see where each path takes us.

Fundamentalism is the logical outcome of *Dominion theology,* which posits that "man" has dominance over the Earth granted to "him" by God after the Flood—*God's charter.* This Biblical theology is ingrained in Western consciousness—the belief that man must control the Earth to provide for humans. However, "Be fruitful and multiply" spells death to Earth; the building battles over food, health, land, birth control, and abortion are intense and primal. Considering potential planetary ecocide, *man* as the central judge selected to fulfill God's charter is suicidal because the patriarchy is blind to the web of life. We all need to employ our brilliant logical minds to rediscover primal survival. Obsession with coming cataclysms prophesied by the angry male God *are necrophilic,* that is, deathly.

New Agers are also infected with their own versions of apocalyptical thought processes, for example, many are obsessed with personal survival amid the "coming Earth changes." Waiting for the apocalypse is always dangerous because it traps us in fear when we are capable of unbounded consciousness. It is nuts to think puny humans cause apocalypses! Asteroids, the cause of many extinctions in the past, aren't caused by a god who throws rocks at our planet because we made him mad! Or if Noah actually did get a real visit from God warning him about the coming Flood, then we should trust our cosmic future.

To me, the real nightmare would be if the people in power refuse to plan for the future based on their Biblical notion that the future is preordained or their focus on personal survival. If this goes on much longer, we *will* experience a human-caused cataclysm by continuing to contribute to the *real danger*—chemical, genetic, and nuclear pollution. Engaged in biological manipulation and war, too many foolishly wait for the Second Coming of Christ. Too bad they're not waiting for their second Saturn Returns! It is time to utilize our knowledge to shatter the mass hypnosis that paralyzes our species.

SEEING IS BELIEVING

Worldwide, body/mind healers are working one-on-one and in workshops to help people clear judgments that block healing. Ecofeminist, Earth-centered communities and households as well as ceremonial events at sacred sites with indigenous people are *grounding a new energy form.* They are reminding us that we *can* live in peace and harmony and experience happiness on Earth again. I know we will, since surely we have not climbed up the long ladder of evolution without a reason. This book is a product of a new revolutionary paradigm—problems start with the individual, and then the outer reality is created by what's inside each person. Even global problems start with individuals. Each person who takes microcosmic responsibility for the universal problem is part of the solution in the macrocosm. It matters if you eat organically, nurture with kindness, and protect the web of life. The film *Avatar* is an advanced exposition of this way of being.

For the past five thousand years human creativity has been funneled into battles and the building of cities and empires. Over time people came to believe that the "enemy" causes the problems. New Agers ask us to stop pointing the blame at the "other" and take responsibility for what is happening ourselves, a great shift in problem solving. Yet those who have attained this new perspective need to be gentle with those trapped in fundamentalism, who deeply fear change and don't know how to stop judging others.

Global awareness is breaking down the idea that there are enemies "out there." Banking disasters make people realize that if one fails, all fail. We must look to *ourselves* for the origination of the problems. Many New Agers avoid politics that are mostly based on control and manipulation. Yet they have found meaningful ways to help society through healing and social action. The idea that we create our own reality—*totally*—is also the source of painful and deep divisions between political types and social reformers because neither group seems to be able to integrate the inner and outer realities. Ironically many social transformers do recognize that how we think creates the polis, but they don't pursue serious personal healing to clear inner pain. They feel they don't have time for personal healing work because they must save the world.

My mentor while I was in graduate school, the theologian Matthew Fox, describes the Catholic Church as a dysfunctional family. The root cause of this dysfunction is the excessive control and violence in Dominion theology. The belief that man is here to control and use the Earth creates the big dysfunctional greedy and competitive family that is gobbling the planet. Well, the United States as an *armed* dysfunctional family creates one new enemy after another because of the need to always blame others, for example, all of the *terrorists* "out there." Is it worth it to go on this way? We hear in 2013 that the wars in Iraq and Afghanistan will cost the U.S. *six trillion dollars!* As long as the United States insists on playing the role of "good guy" (just like God) and using its huge war machine to tell everybody else how to behave, there will be a corresponding enemy who will be assigned to play the role of "bad guy" until the U.S. runs out of money.

Once the breadbasket of the world, the United States is now the *weapons basket* of the world, and these weapons are increasingly being used on families at home. The inner evil shadow of this self-righteous, judgmental nation will be projected on an outside object until Americans admit they've been seduced by awesome collective greed. We need a new global paradigm to help us recover from this dysfunctional patriarchal culture! We will be stuck in the past until we heal our searing inner pain. Right now old thought forms in contemporary culture are creating tremendous resistance to any change; the shift is going to be harder to accomplish than anybody realizes. Various new body/mind therapies could be tremendously therapeutic for fundamentalists, drawing attention to the great need to heal everyone. This is urgent.

Destructive behavior, such as shooting innocent children in schools, erupts out of the unprocessed inner shadows within people's minds. General fear is pervasive in the U.S. because arms manufacturers, like old whores, have sold their goods to anyone who will buy them. Conscious individuals who've done a lot of healing seem to be outside the grip of the mass hypnosis. This is a hard time, when global communications and excessive drugging have rent the veil of hidden and frightening archetypal realms; we need to have great compassion while the angriest ones heal.

THE TURNING POINT

We are now in the time when the outcome seems hopeless, the apex—a series of seven squares between Uranus and Pluto during 2012–2015.

Uranus rules transformation and Pluto rules chaotic change, so we are facing the consequences of five thousand years of patriarchal culture that we have to cleanse. It is hard to imagine how we can do it, so let's turn to indigenous esoteric wisdom for some sense of where to begin.

The 5,125-year-long Mayan Great Calendar just completed itself during 2011–2012, a time of significant change on our planet; these shifts are being processed within each one of us during the Uranus-Pluto squares. Many teachers, such as my Mayan brother Hunbatz Men, say we are in evolutionary time capsules orchestrated from the center of the Milky Way Galaxy. As far as I can see, we are right on schedule for moving into a new time, but the annealing potency of the Uranus-Pluto squares make everything feel horrible! I expect some clarity to come in 2016. My interpretations of events generated by these squares on my website, *handclow2012.com*.

Many indigenous ceremonies and world cultural events that occurred from 1987 to 2012 were based on various readings of the Mayan Calendar as well as the prophecies of indigenous people. Harmonic Convergence in August 1987 began the intense phase ending in 2012. Now we walk paths in a new world. To take Mayan prophecy seriously, you have to realize *the Galactic Center has consciousness.* Hunbatz Men teaches that individual actions affect the Milky Way galaxy, and I have experienced this in the ninth dimension as described in *Alchemy of Nine Dimensions.*[2] It is valuable to realize we are cosmic because it pulls us out of anthropomorphic blindness. We are *erotically involved* with the whole universe. When we surrender our consciousness to our spiraling galaxy, narrow existence dissipates. The universal spiral symbols at megalithic temples such as Newgrange in figure 10.1 suggest galactic consciousness was available to most humans before the patriarchy.

The Mayan scholar José Argüelles says that the evolutionary phases of the Mayan calendar are synchronized with Earth by a beam in space, the "Galactic Synchronization Beam."[3] The end of this long cycle in 2012 releases us to choose conscious participation in other dimensions, such as the Galactic Center. The biologist Terence McKenna suggests

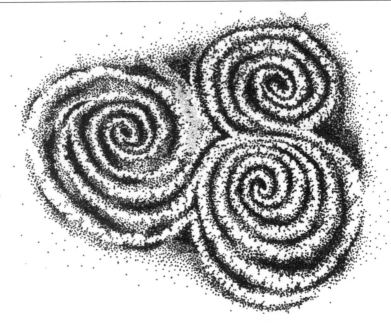

Figure 10.1. Spiral symbols of Newgrange

that the end of the current Mayan Great Cycle indicates we are being pulled to an evolutionary leap by an "attracter"—*divine consciousness directing planetary evolution.* At a lecture at the New York Open Center in 1990, McKenna noted that we might be being *pulled* through history toward some kind of apotheosis—a grand climax of human striving. The biologist Carl Johan Calleman has discovered nine cycles over 16.4 billion years that culminated in 2011, which I wrote about in *The Mayan Code.*

We are observing ourselves within evolutionary flow, thus we are fascinated by creation stories and archaeological discoveries. However, this is a very dangerous time because male-dominant monotheistic world religions resist the idea of the awakened human. This critical leap, so apparent in the dire state of world affairs, means we are in the hardest passage. For example, the patriarchy cannot continue to poison the world economy and structures. We have to reactivate feminine powers and use right-brain skills to counteract this imbalance.

Great power is available to men and women who activate their female side—the creative potential in holistic brain synchronization. When our right brain intuition works in concert with our highly developed left brains, we seek a nonviolent and creative culture that will facilitate the complete evolution of consciousness. We will refuse to be divided by egoistic separation, knowing we are in no way superior to any other elements or species.

The female side, traditionally associated with the right brain, is rich in the archetypes of many dimensions such as animal totems, the crystalline electromagnetic powers of rocks, gems, and plants, and the consciousness that emanates from the stars. These symbiotic parts of self contain the mysteries of nonhuman forms. We need to learn from the other kingdoms to recall harmony with Mother Earth. We will not be able to achieve the next stage of evolution without visualizing, meditating upon, and playing with images of *ourselves within the web of all life*. All species are required for planetary survival.

THE GLOBAL SHAMANIC PARADIGM

The paradigm offered by the Maya is *shamanic,* that is, a culture that intentionally developed synchronistic thought processes, intuition, and multidimensional perceptions. Shamanic cultures revere the female as the source of life and believe it is the role of both the male and female to create respect for all life. Learning how to utilize the key life passages creates balance in human society. Since it is a method that works well in Western cultures, it is a way to cause the mass activation of shamanic powers always lying dormant in our bodies. We are the sacred fire.

Psychic and psychological maturation of members has always been the goal of shamanic cultures. Hunbatz Men notes, "From infancy, the Mayan initiate knows how to manage energy with both the body and mind, for this knowledge is structured in the teaching process. The Maya refer to the spirit as *k'inan,* meaning 'of solar origin.'"[4] When I studied with Hunbatz, I knew he was right about the solar origin, since it is the core of my Cherokee heritage. But I did not understand it scientifically until Dr. Percy Seymour published his theory on solar magnetism as the causal principle of astrology in *Astrology: The Evidence of Science*. Then I realized that the key life passages are triggered by the fluctuations in the solar magnetic field, which activates responses on Earth. Like plants, we grow by the Sun.

Historically, there is great precedent for the idea that the transformation of the individual is at the core of an enlightened society. There are countless examples of ancient cultures that existed in a state of peace and harmony for hundreds and even thousands of years based on this belief. These cultures have left behind artistic, written, and archaeological records of highly developed shamanic techniques. Mayan and Egyptian cultures abound with such evidence, and the Hopi people of the sacred Four Corners region of the American Southwest still maintain a shamanic culture that is thousands of years old. Grandparents taught the Hopi children, while their parents grew corn and managed the village affairs. Around seventy years ago, the U.S. government took the Hopi children away from their grandparents to put them in "schools," but they have still maintained their shamanic initiations.

We are all descended from the people of the Mother Goddess. We still retain the deep memory of how to create and live on the planet in a peaceful, healthy way. From 12,000 to around 3,500 years ago living was primarily peaceful, according to many of the great feminist scholars of our times, including Marija Gimbutas, William Irwin Thompson, Gerda Lerner, Riane Eisler, and Mary Settegast. Birthing and a sense of all things coming from the feminine was at the center of this culture; the women guided birthing.

Modern people retain very few cultural memories from *before* 12,000 years ago due to a series of cataclysms that almost destroyed our planet, but the Goddess culture goes way back into the mists of time. Mary Settegast's descriptions of the Great Mother culture in story and artifacts in *Plato Prehistorian: 10,000 to 5,000 B.C.* are very compelling. The fall of the Minoan culture 3,500 years ago ended the primordial Goddess culture when the eruption of a huge volcano on the Greek island of Santorini threw the Aegean basin into a long dark age. A great fear of the power of nature ensued in the West that eventually led to the idea that God created the world for human usage.

The collective wisdom of the Great Mother culture has much to offer. From what we know of artifacts, art, myths, and sacred sites such as Çatal Hüyuk in Turkey, Avebury in England, and Knossos on Crete, this culture maintained itself for thousands of years by means of *collective agreement and order*. Creativity and respect for all life, not control of resources and acquisition of wealth and power, was the basis of life and culture. The male was the warrior who protected the hearth, and the female owned the land, female body, and the children. The existence of this long phase of prehistory is a hopeful indication that we could choose to create such a culture again if men and women could unify their goals.

With the takeover of the "civilized" world by the patriarchy 3,500 years ago when the last vestiges of the Goddess culture ended at Knossos, control and fear for survival became the basis of society. This suppressed the female and ended trust in the natural cycles of Earth. Now that we've progressed beyond mere survival, many feel *life exists for growth and experience, not for male control*. Consciously flowing with the key cycles of life is the way to choose a full existence. From what we know of the Great Mother culture, the ideal way to live is to create a collective ideal based on honoring the female. This approach never puts males in lesser roles than females, since the male possesses the unique power to inseminate life and protect women and children. But it does downplay *control* and *dominance*.

In our modern world we don't have to recreate the rituals of the Goddess cultures, such as *hieros gamos* (sacred marriage), bull dances, or the yearly death of corn gods at harvest time. But we *can* enjoy the exquisite primal joy of the Goddess by being in tune with the cycles of time and nature and enjoying sex for pleasure, not just for birthing. After all, the world population explosion means women are not needed just for birthing. Based on what we know about Goddess cultures, sex was free, sensual, and based on pleasure and joy; we all have a deep memory of such sexual knowing. You may believe that in the past women birthed constantly, from the onset of fertility until an early death. But even now in secret indigenous teachings there are lunar techniques for controlling fertility. Excessive birthing came from patriarchal control over women's bodies as exemplified in Vatican policy. Now, thankfully, sex just for pleasure is back because of birth control and longer and healthier life spans.

THE JOURNEY INTO DIAMOND BODY

Now we will journey into the Galactic Center, *the dreamtime*. During periods of radical shifting, storytelling often opens new paths into dark forests. This is a story given to me by my Mayan teachers and my Cherokee grandfather. Please breathe and enter into a meditative state before you read it in a quiet place where you will not be interrupted. Get comfortable.

Hear my spinning diamond excellence in space. Remember how to hear me in the center of yourself to receive my energy. Remember you are spinning around my heart, the Milky Way's center. You are acutely conscious of the equinoxes and solstices because you spin on a tilting axis and your solar system journeys around me. Way out in my nether regions, I reach far back into the hallways of your inner mind into your DNA spiral coding. I quicken you in three whirling concentric circles that are eighteen inches above the center of your head (see figure 10.2). Close your eyes for a moment to see those three whirling circles. While you watch them, breathe deeply in and out three times and then open your eyes.

The Galactic Center circle—the fifth-dimensional vortex of your crown chakra—is the highest above your head. Your whole crown chakra is activated now. The lowest of the three circles is where you receive spirit in the third dimension, and that is where we start.

Attune yourself to this spiritual center by closing your eyes, going deep within your skull. Remember to breathe, and ask your personal spirit-knowing to awaken. Notice how your spiritual center spins as if whirled by a bell struck in my center. Hear me now and never forget this: I do not care how you see me—through what religion or image—I care only that you ask for me. I created you so that you could sing to me while I tone in the cosmos. You are one with my spirit, and you hear me when your brain

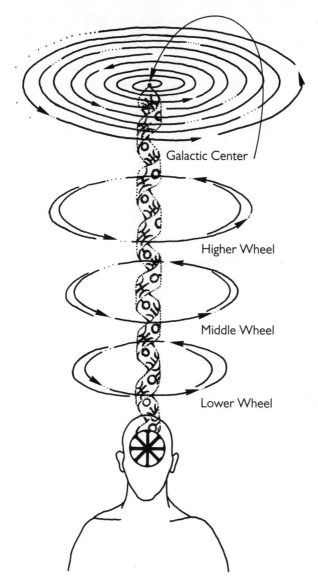

Figure 10.2. The upper dimensions of the crown chakra

pulsates to a high-pitched resonance not audible in the third dimension. You see my beam of light, and you hear me in the divine way that I speak for you.

As your spiritual center enlivens, you hear my tone in the middle wheel of your crown chakra where fifth-dimensional feelings filter down into the *third dimension. In the highest spinning center, nothing is split into black or white, male or female, good or evil—all is unity. But because matter was created and polarized in the third dimension for its evolution in time, my unified and timeless existence needs to be taught to you through the fourth dimension, the middle wheel. For thousands of years your reality has been taken over by fourth-dimensional laws. This causes you to imagine spirits such as gods and devils; one saves you, another damns you. Nothing could be farther from the truth, for they are your teachers. Obsession with duality causes you to miss the divine bridge to my subtle worlds.*

The first dimension is rocks and geologic time, matter without life that holds experiences in time. I exist in emptiness. The second dimension is the plant world where life is injected into matter. Animals live freely in the third, fourth, and fifth dimensions. I say this because you misunderstand animals; you think you are superior to them. But primates do rain dances and baboons wait for the rising of Sirius every summer. Did you know that dolphins swim according to lines of light from Sirius?

As you become more fourth dimensional, you will discover that there is no such thing as the elimination of a species. When you encounter the primal animal sexual force, the jaguar, you realize that all life is potential that can manifest anywhere in the universe. As you eliminate species on Earth in the solid dimension, you destroy your access to the richness of these other realms. Animals do not judge; their dimensional skills are a source of rich diversification in the third dimension. The ancient Egyptian animal totems reveal secrets about human potential needed to develop access to animal genius.

But let us better understand the fourth dimension and how I filter through it continually calling for you through the cycles of time. Most of what you know about the fourth dimension is from religion. Yet there is a hierarchy of fourth-dimensional skills, and your ability to master these skills is going to be the key to your freedom on Earth. Animal theology is more subtle and creative than dividing things into good and evil, dark and light. The third dimension is merely matter's form; the fourth dimension is matter's morphic fields—matter reflecting on itself. Prime access is attunement to electromagnetic fields. Fourth-dimensional skills contact subtle intelligence beyond normal solid reality.

Have you felt me as light? As gravity? As ecstatic power in your body? Religions have small traces of my essence because I go away when you polarize me. Religions have recorded my appearances, yet when I come, you say I am the "burning bush." You find me when you contemplate me as movement and measure, when you feel me as elemental energy in the form of light and waveforms.

The Maya say you are ready to start activating certain survival skills. Are you? Will you confront fear by walking on fire, getting lost in a cave, doing tantra, and meditating with growing plants? Name your powers; remember you really are part of the cosmic plan. *It is time to enjoy magic and divination and to remember the myths and stories about when I've come to Earth. All this can be done by any of you right now, if you just ask for my light. Let us view our present-future from the cosmic, the Mayan, view. Let me tell you how creation came about.*

I have eyes. One day I became fascinated by your solar system seeing Earth emerge from behind the Sun. As I thought about you, an owl opened its eyes in a deep canopied forest and saw flashing bursts of light. A great jaguar in the jungle shivered with my sight of you. A hawk dove through the air layers and sailed. A frog looked into the ethers with luminous, blinking, wet eyes, and a mirror was formed in the sky when obsidian was made in volcanic fire.

For more than an eternity I gazed into that black mirror. It occurred to me, for the first time, to wonder who I am. Gazing into the mirror, I contemplated the trees, vines, flowers, and the belching mountains spewing hot lava into salty water. The more I looked at you, the more I discovered something different from myself; this fascinated me. I realized everything I created is known to me and you can feel me. You are my body, my own cells.

But, as I gazed into the obsidian mirror, I saw that you did not know *me. You do not* know *that I exist in continuous ebb and flow with you. As I exhale, you inhale. Then I realized you could not know me yet for you do not have mind; you are simply my consciousness.*

Intrigued, I contemplated you for another eternity. I saw that you did not experience the divine eros that moves the galaxies. What if there was a form on your planet that was eros, as I am? If such a form existed—exited from me—then this new creation would be sexual and I could feel you. I contemplated you, you felt me, and I wondered what the cosmos would be like if you contemplated me and I felt you. As this thought first came into form, I made your body. I was drawn to you as a new creation to know myself, and now I do! I sent a great bolt of lightning to you, which created magnetism, and light came into form.

In my system of seven powers, seven solar systems, and seven stars, I created orgasm. As I synchronized through sound/word, you were attracted to me through time, and energy centers were born in your spine and brain. In this liquid light I feel you as you feel me. I sent you that electrical spark that made magnetic waves of light that caused a nuclear reaction, the centering of my spinning. As you knew me and I felt you, evolution began in a moment. Neither one of us will ever be satisfied until we are reunified as you ascend your spine.

I attract you, you struggle to arrive, and I shiver with ecstasy. Your crown chakra opens with liquid light—my crystalline matrix for your return.

Just for a moment, close your eyes, breathe, attune to the third and highest vortex of your crown chakra that spins just like the Galactic Center. You are compressed like carbon with all the layers of time, and pressure is building to forge your diamond light body. As I have found my name in the evolution of seven solar systems, you will open your seven powers to name yourself. Your sound causes the cosmos to shiver with the delight of fusion . . .

> In Lak'ech.
> [Yucatec Mayan for "I am Yourself."]
> Galun La'ti
> [Cherokee for "The Mother of the Sky."]

Key Life Passages Tables

THE "KEY LIFE PASSAGES" TABLES show the sign and degree locations of the planets Saturn, Uranus, and Chiron in the birth chart, and they give the timing of Saturn Return, Uranus Opposition, and Chiron Return. Simply find the table that indicates your year of birth and then consult the horizontal line of information after your month of birth.

The first column indicates Saturn's location in your birth chart, and the second column shows the time range of Saturn Return. The third column indicates where Uranus is located in your birth chart, and the fourth column shows the time range of Uranus Opposition. The fifth column indicates Chiron's location in your birth chart, and the last column shows the time range of Chiron Return. Numbers that are out of sequence exist because of the "retrograde" motion of planets, which occurs at certain times of the year when planets appear to move backward in the sky from our viewing perspective on Earth.

In order to get an *exact* timing for these key life passages, an astrologer must be consulted. However the information given here is accurate enough to offer a very close time range. It is important to note that while the time ranges listed here cover the most intense phase of each life-passage period, the influence of these planetary transits on the individual tends to begin approximately a year before the dates listed and to continue for a year after these dates.

For individuals wishing to have a more exact location of planets in their birth charts and timing of these key life passages, an astrologer can be consulted or a free computerized chart can be obtained by going to www.astrotheme.com/horoscope_chart_sign_ascendant .php. Also many fine Apps are available for casting your chart, and you should try a few of them to see which ones work for you. If you need an ephemeris to calculate your Saturn transit, there are many choices online. Have fun!

Note

The tables for Saturn Return and Uranus Opposition give the range in which these two planets arrive at the exact degree and minute of their respective transits to the monthly natal positions indicated, although minutes of degrees are not listed in the tables.

All tables for Chiron give the range in which Chiron arrives at the exact degree of its transits, regardless of the natal or transiting minute of that degree. This is due to the fact that published ephemerides for Chiron at this time are not available that list exact degree and minute positions of Chiron on a daily basis for the years covered in these tables.

All tables are based on planetary positions listed in the following ephemerides: *The American Ephemeris for the 20th Century, 1900 to 2000 at Midnight* by Neil F. Michelsen (San Diego: ACS Publications, 1980); *The American Ephemeris for the 21st Century, 2001 to 2050 at Midnight*, Revised by Neil F. Michelsen (San Diego: ACS Publications, 1982); and *Ephemeris of Chiron, 1890–2000* by James Neely and Eric Tarkington.

KEY LIFE PASSAGES

1940	Saturn	Return	Uranus	Opposition	Chiron	Return
Jan	24°–25° Aries	6/68–3/69	18°–17° Taurus	11/78–9/79	17°–15° Cancer	9/89–7/90
Feb	25°–27° Aries	7/68–4/69	17°–18° Taurus	11/78–9/79	15°–14° Cancer	8/89–6/90
Mar	27° Aries– 1° Taurus	4/69–5/69	18°–19° Taurus	12/78–10/79	14°–13° Cancer	6/89–6/90
April	1°–5° Taurus	5/69–3/70	19°–21° Taurus	12/78–11/79	14°–15° Cancer	8/89–6/90
May	5°–8° Taurus	6/69–4/70	21°–23° Taurus	11/79–9/80	15°–17° Cancer	9/89–7/90
June	8°–11° Taurus	8/69–5/70	23°–24° Taurus	12/79–10/80	17°–20° Cancer	6/90–8/90
July	12°–14° Taurus	5/70	24°–25° Taurus	1/80–11/80	20°–24° Cancer	7/90–6/91
Aug	14° Taurus	5/70	25°–26° Taurus	11/80–8/81	24°–27° Cancer	9/90–7/91
Sept	14°–13° Taurus	5/70	26°–25° Taurus	11/80–8/81	27° Cancer– 0° Leo	10/90–7/91
Oct	13°–11° Taurus	4/70–5/70	25°–24° Taurus	1/80–11/80	0°–1° Leo	7/91–8/91
Nov	11°–9° Taurus	4/70	24°–23° Taurus	12/79–11/80	1° Leo	7/91–8/91
Dec	9°–7° Taurus	7/69–4/70	23°–22° Taurus	12/79–10/80	1° Leo– 29° Cancer	7/91–8/91

1941	Saturn	Return	Uranus	Opposition	Chiron	Return
Jan	7°–8° Taurus	7/69–4/70	22° Taurus	11/79–9/80	29°–27° Cancer	10/90–7/91
Feb	8°–10° Taurus	7/69–4/70	22° Taurus	11/79–9/80	27°–25° Cancer	9/90–7/91
Mar	10°–13° Taurus	4/70–5/70	22°–23° Taurus	12/79–10/80	25° Cancer	9/90–6/91
April	13°–16° Taurus	5/70–2/71	23°–25° Taurus	12/79–11/80	25°–26° Cancer	9/90–6/91
May	16°–20° Taurus	6/70–4/71	25°–26° Taurus	2/80–9/81	26°–28° Cancer	9/90–7/91
June	20°–24° Taurus	7/70–5/71	27°–28° Taurus	12/80–10/81	28° Cancer– 1° Leo	7/91–8/91
July	24°–27° Taurus	5/71	28°–29° Taurus	1/81–11/81	1°–5° Leo	7/91–6/92
Aug	27°–28° Taurus	5/71–6/71	29° Taurus– 0°Gemini	2/81–11/81	5°–8° Leo	9/91–6/92
Sept	28° Taurus	6/71	0° Gemini	2/81–11/81	8°–11° Leo	10/91–7/92
Oct	28°–26° Taurus	5/71–6/71	0° Gemini– 29° Taurus	1/81–11/81	11°–13° Leo	7/92–8/92
Nov	26°–24° Taurus	5/71	29°–27° Taurus	12/80–11/81	13°–14° Leo	8/92
Dec	24°–22° Taurus	8/70–5/71	27°–26° Taurus	12/80–10/81	14°–13° Leo	8/92

KEY LIFE PASSAGES

1942	Saturn	Return	Uranus	Opposition	Chiron	Return
Jan	22°–21° Taurus	8/70–4/71	26° Taurus	11/80–9/81	13°–11° Leo	7/92–8/92
Feb	21°–22° Taurus	8/70–4/71	26° Taurus	11/80–9/81	11°–9° Leo	10/91–7/92
Mar	22°–25° Taurus	4/71–5/71	26°–27° Taurus	11/80–10/81	9°–8° Leo	10/91–7/92
April	25°–28° Taurus	5/71–6/71	27°–29° Taurus	12/80–11/81	8° Leo	10/91–6/92
May	29° Taurus–2° Gemini	6/71–4/72	29° Taurus–0° Gemini	1/81–9/82	8°–10° Leo	10/91–7/92
June	2°–6° Gemini	7/71–5/72	0°–2° Gemini	12/81–10/82	10°–13° Leo	7/92–8/92
July	6°–9° Gemini	8/71–5/72	2°–3° Gemini	12/81–11/82	13°–17° Leo	8/92–5/93
Aug	9°–11° Gemini	5/72–6/72	3°–4° Gemini	1/82–11/82	17°–21° Leo	9/92–7/93
Sept	11°–12° Gemini	6/72	4° Gemini	2/82–11/82	21°–24° Leo	10/92–7/93
Oct	12°–11° Gemini	6/72	4°–3° Gemini	1/82–11/82	24°–27° Leo	7/93–8/93
Nov	11°–9° Gemini	5/72–6/72	3°–2° Gemini	12/81–11/82	27°–29° Leo	8/93–9/93
Dec	9°–6° Gemini	5/72	2°–1° Gemini	12/81–10/82	29° Leo	8/93–9/93

1943	Saturn	Return	Uranus	Opposition	Chiron	Return
Jan	6°–5° Gemini	8/71–5/72	1°–0° Gemini	11/81–9/82	29°–27° Leo	8/93–9/93
Feb	5°–6° Gemini	8/71–4/72	0° Gemini	11/81–9/82	27°–25° Leo	7/93–8/93
Mar	6°–8° Gemini	8/71–5/72	0°–1° Gemini	11/81–9/82	25°–23° Leo	11/92–8/93
April	8°–11° Gemini	5/72–6/72	1°–3° Gemini	12/81–10/82	23°–22° Leo	10/92–7/93
May .	11°–15° Gemini	6/72–3/73	3°–4° Gemini	1/82–11/82	23°–24° Leo	11/92–7/93
June	15°–18° Gemini	7/72–5/73	4°–6° Gemini	11/82–10/83	24°–26° Leo	7/93–8/93
July	18°–22° Gemini	8/72–6/73	6°–7° Gemini	12/82–11/83	26° Leo–0° Virgo	8/93–9/93
Aug	22°–25° Gemini	6/73	8° Gemini	1/83–11/83	0°–4° Virgo	9/93–6/94
Sept	25°–26° Gemini	6/73–7/73	8° Gemini	2/83–11/83	4°–8° Virgo	10/93–7/94
Oct	26° Gemini	7/73	8° Gemini	1/83–11/83	8°–12° Virgo	11/93–8/94
Nov	26°–24° Gemini	6/73–7/73	7°–6° Gemini	12/82–11/83	12°–14° Virgo	8/94–9/94
Dec	26°–24° Gemini	6/73–7/73	7°–6° Gemini	12/82–11/83	12°–14° Virgo	8/94–9/94

KEY LIFE PASSAGES

1944	Saturn	Return	Uranus	Opposition	Chiron	Return
Jan	21°–20° Gemini	9/72–5/73	5°–4° Gemini	11/82–9/83	15°–14° Virgo	9/94
Feb	20°–19° Gemini	8/72–5/73	4° Gemini	11/82	14°–12° Virgo	8/94–9/94
Mar	19°–21° Gemini	8/72–5/73	4°–5° Gemini	11/82–9/83	12°–10° Virgo	8/94
April	21°–23° Gemini	5/73–6/73	5°–7° Gemini	12/82–10/83	10°–9° Virgo	12/93–8/94
May	23°–27° Gemini	6/73–7/73	7°–8° Gemini	1/83–11/83	9° Virgo	12/93–8/94
June	27° Gemini– 1° Cancer	7/73–5/74	9°–10° Gemini	2/83–10/84	9°–11° Virgo	12/93–8/94
July	1°–5° Cancer	8/73–6/74	10°–12° Gemini	12/83–11/84	11°–15° Virgo	8/94–9/94
Aug	5°–8° Cancer	6/74–7/74	12° Gemini	1/84–11/84	15°–19° Virgo	9/94–10/94
Sept	8°–10° Cancer	6/74–7/74	13° Gemini	2/84–11/84	19°–23° Virgo	10/94–7/95
Oct	10° Cancer	7/74	13°–12° Gemini	1/84–11/84	23°–28° Virgo	11/94–9/95
Nov	10°–9° Cancer	7/74	12°–11° Gemini	1/84–11/84	28° Virgo– 1° Libra	8/95–9/95
Dec	9°–7° Cancer	6/74–7/74	11°–10° Gemini	12/83–10/84	1°–3° Libra	9/95–10/95

1945	Saturn	Return	Uranus	Opposition	Chiron	Return
Jan	7°–4° Cancer	6/74	9° Gemini	11/83–9/84	3° Libra	9/95–10/95
Feb	4°–3° Cancer	9/73–6/74	9° Gemini	3/83–12/83	3°–1° Libra	9/95–10/95
Mar	3°–4° Cancer	9/73–6/74	9° Gemini	11/83–9/84	1° Libra– 29° Virgo	9/95
April	4°–6° Cancer	9/73–6/74	9°–11° Gemini	12/83–10/84	29°–27° Virgo	8/95–9/95
May	6°–9° Cancer	6/74–7/74	11°–12° Gemini	1/84–11/84	27°–26° Virgo	12/94–8/95
June	9°–13° Cancer	7/74–4/75	13°–14° Gemini	2/84–10/85	26°–28° Virgo	12/94–9/95
July	13°–17° Cancer	8/74–6/75	14°–16° Gemini	12/84–11/85	28° Virgo– 0° Libra	8/95–9/95
Aug	17°–21° Cancer	9/74–7/75	16°–17° Gemini	1/85–11/85	0°–4° Libra	9/95–10/95
Sept	21°–23° Cancer	7/75	17° Gemini	2/85–11/85	4°–9° Libra	10/95–7/96
Oct	23°–24° Cancer	7/75–8/75	17°–16° Gemini	1/85–11/85	9°–13° Libra	11/95–8/96
Nov	24° Cancer	7/75–8/75	16°–15° Gemini	1/85–11/85	13°–17° Libra	12/95–9/96
Dec	24°–22° Cancer	7/75	15°–14° Gemini	12/84–10/85	17°–20° Libra	9/96–10/96

KEY LIFE PASSAGES

1946	Saturn	Return	Uranus	Opposition	Chiron	Return
Jan	22°–19° Cancer	6/75–7/75	14°–13° Gemini	3/84–9/85	20°–21° Libra	10/96
Feb	19°–18° Cancer	10/74–6/75	13° Gemini	2/84–12/84	21°–20° Libra	10/96
Mar	18°–17° Cancer	9/74–6/75	13°–14° Gemini	3/84–11/84	20°–18° Libra	9/96–10/96
April	18°–19° Cancer	10/74–6/75	14°–15° Gemini	12/84–10/85	18°–16° Libra	9/96–10/96
May	19°–22° Cancer	6/75–7/75	15°–17° Gemini	12/84–11/85	16°–15° Libra	9/96
June	22°–25° Cancer	7/75–8/75	17°–18° Gemini	2/85–9/86	15°–14° Libra	8/96–9/96
July	25°–29° Cancer	8/75–6/76	18°–20° Gemini	12/85–11/86	15°–17° Libra	9/96
Aug	29° Cancer–3° Leo	9/75–7/76	20°–21° Gemini	1/86–11/86	17°–20° Libra	9/96–10/96
Sept	3°–6° Leo	7/76	21° Gemini	2/86–12/86	20°–24° Libra	10/96–11/96
Oct	6°–8° Leo	7/76–8/76	21° Gemini	2/86–12/86	24°–28° Libra	11/96–8/97
Nov	8° Leo	8/76	21°–20° Gemini	1/86–11/86	28° Libra–2° Scorpio	12/96–9/97
Dec	8°–7° Leo	8/76	20°–18° Gemini	12/85–11/86	2°–6° Scorpio	2/97–10/97

1947	Saturn	Return	Uranus	Opposition	Chiron	Return
Jan	7°–5° Leo	7/76–8/76	18° Gemini	12/85–10/86	6°–8° Scorpio	10/97–11/97
Feb	4°–3° Leo	7/76	17° Gemini	2/85–12/85	8° Scorpio	11/97
Mar	2°–1° Scorpio	10/75–7/76	17°–18° Gemini	2/85–12/85	8°–7° Leo	10/97–11/97
April	1°–2° Leo	10/75–6/76	18°–19° Gemini	12/85–10/86	7°–5° Scorpio	10/97–11/97
May	2°–4° Leo	10/75–7/76	19°–21° Gemini	12/85–11/86	5°–3° Scorpio	9/97–10/97
June	4°–7° Leo	7/76–8/76	21°–22° Gemini	2/86–9/87	3°–2° Scorpio	2/97–10/97
July	7°–11° Leo	8/76–5/77	22°–24° Gemini	12/86–11/87	2°–3° Scorpio	2/97–10/97
Aug	11°–15° Leo	9/76–7/77	24°–25° Gemini	1/87–11/87	3°–5° Scorpio	9/97–10/97
Sept	15°–19° Leo	10/76–8/77	25°–26° Gemini	2/87–12/87	5°–8° Scorpio	10/97–11/97
Oct	19°–21° Leo	8/77	26°–25° Gemini	2/87–12/87	8°–13° Scorpio	11/97–8/98
Nov	21°–22° Leo	8/77	25°–24° Gemini	1/87–12/87	13°–17° Scorpio	12/97–10/98
Dec	22° Leo	8/77–9/77	24°–23° Gemini	12/86–11/87	17°–20° Scorpio	1/98–10/98

KEY LIFE PASSAGES

1948	Saturn	Return	Uranus	Opposition	Chiron	Return
Jan	21°–19° Leo	8/77	23°–22° Gemini	12/86–10/87	20°–23° Scorpio	10/98–11/98
Feb	19°–17° Leo	7/77–8/77	22° Gemini	3/86–12/86	23°–24° Scorpio	11/98
Mar	17°–16° Leo	10/76–7/77	22° Gemini	3/86–12/86	24° Scorpio	11/98
April	15° Leo	10/76–7/77	22°–23° Gemini	12/86–10/87	24°–22° Scorpio	11/98
May	15°–17° Leo	10/76–7/77	23°–25° Gemini	1/87–11/87	22°–20° Scorpio	10/98–11/98
June	17°–20° Leo	7/77–8/77	25°–27° Gemini	2/87–9/88	20°–18° Scorpio	2/98–10/98
July	20°–23° Leo	8/77–5/78	27°–28° Gemini	12/87–11/88	18° Scorpio	2/98–10/98
Aug	23°–27° Leo	9/77–7/78	28° Gemini–0° Cancer	1/88–12/88	18°–20° Scorpio	2/98–10/98
Sept	27° Leo–1° Virgo	10/77–8/78	0° Cancer	2/88–12/88	20°–22° Scorpio	10/98–11/98
Oct	1°–4° Virgo	8/78	0° Cancer	2/88–12/88	22°–26° Scorpio	11/98–12/98
Nov	4°–5° Virgo	8/78–9/78	0° Cancer–29° Gemini	2/88–12/88	26° Scorpio–0° Sagittarius	12/98–10/99
Dec	5°–6° Virgo	9/78	29°–28° Gemini	1/88–11/88	0°–4° Sagittarius	1/99–11/99

1949	Saturn	Return	Uranus	Opposition	Chiron	Return
Jan	5°–4° Virgo	8/78–9/78	28°–26° Gemini	12/87–10/88	4°–7° Sagittarius	10/99–12/99
Feb	4°–2° Virgo	8/78	26° Gemini	3/87–12/87	7°–8° Sagittarius	11/99–12/99
Mar	2°–0° Virgo	11/77–8/78	26° Gemini	3/87–12/87	8°–9° Sagittarius	12/99
April	0° Virgo–29° Leo	11/77–7/78	26°–27° Gemini	12/87–10/88	9°–7° Sagittarius	11/99–12/99
May	29° Leo–0° Virgo	11/77–7/78	27°–29° Gemini	12/87–11/88	7°–5° Sagittarius	11/99–12/99
June	0°–2° Virgo	11/77–8/78	29° Gemini–1° Cancer	2/88–12/88	5°–3° Sagittarius	2/99–11/99
July	2°–5° Cancer	8/78–9/78	1°–2° Virgo	12/88–11/89	3°–2° Sagittarius	1/99–10/99
Aug	5°–9° Virgo	9/78–6/79	2°–4° Cancer	1/89–12/89	2°–3° Sagittarius	1/99–10/99
Sept	9°–12° Virgo	10/78–8/79	4° Cancer	2/89–12/89	3°–5° Sagittarius	2/99–11/99
Oct	13°–16° Virgo	11/78–9/79	4°–5° Cancer	3/89–12/89	5°–8° Sagittarius	11/99–12/99
Nov	16°–18° Virgo	9/79	4° Cancer	2/89–12/89	8°–12° Sagittarius	12/99–9/00
Dec	18°–19° Virgo	9/79	3°–2° Cancer	1/89–12/89	12°–15° Sagittarius	1/00–11/00

KEY LIFE PASSAGES

1950	Saturn	Return	Uranus	Opposition	Chiron	Return
Jan	19°–18° Virgo	9/79	2°–1° Cancer	12/88–11/89	15°–18° Sagittarius	2/00–12/00
Feb	18°–16° Virgo	9/79	1°–0° Cancer	3/88–10/89	18°–20° Sagittarius	11/00–12/00
Mar	16°–14° Virgo	8/79–9/79	0°–1° Cancer	3/88–12/88	20°–21° Sagittarius	12/00
April	14°–12° Virgo	11/78–8/79	1°–2° Cancer	12/88–10/89	21° Sagittarius	12/00
May	12° Virgo	11/78–8/79	2°–3° Cancer	1/89–11/89	21°–19° Sagittarius	12/00
June	12°–14° Virgo	11/78–8/79	3°–5° Cancer	2/89–12/89	19°–17° Sagittarius	3/00–12/00
July	14°–17° Virgo	8/79–9/79	5°–7° Cancer	4/89–11/90	17°–15° Sagittarius	2/00–11/00
Aug	17°–20° Virgo	9/79–6/80	7°–8° Cancer	1/90–12/90	15° Sagittarius	2/00–11/00
Sept	20°–24° Virgo	10/79–8/80	8°–9° Cancer	2/90–12/90	15°–17° Sagittarius	2/00–11/00
Oct	24°–28° Virgo	11/79–9/80	9° Cancer	3/90–12/90	17°–19° Sagittarius	3/00–12/00
Nov	28° Virgo–0° Libra	9/80	9°–8° Cancer	2/90–12/90	19°–22° Sagittarius	12/00–9/01
Dec	0°–2° Libra	9/80–10/80	8°–7° Cancer	1/90–12/90	22°–26° Sagittarius	12/00–11/01

1951	Saturn	Return	Uranus	Opposition	Chiron	Return
Jan	2° Libra	10/80	7°–6° Cancer	1/90–11/90	26°–29° Sagittarius	2/01–12/01
Feb	2°–0° Libra	9/80–10/80	6°–5° Cancer	12/89–10/90	29° Sagittarius–1° Capricorn	4/01–12/01
Mar	0° Libra–28° Virgo	9/80	5° Cancer	12/89	1°–2° Capricorn	12/01–1/02
April	28°–26° Virgo	12/79–9/80	5°–6° Cancer	12/89–10/90	2° Capricorn	12/01–1/02
May	26°–25° Virgo	11/79–8/80	6°–7° Cancer	1/90–11/90	2°–1° Capricorn	12/01–1/02
June	25°–26° Virgo	11/79–8/80	7°–9° Cancer	2/90–12/90	1° Capricorn–29° Sagittarius	4/01–12/01
July	26°–28° Virgo	12/79–9/80	9°–11° Cancer	4/90–11/91	29°–27° Sagittarius	2/01–12/01
Aug	28° Virgo–1° Libra	9/80–10/80	11°–12° Cancer	1/91–12/91	27°–26° Sagittarius	2/01–11/01
Sept	2°–5° Libra	10/80–8/81	12°–13° Cancer	3/91–1/92	26°–27° Sagittarius	2/01–11/01
Oct	5°–9° Libra	11/80–9/81	13° Cancer	4/91–1/92	27°–29° Sagittarius	2/01–12/01
Nov	9°–12° Libra	12/80–10/81	13° Cancer	3/91–1/92	29° Sagittarius–2° Capricorn	4/01–1/02
Dec	12°–14° Libra	10/81	13°–12° Cancer	2/91–12/91	2°–5° Capricorn	12/01–11/02

KEY LIFE PASSAGES

1952	Saturn	Return	Uranus	Opposition	Chiron	Return
Jan	14° Libra	10/81	12°–10° Cancer	1/91–12/91	5°–8° Capricorn	1/02–12/02
Feb	14°–13° Libra	10/81	10° Cancer	1/91–11/91	8°–10° Capricorn	3/02–1/03
Mar	13°–11° Libra	9/81–10/81	10°–9° Cancer	1/91–10/91	10°–12° Capricorn	12/02–10/03
April	11°–9° Libra	1/81–9/81	9°–10° Cancer	1/91–11/91	12° Capricorn	1/03–10/03
May	9°–8° Libra	12/80–9/81	10°–12° Cancer	1/91–12/91	12°–11° Capricorn	1/03–10/03
June	8° Libra	12/80–8/81	12°–13° Cancer	2/91–1/92	11°–9° Capricorn	4/02–1/03
July	8°–10° Libra	12/80–9/81	13°–15° Cancer	4/91–11/92	9°–7° Capricorn	2/02–12/02
Aug	10°–13° Libra	9/81–10/81	15°–17° Cancer	2/92–12/92	7°–6° Capricorn	2/02–12/02
Sept	13°–16° Libra	10/81–7/82	17°–18° Cancer	3/92–10/93	6° Capricorn	2/02–11/02
Oct	16°–20° Libra	11/81–9/82	18° Cancer	1/93–10/93	6°–8° Capricorn	2/02–12/02
Nov	20°–23° Libra	12/81–10/82	18°–17° Cancer	4/92–10/93	8°–10° Capricorn	3/02–1/03
Dec	23°–26° Libra	10/82–11/82	17°–16° Cancer	2/92–1/93	10°–13° Capricorn	12/02–11/03

1953	Saturn	Return	Uranus	Opposition	Chiron	Return
Jan	26°–27° Libra	10/82–7/83	16°–15° Cancer	1/92–12/92	13°–16° Capricorn	1/03–12/03
Feb	27°–26° Libra	10/82–7/83	15°–14° Cancer	1/92–11/92	16°–18° Capricorn	2/03–1/04
Mar	26°–25° Libra	10/82–11/82	14° Cancer	1/92–11/92	18°–20° Capricorn	4/03–10/04
April	25°–22° Libra	1/82–10/82	14°–15° Cancer	1/92–11/92	20°–21° Capricorn	1/04–11/04
May	22°–21° Libra	12/81–9/82	15°–16° Cancer	1/92–12/92	21°–20° Capricorn	1/04–11/04
June	20° Libra	12/81–9/82	16°–18° Cancer	2/92–1/93	20°–18° Capricorn	4/03–10/04
July	20°–21° Libra	12/81–9/82	18°–19° Cancer	1/93–12/93	18°–16° Capricorn	2/03–1/04
Aug	21°–24° Libra	1/82–10/82	20°–21° Cancer	2/93–1/94	16°–15° Capricorn	2/03–12/03
Sept	24°–27° Libra	10/82–11/82	21°–22° Cancer	3/93–11/94	15° Capricorn	2/03–12/03
Oct	27° Libra–1° Scorpio	11/82–9/83	22°–23° Cancer	1/94–11/94	15°–16° Capricorn	2/03–12/03
Nov	1°–4° Scorpio	12/82–10/83	23°–22° Cancer	1/94–11/94	16°–18° Capricorn	2/03–1/04
Dec	4°–7° Scorpio	1/83–11/83	22°–21° Cancer	3/93–10/94	18°–20° Capricorn	4/03–10/04

KEY LIFE PASSAGES

1954	Saturn	Return	Uranus	Opposition	Chiron	Return
Jan	7°–9° Scorpio	11/83	21°–20° Cancer	2/93–12/93	20°–23° Capricorn	1/04–12/04
Feb	9° Scorpio	11/83	20°–19° Cancer	1/93–12/93	23°–26° Capricorn	2/04–1/05
Mar	9°–7° Scorpio	11/83	19° Cancer	1/93–11/93	26°–27° Capricorn	4/04–10/05
April	7°–5° Scorpio	10/83–11/83	19° Cancer	1/93–11/93	27°–28° Capricorn	1/05–11/05
May	5°–3° Scorpio	1/83–10/83	19°–20° Cancer	2/93–12/93	28° Capricorn	1/05–11/05
June	3°–2° Scorpio	12/82–10/83	20°–22° Cancer	2/93–10/94	28°–26° Capricorn	4/04–11/05
July	2°–3° Scorpio	12/82–9/83	22°–24° Cancer	1/94–12/94	26°–25° Capricorn	3/04–1/05
Aug	3°–5° Scorpio	1/83–10/83	24°–25° Cancer	2/94–1/95	25°–23° Capricorn	2/04–1/05
Sept	5°–7° Scorpio	10/83–11/83	26°–27° Cancer	4/94–11/95	23° Capricorn	2/04–12/04
Oct	8°–11° Scorpio	11/83–8/84	27° Cancer	1/95–11/95	23° Capricorn	2/04–12/04
Nov	11°–15° Scorpio	12/83–10/84	27° Cancer	2/95–11/95	23°–25° Capricorn	2/04–1/05
Dec	15°–18° Scorpio	1/84–11/84	27°–26° Cancer	4/94–11/95	25°–27° Capricorn	3/04–10/05

1955	Saturn	Return	Uranus	Opposition	Chiron	Return
Jan	18°–20° Scorpio	11/84	26°–25° Cancer	3/94–1/95	27° Capricorn– 0° Aquarius	1/05–12/05
Feb	20°–21° Scorpio	11/84	25°–24° Cancer	2/94–12/94	0°–2° Aquarius	2/05–1/06
Mar	21°–20° Scorpio	11/84	24°–23° Cancer	2/94–12/94	2°–4° Aquarius	3/05–11/06
April	20°–18° Scorpio	11/84	23° Cancer	2/94–12/94	4°–5° Aquarius	1/06–12/06
May	18°–16° Scorpio	2/84–11/84	23°–25° Cancer	2/94–12/94	5° Aquarius	2/06–12/06
June	16°–14° Scorpio	1/84–10/84	25°–26° Cancer	3/94–1/95	5°–4° Aquarius	1/06–12/06
July	14° Scorpio	1/84–10/84	26°–28° Cancer	1/95–12/95	4°–2° Aquarius	3/05–11/06
Aug	14°–15° Scorpio	1/84–10/84	28° Cancer– 0° Leo	2/95–1/96	2°–0° Aquarius	2/05–1/06
Sept	16°–18° Scorpio	2/84–11/84	0°–1° Leo	4/95–11/96	0° Aquarius	2/05–12/05
Oct	18°–21° Scorpio	11/84–8/85	1°–2° Leo	2/96–12/96	0° Aquarius	2/05–12/05
Nov	21°–25° Scorpio	12/84–10/85	2° Leo	2/96–12/96	0°–1° Aquarius	2/05–1/06
Dec	25°–28° Scorpio	1/85–11/85	2°–1° Leo	2/96–12/96	1°–3° Aquarius	3/05–1/06

KEY LIFE PASSAGES

1956	Saturn	Return	Uranus	Opposition	Chiron	Return
Jan	28° Scorpio–1° Sagittarius	11/85	1° Leo–29° Cancer	3/95–11/96	3°–6° Aquarius	4/05–12/06
Feb	1°–2° Sagittarius	11/85–12/85	29°–28° Cancer	2/95–1/96	6°–8° Aquarius	2/06–1/07
Mar	2° Sagittarius	12/85	28° Cancer	2/95–12/95	8°–10° Aquarius	3/06–11/07
April	2°–1° Sagittarius	11/85–12/85	28° Cancer	2/95–12/95	10°–11° Aquarius	1/07–12/07
May	0° Sagittarius–28° Scorpio	11/85	28°–29° Cancer	2/95–1/96	11° Aquarius	2/07–12/07
June	28°–26° Scorpio	1/85–11/85	29° Cancer–1° Leo	3/95–11/96	11°–10° Aquarius	1/07–12/07
July	26° Scorpio	1/85–10/85	1°–2° Leo	1/96–12/96	10°–9° Aquarius	4/06–11/07
Aug	26° Scorpio	1/85–10/85	3°–4° Leo	3/96–10/97	9°–7° Aquarius	3/06–1/07
Sept	26°–29° Scorpio	1/85–11/85	4°–6° Leo	1/97–12/97	7°–6° Aquarius	2/06–1/07
Oct	29° Scorpio–2° Sagittarius	11/85–12/85	6° Leo	2/97–12/97	6° Aquarius	2/06–12/06
Nov	2°–5° Sagittarius	12/85–10/86	6° Leo	3/97–12/97	6°–7° Aquarius	2/06–1/07
Dec	5°–9° Sagittarius	1/86–11/86	6°–5° Leo	2/97–12/97	7°–9° Aquarius	3/06–1/07

1957	Saturn	Return	Uranus	Opposition	Chiron	Return
Jan	9°–12° Sagittarius	2/86–12/86	5°–4° Leo	1/97–12/97	9°–11° Aquarius	4/06–12/07
Feb	12°–13° Sagittarius	12/86	4°–3° Leo	3/96–1/97	11°–14° Aquarius	2/07–1/08
Mar	13°–14° Sagittarius	12/86	3°–2° Leo	3/96–1/97	14°–16° Aquarius	3/07–12/08
April	14°–13° Sagittarius	12/86	2°–3° Leo	3/96–12/96	16°–17° Aquarius	2/08–12/08
May	13°–11° Sagittarius	11/86–12/86	3° Leo	3/96–1/97	17° Aquarius	2/08–12/08
June	11°–9° Sagittarius	2/86–11/86	4°–5° Leo	4/96–11/97	17°–16° Aquarius	2/08–12/08
July	9°–7° Sagittarius	1/86–11/86	5°–7° Leo	2/97–1/98	16°–15° Aquarius	4/07–12/08
Aug	7° Sagittarius	1/86–10/86	7°–9° Leo	3/97–11/98	15°–13° Aquarius	3/07–2/08
Sept	8°–9° Sagittarius	2/86–11/86	9°–10° Leo	2/98–12/98	13°–12° Aquarius	2/07–1/08
Oct	9°–12° Sagittarius	3/86–12/86	10°–11° Leo	3/98–1/99	12° Aquarius	2/07–12/07
Nov	12°–15° Sagittarius	12/86–9/87	11° Leo	3/98–1/99	12°–13° Aquarius	2/07–1/08
Dec	15°–19° Sagittarius	1/87–11/87	11°–10° Leo	3/98–1/99	13°–14° Aquarius	3/07–1/08

KEY LIFE PASSAGES

1958	Saturn	Return	Uranus	Opposition	Chiron	Return
Jan	19°–22° Sagittarius	2/87–12/87	10°–9° Leo	2/98–12/98	14°–17° Aquarius	3/07–12/08
Feb	22°–24° Sagittarius	12/87	9°–8° Leo	4/97–12/98	17°–19° Aquarius	2/08–1/09
Mar	24°–25° Sagittarius	12/87–1/88	8°–7° Leo	3/97–1/98	19°–21° Aquarius	3/08–12/09
April	25° Sagittarius	12/87–1/88	7° Leo	3/97–1/98	21°–22° Aquarius	5/08–12/09
May	25°–23° Sagittarius	12/87	7°–8° Leo	3/97–1/98	22° Aquarius	2/09–12/09
June	23°–21° Sagittarius	11/87–12/87	8°–9° Leo	4/97–12/98	22° Aquarius	2/09–12/09
July	21°–19° Sagittarius	2/87–11/87	9°–11° Leo	2/98–1/99	22°–20° Aquarius	4/08–12/09
Aug	19° Sagittarius	2/87–11/87	11°–13° Leo	3/98–12/99	20°–19° Aquarius	3/08–2/09
Sept	19°–20° Sagittarius	2/87–11/87	13°–15° Leo	2/99–1/00	19°–18° Aquarius	3/08–1/09
Oct	20°–22° Sagittarius	2/87–12/87	15°–16° Leo	3/99–1/00	18°–17° Aquarius	2/08–1/09
Nov	22°–25° Sagittarius	12/87–1/88	16° Leo	4/99–1/00	17°–18° Aquarius	2/08–1/09
Dec	25°–29° Sagittarius	1/88–11/88	16°–15° Leo	3/99–1/00	18°–19° Aquarius	3/08–1/09

1959	Saturn	Return	Uranus	Opposition	Chiron	Return
Jan	29° Sagittarius–2° Capricorn	2/88–12/88	15°–14° Leo	3/99–1/00	19°–21° Aquarius	3/08–12/09
Feb	2°–5° Capricorn	3/88–1/89	14°–13° Leo	2/99–12/99	21°–23° Aquarius	5/08–1/10
Mar	5°–6° Capricorn	12/88–1/89	13°–12° Leo	4/98–11/99	23°–25° Aquarius	3/09–2/10
April	6°–7° Capricorn	1/89	12° Leo	4/98–1/99	25°–27° Aquarius	09–1/11
May	6°–5° Capricorn	12/88–1/89	12° Leo	4/98–11/99	27° Aquarius	3/10–1/11
June	5°–3° Capricorn	12/88–1/89	12°–14° Leo	2/99–12/99	27° Aquarius	3/10–1/11
July	3°–1° Capricorn	3/88–12/88	14°–16° Leo	3/99–1/00	27°–26° Aquarius	5/09–1/11
Aug	1°–0° Capricorn	2/88–11/88	16°–17° Leo	4/99–12/00	26°–24° Aquarius	3/09–12/10
Sept	0° Capricorn	2/88–11/88	18°–19° Leo	2/00–1/01	24°–23° Aquarius	3/09–1/10
Oct	1°–2° Capricorn	2/88–12/88	19°–20° Leo	3/00–2/01	23°–22° Aquarius	2/09–1/10
Nov	2°–5° Capricorn	12/88–1/89	20°–21° Leo	5/00–11/01	22°–23° Aquarius	2/09–1/10
Dec	5°–9° Capricorn	1/89–11/89	21°–20° Leo	4/00–11/01	23°–24° Aquarius	3/09–1/10

KEY LIFE PASSAGES

1960	Saturn	Return	Uranus	Opposition	Chiron	Return
Jan	9°–12° Capricorn	2/89–12/89	20°–19° Leo	3/00–2/01	24°–26° Aquarius	3/09–12/10
Feb	13°–15° Capricorn	3/89–1/90	19°–18° Leo	3/00–1/01	26°–28° Aquarius	5/09–1/11
Mar	15°–17° Capricorn	1/90	18°–17° Leo	2/00–12/00	28° Aquarius– 0° Pisces	3/10–12/11
April	17°–18° Capricorn	1/90	17°–16° Leo	2/00–11/00	0°–1° Pisces	4/10–1/12
May	18°–17° Capricorn	1/90	16°–17° Leo	2/00–12/00	1°–2° Pisces	2/11–1/12
June	17°–15° Capricorn	1/90	17°–18° Leo	2/00–1/01	2°–1° Pisces	2/11–1/12
July	15°–13° Capricorn	3/89–1/90	18°–20° Leo	3/00–2/01	1°–0° Pisces	4/10–1/12
Aug	13°–12° Capricorn	3/89–12/89	20°–22° Leo	4/00–1/02	0° Pisces– 29° Aquarius	3/10–12/11
Sept	12°–11° Capricorn	3/89–12/89	22°–24° Leo	3/01–2/02	29°–28° Aquarius	3/10–2/11
Oct	12°–13° Capricorn	3/89–12/89	24°–25° Leo	4/01–12/02	28°–27° Aquarius	3/10–1/11
Nov	13°–16° Capricorn	3/89–1/90	25° Leo	2/02–12/02	27° Aquarius	3/10–1/11
Dec	16°–19° Capricorn	1/90–10/90	25° Leo	2/02–12/02	27°–28° Aquarius	3/10–2/11

1961	Saturn	Return	Uranus	Opposition	Chiron	Return
Jan	19°–23° Capricorn	2/90–12/90	25°–24° Leo	4/01–12/02	28° Aquarius– 0° Pisces	3/10–12/11
Feb	23°–26° Capricorn	3/90–1/91	24°–23° Leo	3/01–2/02	0°–2° Pisces	4/10–1/12
Mar	26°–28° Capricorn	1/91	23°–22° Leo	3/01–1/02	2°–4° Pisces	3/11–2/12
April	28°–29° Capricorn	1/91–2/91	22°–21° Leo	2/01–12/01	4°–5° Pisces	4/11–12/12
May	29° Capricorn	2/91	21°–22° Leo	2/01–12/01	5°–6° Pisces	5/11–1/13
June	29°–27° Capricorn	1/91–2/91	22°–23° Leo	3/01–1/02	6° Pisces	3/12–1/13
July	27°–25° Capricorn	4/90–1/91	23°–24° Leo	3/01–11/02	6°–5° Pisces	5/11–1/13
Aug	25°–23° Capricorn	3/90–1/91	25°–26° Leo	2/02–1/03	5°–4° Pisces	4/11–12/12
Sept	23° Capricorn	3/90–12/90	26°–28° Leo	3/02–2/03	4°–2° Pisces	3/11–2/12
Oct	23°–24° Capricorn	3/90–12/90	28°–29° Leo	5/02–12/03	2°–1° Pisces	2/11–1/12
Nov	24°–26° Capricorn	3/90–1/91	29° Leo– 0° Virgo	3/03–1/04	1°–2° Pisces	2/11–1/12
Dec	26°–29° Capricorn	1/91–2/91	0° Virgo	3/03–1/04	2°–3° Pisces	3/11–2/12

KEY LIFE PASSAGES

1962	Saturn	Return	Uranus	Opposition	Chiron	Return
Jan	29° Capricorn–3° Aquarius	2/91–12/91	0° Virgo–29° Leo	2/03–1/04	3°–4° Pisces	3/11–2/12
Feb	3°–6° Aquarius	3/91–1/92	29°–28° Leo	4/02–12/03	4°–6° Pisces	4/11–1/13
Mar	6°–9° Aquarius	4/91–1/92	28°–26° Leo	3/02–2/03	6°–8° Pisces	3/12–2/13
April	9°–11° Aquarius	1/92–2/92	26° Leo	3/02–1/03	8°–9° Pisces	4/12–1/14
May	11° Aquarius	2/92	26° Leo	3/02–1/03	9°–10° Pisces	5/12–1/14
June	11°–10° Aquarius	2/92	26°–27° Leo	3/02–1/05	10° Pisces	3/13–1/14
July	10°–8° Aquarius	1/92–2/92	27°–29° Leo	4/02–12/03	10°–9° Pisces	5/12–1/14
Aug	8°–5° Aquarius	4/91–1/92	29° Leo–1° Virgo	2/03–1/04	9°–8° Pisces	4/12–1/14
Sept	5°–4° Aquarius	3/91–1/92	1°–3° Virgo	4/03–12/04	8°–7° Pisces	3/12–2/13
Oct	4°–5° Aquarius	3/91–12/91	3°–4° Virgo	2/04–1/05	7°–6° Pisces	3/12–2/13
Nov	5°–6° Aquarius	4/91–1/92	4°–5° Virgo	3/04–1/05	6° Pisces	3/12–1/13
Dec	6°–9° Aquarius	4/91–2/92	5° Virgo	4/04–1/05	6°–7° Pisces	3/12–2/13

1963	Saturn	Return	Uranus	Opposition	Chiron	Return
Jan	9°–13° Aquarius	2/92–11/92	5°–4° Virgo	3/04–1/05	7°–8° Pisces	3/12–2/13
Feb	13°–16° Aquarius	3/92–1/93	4°–3° Virgo	2/04–1/05	8°–10° Pisces	4/12–1/14
Mar	16°–19° Aquarius	4/92–2/93	2°–1° Virgo	4/03–11/04	10°–12° Pisces	3/13–2/14
April	20°–22° Aquarius	2/93	1° Virgo	4/03–2/04	12°–13° Pisces	4/13–1/15
May	22°–23° Aquarius	2/93	1° Virgo	4/03–1/04	13°–14° Pisces	5/13–1/15
June	23°–22° Aquarius	2/93	1°–2° Virgo	4/03–2/04	14° Pisces	3/14–1/15
July	22°–20° Aquarius	2/93	2°–3° Virgo	5/03–1/05	14° Pisces	3/14–1/15
Aug	20°–18° Aquarius	5/92–2/93	3°–5° Virgo	3/04–2/05	14°–12° Pisces	4/13–1/15
Sept	18°–16° Aquarius	4/92–1/93	5°–7° Virgo	4/04–12/05	12°–11° Pisces	3/13–2/14
Oct	16° Aquarius	4/92–1/93	7°–9° Virgo	3/05–2/06	11°–10° Pisces	3/13–1/14
Nov	16°–17° Aquarius	4/92–1/93	9° Virgo	4/05–2/06	10° Pisces	3/13–1/14
Dec	17°–20° Aquarius	4/92–2/93	9°–10° Virgo	4/05–2/06	10° Pisces	3/13–1/14

KEY LIFE PASSAGES

1964	Saturn	Return	Uranus	Opposition	Chiron	Return
Jan	20°–23° Aquarius	2/93–11/93	9° Virgo	4/05–2/06	10°–12° Pisces	3/13–2/14
Feb	23°–27° Aquarius	3/93–1/94	9°–7° Virgo	3/05–2/06	12°–14° Pisces	4/13–1/15
Mar	27° Aquarius– 0° Pisces	4/93–2/94	7°–6° Virgo	5/04–1/06	14°–16° Pisces	3/14–12/15
April	0°–3° Pisces	2/94–3/94	6°–5° Virgo	4/04–2/05	16°–17° Pisces	4/14–1/16
May	3°–4° Pisces	2/94–3/94	5°–6° Virgo	4/04–2/05	17°–18° Pisces	5/14–2/16
June	4°–5° Pisces	3/94	6° Virgo	4/04–11/05	18° Pisces	3/15–2/16
July	4°–3° Pisces	2/94–3/94	6°–8° Virgo	2/05–1/06	18° Pisces	3/15–2/16
Aug	3°–1° Pisces	2/94	8°–10° Virgo	3/05–2/06	18°–16° Pisces	4/14–2/16
Sept	1° Pisces– 29° Aquarius	5/93–2/94	10°–12° Virgo	5/05–1/07	16°–15° Pisces	3/14–12/15
Oct	29°–28° Aquarius	4/93–1/94	12°–13° Virgo	3/06–2/07	15°–14° Pisces	3/14–1/15
Nov	28°–29° Aquarius	4/93–1/94	13°–14° Virgo	4/06–3/07	14° Pisces	3/14–1/15
Dec	29° Aquarius– 1° Pisces	5/93–2/94	14° Virgo	6/06–12/07	14° Pisces	3/14–1/15

1965	Saturn	Return	Uranus	Opposition	Chiron	Return
Jan	1°–4° Pisces	2/94–3/94	14° Virgo	5/06–12/07	14°–16° Pisces	3/14–12/15
Feb	4°–7° Pisces	3/94–12/94	14°–12° Virgo	4/06–2/07	16°–17° Pisces	4/14–1/16
Mar	7°–11° Pisces	4/94–2/95	12°–11° Virgo	3/06–2/07	17°–19° Pisces	5/14–2/16
April	11°–14° Pisces	5/94–3/95	11°–10° Virgo	3/06–1/07	19°–21° Pisces	4/15–1/17
May	14°–16° Pisces	3/95	10° Virgo	5/05–11/06	21°–22° Pisces	5/15–2/17
June	16°–17° Pisces	3/95	10°–11° Virgo	6/05–12/06	22° Pisces	3/16–2/17
July	17°–16° Pisces	3/95	11°–12° Virgo	3/06–2/07	22°–21° Pisces	5/15–2/17
Aug	16°–14° Pisces	2/95–3/95	12°–14° Virgo	4/06–12/07	21°–20° Pisces	4/15–1/17
Sept	14°–12° Pisces	6/94–2/95	14°–16° Virgo	6/06–2/08	20°–19° Pisces	4/15–12/16
Oct	12°–10° Pisces	5/94–2/95	16°–18° Virgo	4/07–3/08	19°–18° Pisces	3/15–2/16
Nov	10° Pisces	5/94–1/95	18°–19° Virgo	5/07–1/09	18°–17° Pisces	5/14–2/16
Dec	10°–12° Pisces	5/94–2/95	19° Virgo	3/08–1/09	17°–18° Pisces	5/14–2/16

KEY LIFE PASSAGES

1966	Saturn	Return	Uranus	Opposition	Chiron	Return
Jan	12°–15° Pisces	6/94–3/95	19° Virgo	3/08–1/09	18°–19° Pisces	3/15–2/16
Feb	15°–18° Pisces	3/95–12/95	19°–17° Virgo	5/07–12/08	19°–21° Pisces	4/15–1/17
Mar	18°–22° Pisces	4/95–2/96	17°–16° Virgo	4/07–2/08	21°–23° Pisces	5/15–3/17
April	22°–25° Pisces	5/95–3/96	16°–15° Virgo	3/07–2/08	23°–24° Pisces	4/16–1/18
May	25°–28° Pisces	3/96	15° Virgo	3/07–1/08	24°–25° Pisces	5/16–2/18
June	28°–29° Pisces	3/96–4/96	15°–16° Virgo	3/07–1/08	25°–26° Pisces	6/16–2/18
July	29° Pisces	4/96	16°–17° Virgo	3/07–2/08	26°–25° Pisces	6/16–2/18
Aug	29°–27° Pisces	3/96–4/96	17°–19° Virgo	4/07–1/09	25°–24° Pisces	5/16–2/18
Sept	27°–25° Pisces	3/96	19°–21° Virgo	3/08–2/09	24°–23° Pisces	4/16–1/18
Oct	25°–23° Pisces	5/95–3/96	21°–22° Virgo	4/08–12/09	23°–22° Pisces	3/16–3/17
Nov	23°–22° Pisces	5/95–2/96	22°–23° Virgo	3/09–1/10	22°–21° Pisces	5/15–2/17
Dec	22°–23° Pisces	5/95–2/96	24° Virgo	4/09–2/10	21°–22° Pisces	5/15–2/17

1967	Saturn	Return	Uranus	Opposition	Chiron	Return
Jan	24°–26° Pisces	6/95–3/96	24°–23° Virgo	4/09–2/10	22°–23° Pisces	3/16–3/17
Feb	26°–29° Pisces	3/96–4/96	23°–22° Virgo	3/09–1/10	23°–24° Pisces	4/16–1/18
Mar	29° Pisces– 3° Aries	4/96–1/97	22°–21° Virgo	5/08–12/09	24°–26° Pisces	5/16–2/18
April	3°–6° Aries	5/96–3/97	21°–20° Virgo	4/08–2/09	26°–28° Pisces	4/17–1/19
May	7°–10° Aries	6/96–3/97	20° Virgo	4/08–2/09	28°–29° Pisces	5/17–2/19
June	10°–11° Aries	3/97–4/97	20° Virgo	4/08–2/09	29° Pisces	3/18–2/19
July	11°–12° Aries	4/97	20°–21° Virgo	4/08–3/09	29° Pisces	3/18–2/19
Aug	12°–11° Aries	4/97	21°–23° Virgo	5/08–1/10	29°–28° Virgo	5/17–2/19
Sept	11°–9° Aries	3/97–4/97	23°–25° Virgo	4/09–2/10	28°–27° Pisces	4/17–1/19
Oct	9°–6° Aries	6/96–3/97	25°–27° Virgo	5/09–1/11	27°–25° Pisces	6/16–12/18
Nov	6°–5° Aries	6/96–3/97	27°–28° Virgo	3/10–2/11	25° Pisces	6/16–2/18
Dec	5°–6° Aries	6/96–2/97	28°–29° Virgo	4/10–2/11	25° Pisces	6/16–2/18

KEY LIFE PASSAGES

1968	Saturn	Return	Uranus	Opposition	Chiron	Return
Jan	6°–8° Aries	6/96–3/97	29° Virgo	4/10–3/11	25°–26° Pisces	6/16–2/18
Feb	8°–11° Aries	3/97–4/97	29°–28° Virgo	4/10–2/11	26°–28° Pisces	4/17–1/19
Mar	11°–15° Aries	4/97–2/98	28°–27° Virgo	9/10–2/11	28° Pisces– 0° Aries	6/17–3/19
April	15°–18° Aries	5/97–3/98	27°–26° Virgo	3/10–2/11	0°–1° Aries	4/18–1/20
May	18°–22° Aries	6/97–4/98	26°–25° Virgo	4/09–3/10	1°–3° Aries	5/18–3/20
June	22°–24° Aries	4/98	25° Virgo	4/09–3/10	3° Aries	4/19–3/20
July	24°–26° Aries	4/98–5/98	25°–27° Virgo	4/09–2/11	3° Aries	4/19–3/20
Aug	26°–25° Aries	4/98–1/99	27°–28° Virgo	3/10–2/11	3°–2° Aries	5/18–3/20
Sept	25°–23° Aries	4/98–5/98	28° Virgo– 0° Libra	4/10–12/12	2°–1° Aries	4/18–2/20
Oct	23°–21° Aries	3/98–4/98	0°–2° Libra	4/10–1/12	1° Aries– 29° Pisces	6/17–1/20
Nov	21°–19° Aries	6/97–3/98	2°–3° Libra	4/11–3/12	29° Pisces	6/17–2/19
Dec	19° Aries	6/97–3/98	3°–4° Libra	5/11–1/13	29° Pisces	6/17–2/19

1969	Saturn	Return	Uranus	Opposition	Chiron	Return
Jan	19°–20° Aries	6/97–3/98	4° Libra	6/11–1/13	29° Pisces– 0° Aries	6/17–3/19
Feb	20°–23° Aries	7/97–4/98	4°–3° Libra	5/11–1/13	0°–1° Aries	4/18–1/20
Mar	23°–26° Aries	4/98–1/99	3°–2° Libra	4/11–3/12	1°–3° Aries	5/18–3/20
April	26° Aries– 0° Taurus	5/98–3/99	2°–0° Libra	4/10–1/12	3°–5° Aries	4/19–2/21
May	0°–4° Taurus	6/98–4/99	0° Libra– 29° Virgo	5/10–1/12	5°–6° Aries	6/19–2/21
June	4°–7° Taurus	4/99–5/99	29° Virgo– 0° Libra	5/10–1/12	6°–7° Aries	7/19–3/21
July	7°–9° Taurus	4/99–5/99	0°–1° Libra	4/10–2/12	7° Aries	4/20–3/21
Aug	9° Taurus	5/99	1°–3° Libra	2/11–3/12	7°–6° Aries	7/19–3/21
Sept	9°–8° Taurus	5/99	3°–5° Libra	5/11–2/13	6°–4° Aries	5/19–2/21
Oct	8°–5° Taurus	4/99–5/99	5°–6° Libra	4/12–3/13	4°–3° Aries	4/19–12/20
Nov	5°–3° Taurus	7/98–4/99	6°–8° Libra	4/12–1/14	3°–2° Aries	5/18–3/20
Dec	3°–2° Taurus	7/98–4/99	8°–9° Libra	6/12–2/14	2° Aries	5/18–2/20

KEY LIFE PASSAGES

1970	Saturn	Return	Uranus	Opposition	Chiron	Return
Jan	2°–3° Taurus	7/98–4/99	9° Libra	4/13–2/14	2°–3° Aries	5/18–5/20
Feb	3°–5° Taurus	7/98–4/99	9°–8° Libra	6/12–2/14	3°–5° Aries	4/19–2/21
Mar	5°–8° Taurus	4/99–5/99	8°–7° Libra	5/12–1/14	5°–7° Aries	6/19–3/21
April	8°–12° Taurus	5/99–3/00	7°–5° Libra	4/12–3/13	7°–8° Aries	4/20–1/22
May	12°–16° Taurus	6/99–4/00	5° Libra	4/12–2/13	8°–10° Aries	5/20–3/22
June	16°–19° Taurus	7/99–5/00	5° Libra	4/12–2/13	10° Aries	4/21–3/22
July	19°–22° Taurus	4/00–5/00	5°–6° Libra	4/12–3/13	10° Aries	4/21–3/22
Aug	22°–23° Taurus	5/00–6/00	6°–7° Libra	4/12–3/13	10°–9° Aries	6/20–3/22
Sept	23°–22° Taurus	5/00–6/00	7°–9° Libra	5/12–2/14	9°–8° Aries	5/20–2/22
Oct	22°–20° Taurus	5/00	9°–11° Libra	4/13–3/14	8°–7° Aries	4/20–1/22
Nov	20°–18° Taurus	3/00–5/00	11°–12° Libra	5/13–1/15	7°–6° Aries	7/19–3/21
Dec	18°–16° Taurus	7/99–4/00	12°–13° Libra	6/13–2/15	6° Aries	7/19–2/21

1971	Saturn	Return	Uranus	Opposition	Chiron	Return
Jan	16° Taurus	7/99–4/00	13° Libra	4/14–2/15	6°–7° Aries	7/19–3/21
Feb	16°–17° Taurus	7/99–4/00	13° Libra	4/14–2/15	7°–8° Aries	4/20–1/22
Mar	17°–20° Taurus	8/99–6/00	13°–12° Libra	6/13–2/15	8°–10° Aries	5/20–3/22
April	20°–24° Taurus	8/99–2/01	12°–10° Libra	4/13–1/15	10°–12° Aries	4/21–2/23
May	24°–28° Taurus	6/00–4/01	10° Libra	4/13–3/14	12°–13° Aries	5/21–3/23
June	28° Taurus–1° Gemini	7/00–5/01	10°–9° Libra	4/13–3/14	13°–14° Aries	6/21–3/23
July	1°–4° Gemini	8/00–5/01	9°–10° Libra	4/13–3/14	14° Aries	5/22–3/23
Aug	4°–6° Gemini	5/01–6/01	10°–12° Libra	4/13–1/15	14°–13° Aries	6/21–3/23
Sept	6° Gemini	6/01	12°–13° Libra	6/13–2/15	13°–12° Aries	5/21–3/23
Oct	6°–5° Gemini	5/01–6/01	13°–15° Libra	4/14–3/15	12°–10° Aries	4/21–2/23
Nov	5°–3° Gemini	5/01–6/01	15°–17° Libra	5/14–2/16	10° Aries	4/21–3/22
Dec	3°–0° Gemini	8/00–5/01	17°–18° Libra	4/15–3/16	10°–9° Aries	6/20–3/22

KEY LIFE PASSAGES

1972	Saturn	Return	Uranus	Opposition	Chiron	Return
Jan	0° Gemini	8/00–4/01	18° Libra	5/15–3/16	9°–10° Aries	6/20–3/22
Feb	0° Gemini	8/00–4/01	18° Libra	5/15–3/16	10°–11° Aries	4/21–1/23
Mar	0°–3° Gemini	8/00–5/01	18°–17° Libra	4/15–3/16	11°–13° Aries	4/21–3/23
April	3°–6° Gemini	5/01–6/01	17°–15° Libra	5/14–2/16	13°–15° Aries	6/21–1/24
May	6°–10° Gemini	6/01–4/02	15°–14° Libra	4/14–3/15	15°–16° Aries	5/22–2/24
June	10°–14° Gemini	7/01–5/02	14° Libra	4/14–3/15	16°–17° Aries	6/22–3/24
July	14°–17° Gemini	8/01–6/02	14°–15° Libra	4/14–3/15	17° Aries	4/23–3/24
Aug	17°–20° Gemini	5/02–6/02	15°–16° Libra	5/14–1/16	17° Aries	4/23–3/24
Sept	20°–21° Gemini	6/02–7/02	16°–18° Libra	6/14–3/16	17°–15° Aries	5/22–3/24
Oct	21°–20° Gemini	6/02–7/02	18°–20° Libra	5/15–1/17	15°–14° Aries	5/22–1/24
Nov	20°–18° Gemini	6/02	20°–22° Libra	6/15–3/17	14°–13° Aries	6/21–4/23
Dec	18°–15° Gemini	9/01–6/02	22°–23° Libra	5/16–4/17	13° Aries	6/21–4/23

1973	Saturn	Return	Uranus	Opposition	Chiron	Return
Jan	15°–14° Gemini	8/01–5/02	23° Libra	5/16–4/17	13°–14° Aries	6/21–4/23
Feb	14° Gemini	8/01–5/02	23° Libra	5/16–4/17	14°–15° Aries	5/22–1/24
Mar	14°–15° Gemini	8/01–5/02	23°–22° Libra	5/16–4/17	15°–16° Aries	5/22–2/24
April	15°–18° Gemini	9/01–6/02	21°–20° Libra	6/15–2/17	16°–18° Aries	6/22–12/24
May	18°–22° Gemini	6/02–3/03	20°–19° Libra	5/15–1/17	18°–20° Aries	5/23–3/25
June	22°–26° Gemini	7/02–5/03	19° Libra	5/15–4/16	20°–21° Aries	7/23–3/25
July	26° Gemini–0° Cancer	8/02–6/03	19° Libra	5/15–4/16	21° Aries	4/24–3/25
Aug	0°–3° Cancer	6/03–7/03	19°–21° Libra	5/15–2/17	21°–20° Aries	7/23–3/25
Sept	3°–4° Cancer	6/03–7/03	21°22° Libra	4/16–3/17	20°–19° Aries	6/23–3/25
Oct	4°–5° Cancer	7/03	22°–24° Libra	5/16–2/18	19°–18° Aries	5/23–2/25
Nov	5°–3° Cancer	6/03–7/03	24°–26° Libra	6/16–3/18	18°–17° Aries	4/23–12/24
Dec	3°–1° Cancer	6/03–7/03	26°–27° Libra	5/17–4/18	17°–16° Aries	6/22–3/24

KEY LIFE PASSAGES

1974	Saturn	Return	Uranus	Opposition	Chiron	Return
Jan	1° Cancer–28° Gemini	8/02–6/03	27°–28° Libra	6/17–2/19	16°–17° Aries	6/22–3/24
Feb	28° Gemini	9/02–5/03	28°–27° Libra	6/17–2/19	17°–18° Aries	4/23–12/24
Mar	28°–29° Gemini	9/02–6/03	27°–26° Libra	5/17–4/18	18°–20° Aries	5/23–3/25
April	29° Gemini–1° Cancer	9/02–6/03	26°–25° Libra	4/17–3/18	20°–22° Aries	7/23–1/26
May	1°–4° Cancer	6/03–7/03	25°–24° Libra	6/16–3/18	22°–23° Aries	5/24–2/26
June	4°–8° Cancer	7/03–5/04	24° Libra	6/16–2/18	23°–24° Aries	6/24–3/26
July	8°–12° Cancer	8/03–6/04	24° Libra	6/16–2/18	24° Aries	4/25–3/26
Aug	12°–16° Cancer	9/03–7/04	24°–25° Libra	6/16–3/18	24° Aries	4/25–3/26
Sept	16°–18° Cancer	7/04–8/04	25°–27° Libra	4/17–4/18	24°–23° Aries	6/24–3/26
Oct	18°–19° Cancer	7/04–8/04	27°–29° Libra	6/17–3/19	23°–21° Aries	5/24–2/26
Nov	19°–18° Cancer	7/04–8/04	29° Libra–0° Scorpio	4/18–3/19	21°–20° Aries	7/23–3/25
Dec	18°–16° Cancer	7/04–8/04	1°–2° Scorpio	6/18–2/20	20° Aries	7/23–3/25

1975	Saturn	Return	Uranus	Opposition	Chiron	Return
Jan	16°–14° Cancer	6/04–7/04	2° Scorpio	7/18–2/20	20° Aries	7/23–3/25
Feb	14°–12° Cancer	9/03–6/04	2° Scorpio	7/18–2/20	20°–21° Aries	7/23–3/25
Mar	12° Cancer	9/03–6/04	2°–1° Scorpio	6/18–2/20	21°–23° Aries	5/24–2/26
April	12°–14° Cancer	9/03–6/04	1°–0° Scorpio	5/18–4/19	23°–25° Aries	6/24–4/26
May	14°–17° Cancer	6/04–7/04	0° Scorpio–29° Libra	4/18–3/19	25°–27° Aries	5/25–3/27
June	17°–20° Cancer	7/04	29°–28° Libra	6/17–3/19	27°–28° Aries	7/25–3/27
July	20°–24° Cancer	7/04–6/05	28° Libra	6/17–3/19	28° Aries	5/26–3/27
Aug	24°–28° Cancer	9/04–7/05	28°–29° Libra	6/17–3/19	28° Aries	5/26–3/27
Sept	28° Cancer–1° Leo	6/05–7/05	29° Libra–1° Scorpio	4/18–4/19	28°–27° Aries	7/25–3/27
Oct	1°–3° Leo	7/05–8/05	1°–3° Scorpio	6/18–3/20	27°–25° Aries	5/25–3/27
Nov	3° Leo	8/05	3°–5° Scorpio	5/19–4/20	25°–24° Aries	4/25–4/26
Dec	3°–1° Leo	7/05–8/05	5°–6° Scorpio	6/19–2/21	24° Aries	4/25–3/26

KEY LIFE PASSAGES

1976	Saturn	Return	Uranus	Opposition	Chiron	Return
Jan	1° Leo–29° Cancer	7/05–8/05	6°–7° Scorpio	7/19–3/21	24° Aries	4/25–3/26
Feb	29°–27° Cancer	10/04–7/05	7° Scorpio	5/20–3/21	24°–25° Aries	4/25–4/26
Mar	27°–26° Cancer	9/04–6/05	7°–6° Scorpio	7/19–3/21	25°–27° Aries	5/25–3/27
April	26°–27° Cancer	9/04–6/05	6°–5° Scorpio	6/19–2/21	27°–28° Aries	7/25–3/27
May	27°–29° Cancer	10/04–7/05	5°–4° Scorpio	5/19–4/20	28° Aries–0° Taurus	5/26–2/28
June	29° Cancer–3° Leo	7/05–8/05	4°–3° Scorpio	5/19–3/20	0°–1° Taurus	6/26–3/28
July	3°–7° Leo	8/05–6/06	3° Scorpio	5/19–3/20	1°–2° Taurus	8/26–4/28
Aug	7°–11° Leo	9/05–7/06	3°–4° Scorpio	5/19–3/20	2° Taurus	5/27–4/28
Sept	11°–14° Leo	11/05–8/06	4°–6° Scorpio	5/19–2/21	2°–1° Taurus	8/26–4/28
Oct	14°–16° Leo	8/06	6°–8° Scorpio	7/19–3/21	1° Taurus–29° Aries	5/26–3/28
Nov	16°–17° Leo	8/06–9/06	8°–9° Scorpio	5/20–4/21	29°–28° Aries	5/26–4/27
Dec	17°–16° Leo	8/06–9/06	9°–11° Scorpio	6/20–3/22	28°–27° Aries	7/25–3/27

1977	Saturn	Return	Uranus	Opposition	Chiron	Return
Jan	16°–14° Leo	8/06	11°–12° Scorpio	5/21–4/22	27°–28° Aries	7/25–3/27
Feb	14°–11° Leo	11/05–8/06	12° Scorpio	5/21–4/22	28°–29° Aries	5/26–4/27
Mar	11°–10° Leo	10/05–7/06	12°–11° Scorpio	5/21–4/22	29° Aries–0° Taurus	5/26–2/28
April	10° Leo	10/05–7/06	11°–10° Scorpio	7/20–3/22	0°–2° Taurus	6/26–4/28
May	10°–12° Leo	10/05–7/06	10–9° Scorpio	6/20–2/22	2°–4° Taurus	5/27–3/29
June	12°–15° Leo	7/06–8/06	9°–8° Scorpio	5/20–4/21	4°–5° Taurus	6/27–3/29
July	15°–19° Leo	8/06–6/07	8° Scorpio	5/20–3/21	5°–6° Taurus	5/28–4/29
Aug	19°–23° Leo	9/06–7/07	8°–9° Scorpio	5/20–4/21	6° Taurus	5/28–4/29
Sept	23°–26° Leo	10/06–8/07	9°–10° Scorpio	6/20–2/22	6°–5° Taurus	5/28–4/29
Oct	26°–29° Leo	8/07–9/07	10°–12° Scorpio	7/20–4/22	5°–3° Taurus	6/27–3/29
Nov	29° Leo–0° Virgo	8/07–9/07	12°–14° Scorpio	5/21–2/23	3°–2° Taurus	5/27–1/29
Dec	0° Virgo	9/07	14°–15° Scorpio	8/21–2/23	2°–1° Taurus	8/26–4/28

KEY LIFE PASSAGES

1978	Saturn	Return	Uranus	Opposition	Chiron	Return
Jan	0° Virgo–28° Leo	8/07–9/07	15°–16° Scorpio	5/22–4/23	1° Taurus	8/26–3/28
Feb	28°–26° Leo	8/07	16° Scorpio	5/22–4/23	1°–2° Taurus	8/26–4/28
Mar	26°–24° Leo	11/06–8/07	16° Scorpio	5/22–4/23	2°–4° Taurus	5/27–3/29
April	24° Leo	11/06–7/07	16°–15° Scorpio	5/22–4/23	4°–6° Taurus	6/27–4/29
May	24°–25° Leo	11/06–8/07	15°–13° Scorpio	6/21–2/23	6°–7° Taurus	5/28–1/30
June	25°–27° Leo	11/06–8/07	13°–12° Scorpio	5/21–4/22	7°–9° Taurus	6/28–3/30
July	27° Leo–1° Virgo	8/07–5/08	12° Scorpio	5/21–4/22	9°–10° Taurus	8/28–4/30
Aug	1°–4° Virgo	9/07–7/08	12°–13° Scorpio	5/21–4/22	10° Taurus	5/29–4/30
Sept	4°–8° Virgo	10/07–8/08	13°–14° Scorpio	6/21–2/23	10°–9° Taurus	8/28–4/30
Oct	8°–11° Virgo	11/07–9/08	14°–16° Scorpio	7/21–4/23	9°–7° Taurus	6/28–3/30
Nov	11°–13° Virgo	8/08–9/08	16°–18° Scorpio	5/22–5/23	7°–6° Taurus	5/28–1/30
Dec	13°–14° Virgo	9/08–5/09	18°–20° Scorpio	7/22–4/24	6°–5° Taurus	5/28–4/29

1979	Saturn	Return	Uranus	Opposition	Chiron	Return
Jan	14°–13° Virgo	9/08–5/09	20°–21° Scorpio	5/23–4/24	5° Taurus	5/28–4/29
Feb	13°–11° Virgo	8/08–9/08	21° Scorpio	6/23–4/24	5°–6° Taurus	5/28–4/29
Mar	11°–8° Virgo	11/07–9/08	21°–20° Scorpio	5/23–4/24	6°–8° Taurus	5/28–3/30
April	8°–9° Virgo	11/07–8/08	20°–19° Scorpio	5/23–4/24	8°–9° Taurus	7/28–3/30
May	7° Virgo	11/07–8/08	19°–18° Scorpio	7/22–3/24	9°–11° Taurus	8/28–1/31
June	7°–9° Virgo	11/07–8/08	18°–17° Scorpio	6/22–5/23	11°–13° Taurus	6/29–3/31
July	9°–12° Virgo	8/08–9/08	17° Scorpio	6/22–4/23	13°–14° Taurus	5/30–4/31
Aug	12°–16° Virgo	9/08–7/09	17° Scorpio	6/22–4/23	14° Taurus	5/30–4/31
Sept	16°–20° Virgo	10/08–8/09	17°–19° Scorpio	6/22–3/24	14°–13° Taurus	5/30–4/31
Oct	20°–23° Virgo	11/08–9/09	19°–20° Scorpio	5/23–4/24	13°–12° Taurus	7/29–3/31
Nov	23°–26° Virgo	9/09	20°–22° Scorpio	5/23–4/24	12°–10° Taurus	5/29–3/31
Dec	26°–27° Virgo	9/09–6/10	22°–24° Scorpio	7/23–4/25	10°–9° Taurus	8/28–4/30

KEY LIFE PASSAGES

1980	Saturn	Return	Uranus	Opposition	Chiron	Return
Jan	27°–26° Virgo	9/09–6/10	24°–25° Scorpio	5/24–4/25	9° Taurus	8/28–3/30
Feb	26°–25° Virgo	9/09–10/09	25°–26° Scorpio	6/24–5/25	9°–10° Taurus	8/28–4/30
Mar	25°–22° Virgo	8/09–9/09	26°–25° Scorpio	6/24–5/25	10°–11° Taurus	5/29–1/31
April	22°–21° Virgo	12/08–8/09	25°–24° Scorpio	5/24–4/25	12°–13° Taurus	7/29–3/31
May	21°–20° Virgo	11/08–8/09	24°–23° Scorpio	8/23–4/25	13°–15° Taurus	5/30–4/31
June	20°–21° Virgo	11/08–8/09	23°–22° Scorpio	7/23–4/25	15°–17° Taurus	6/30–3/32
July	21°–24° Virgo	12/08–10/09	22°–21° Scorpio	6/23–5/24	17°–18° Taurus	8/30–3/32
Aug	24°–27° Virgo	9/09–6/10	21°–22° Scorpio	6/23–5/24	18° Taurus	5/31–3/32
Sept	27° Virgo– 1° Libra	10/09–8/10	22°–23° Scorpio	7/23–4/25	18° Taurus	5/31–3/32
Oct	1°–5° Libra	11/09–9/10	23°–25° Scorpio	8/23–4/25	18°–16° Taurus	7/30–3/32
Nov	5°–8° Libra	9/10–10/10	25°–27° Scorpio	6/24–3/26	16°–15° Taurus	6/30–2/32
Dec	8°–9° Libra	10/10	27°–28° Scorpio	8/24–4/26	15°–14° Taurus	5/30–4/31

1981	Saturn	Return	Uranus	Opposition	Chiron	Return
Jan	9°–10° Libra	10/10–7/11	28°–29° Scorpio	5/25–4/26	14°–13° Taurus	5/30–4/31
Feb	10°–8° Libra	10/10–7/11	0° Sagittarius	7/25–5/26	13°–14° Taurus	5/30–4/31
Mar	8°–6° Libra	9/10–10/10	0° Sagittarius	7/25–5/26	14°–16° Taurus	5/30–2/32
April	6°–4° Libra	12/09–10/10	0° Sagittarius– 29° Scorpio	6/25–5/26	16°–17° Taurus	7/30–3/32
May	4°–3° Libra	12/09–9/10	29°–28° Scorpio	5/25–4/26	17°–20° Taurus	8/30–1/33
June	3° Libra	12/09–8/10	28°–27° Scorpio	8/24–4/26	20°–21° Taurus	7/31–3/33
July	3°–5° Libra	12/09–10/10	27°–26° Scorpio	7/24–3/26	21°–23° Taurus	7/31–4/33
Aug	5°–9° Libra	9/10–10/10	26° Scorpio	7/24–4/25	23° Taurus	6/32–4/33
Sept	9°–12° Libra	10/10–8/11	26°–27° Scorpio	7/24–3/26	23°–22° Taurus	5/32–4/33
Oct	12°–16° Libra	11/10–9/11	27°–29° Scorpio	8/24–4/26	22°–21° Taurus	7/31–3/33
Nov	16°–19° Libra	12/10–10/11	29° Scorpio– 1° Sagittarius	6/25–5/26	21°–19° Taurus	6/31–3/33
Dec	19°–21° Libra	10/11	1°–3° Sagittarius	8/25–4/27	19°–18° Taurus	5/31–4/32

KEY LIFE PASSAGES

1982	Saturn	Return	Uranus	Opposition	Chiron	Return
Jan	21°–22° Libra	10/11–7/12	3°–4° Sagittarius	6/26–5/27	18° Taurus	5/31–4/32
Feb	22°–21° Libra	10/11–7/12	4°–5° Sagittarius	6/26–5/27	18° Taurus	5/31–4/32
Mar	21°–19° Libra	10/11	5°–4° Sagittarius	6/26–5/27	18°–20° Taurus	5/31–5/32
April	19°–17° Libra	1/11–10/11	4°–3° Sagittarius	6/26–5/27	20°–22° Taurus	7/31–3/33
May	17°–16° Libra	12/10–9/11	3°–2° Sagittarius	5/26–4/27	22°–24° Taurus	5/32–5/33
June	16°–15° Libra	12/10–9/11	2°–1° Sagittarius	7/25–4/27	24°–26° Taurus	6/32–3/34
July	16°–17° Libra	12/10–9/11	1° Sagittarius	8/25–5/26	26°–27° Taurus	8/32–4/34
Aug	17°–20° Libra	1/11–10/11	1° Sagittarius	8/25–5/26	27°–28° Taurus	5/33–4/34
Sept	20°–23° Libra	10/11–7/12	1°–2° Sagittarius	7/25–4/27	28°–27° Taurus	5/33–4/34
Oct	23°–27° Libra	11/11–9/12	2°–3° Sagittarius	5/26–4/27	27°–26° Taurus	8/32–4/34
Nov	27° Libra–0° Scorpio	12/11–10/12	3°–5° Sagittarius	6/26–5/27	26°–24° Taurus	6/32–3/34
Dec	0°–3° Scorpio	10/12–11/12	5°–7° Sagittarius	8/26–4/28	24°–23° Taurus	6/32–5/33

1983	Saturn	Return	Uranus	Opposition	Chiron	Return
Jan	3°–4° Scorpio	10/12–7/13	7°–8° Sagittarius	6/27–5/28	23° Taurus	6/32–4/33
Feb	4° Scorpio	10/12–7/13	8°–9° Sagittarius	6/27–5/28	23° Taurus	6/32–4/33
Mar	4°–3° Scorpio	10/12–7/13	9° Sagittarius	7/27–5/28	23°–24° Taurus	6/32–5/33
April	3°–0° Scorpio	10/12–11/12	9°–8° Sagittarius	6/27–5/28	24°–26° Taurus	6/32–3/34
May	0° Scorpio–28° Libra	10/11–10/12	7°–8° Sagittarius	6/27–5/28	26°–29° Taurus	8/32–5/34
June	28° Libra	12/11–9/12	7°–6° Sagittarius	5/27–4/28	29° Taurus–0° Gemini	6/33–5/34
July	28° Libra	12/11–9/12	6°–5° Sagittarius	8/26–4/28	0°–2° Gemini	7/33–4/35
Aug	28° Libra–1° Scorpio	12/11–10/12	5° Sagittarius	8/26–5/27	2°–3° Gemini	5/34–4/35
Sept	1°–4° Scorpio	10/12–7/13	5°–6° Sagittarius	8/26–4/28	3° Gemini	6/34–4/35
Oct	4°–7° Scorpio	11/12–9/13	6°–7° Sagittarius	5/27–4/28	3°–2° Gemini	5/34–4/35
Nov	7°–11° Scorpio	12/12–10/13	7°–9° Sagittarius	6/27–5/28	2° Gemini–29° Taurus	6/33–4/35
Dec	11°–14° Scorpio	1/13–11/13	9°–11° Sagittarius	5/27–4/28	29°–28° Taurus	6/33–5/34

KEY LIFE PASSAGES

1984

	Saturn	Return	Uranus	Opposition	Chiron	Return
Jan	14°–16° Scorpio	11/13–8/14	11°–13° Sagittarius	6/28–5/29	28° Taurus	6/33–4/34
Feb	16° Scorpio	11/13–8/14	13° Sagittarius	7/28–5/29	28° Taurus	6/33–4/34
Mar	16°–15° Scorpio	11/13–8/14	13°–14° Sagittarius	7/28–2/30	28°–29° Taurus	6/33–5/34
April	15°–13° Scorpio	10/13–11/13	13° Sagittarius	7/28–5/29	29° Taurus – 1° Gemini	6/33–3/35
May	13°–11° Scorpio	1/13–10/13	13°–12° Sagittarius	6/28–5/29	1°–4° Gemini	8/33–5/35
June	11°–10° Scorpio	1/13–10/13	12°–10° Sagittarius	5/28–5/29	4°–6° Gemini	6/34–2/36
July	10° Scorpio	1/13–10/13	10° Sagittarius	8/27–3/29	6°–8° Gemini	8/34–4/36
Aug	10°–12° Scorpio	1/13–10/13	10° Sagittarius	8/27–3/29	8° Gemini	6/35–4/36
Sept	12°–14° Scorpio	10/13–11/13	10° Sagittarius	8/27–3/29	8° Gemini	6/35–4/36
Oct	14°–18° Scorpio	11/13–9/14	10°–12° Sagittarius	5/28–5/29	8°–7° Gemini	5/35–4/36
Nov	18°–21° Scorpio	12/13–10/14	12°–13° Sagittarius	6/28–5/29	7°–6° Gemini	8/34–3/36
Dec	21°–25° Scorpio	1/14–11/14	13°–15° Sagittarius	7/28–4/30	6°–4° Gemini	7/34–2/36

1985

	Saturn	Return	Uranus	Opposition	Chiron	Return
Jan	25°–27° Scorpio	11/14–12/14	15°–17° Sagittarius	6/29–5/30	4°–3° Gemini	6/34–5/35
Feb	27°–28° Scorpio	11/14–9/15	17°–18° Sagittarius	7/29–2/31	3° Gemini	6/34–4/35
Mar	28° Scorpio	12/14–9/15	18° Sagittarius	8/29–2/31	3°–5° Gemini	6/34–5/35
April	28°–26° Scorpio	11/14–9/15	18°–17° Sagittarius	7/29–2/31	5°–7° Gemini	7/34–3/36
May	26°–24° Scorpio	11/14	17°–16° Sagittarius	6/29–5/30	7°–9° Gemini	9/34–4/36
June	24°–22° Scorpio	1/14–11/14	16°–15° Sagittarius	6/29–4/30	9°–11° Gemini	6/35–5/36
July	22°–21° Scorpio	1/14–10/14	15°–14° Sagittarius	8/28–4/30	11°–13° Gemini	7/35–3/37
Aug	21°–23° Scorpio	1/14–10/14	14° Sagittarius	8/28–4/30	13°–14° Gemini	6/36–4/37
Sept	23°–25° Scorpio	2/14–11/14	14°–15° Sagittarius	8/28–4/30	14°–15° Gemini	6/36–4/37
Oct	25°–28° Scorpio	11/14–8/15	15°–16° Sagittarius	6/29–4/30	15°–14° Gemini	6/36–4/37
Nov	28° Scorpio – 2° Sagittarius	12/14–10/15	16°–18° Sagittarius	6/29–2/31	14°–12° Gemini	8/35–4/37
Dec	2°–5° Sagittarius	1/15–11/15	18°–19° Sagittarius	8/29–4/31	12°–10° Gemini	7/35–6/36

KEY LIFE PASSAGES

1986	Saturn	Return	Uranus	Opposition	Chiron	Return
Jan	5°–8° Sagittarius	2/15–12/15	19°–21° Sagittarius	9/29–5/31	10°–9° Gemini	6/35–5/36
Feb	8°–9° Sagittarius	12/15–8/16	21°–22° Sagittarius	7/30–6/31	9° Gemini	6/35–4/36
Mar	9°–10° Sagittarius	12/15–9/16	22° Sagittarius	8/30–6/31	9°–10° Gemini	6/35–5/36
April	10°–8° Sagittarius	12/15–9/16	22° Sagittarius	8/30–6/31	10°–12° Gemini	7/35–6/36
May	8°–6° Sagittarius	11/15–12/15	22°–21° Sagittarius	7/30–6/31	12°–15° Gemini	8/35–4/37
June	6°–4° Sagittarius	2/15–11/15	21°–20° Sagittarius	7/30–5/31	15°–17° Gemini	6/36–5/37
July	4°–3° Sagittarius	1/15–11/15	20°–19° Sagittarius	9/29–5/31	17°–19° Gemini	7/36–6/37
Aug	3°–4° Sagittarius	1/15–11/15	19°–18° Sagittarius	8/29–4/31	19°–21° Gemini	9/36–4/38
Sept	4°–5° Sagittarius	2/15–11/15	18°–19° Sagittarius	8/29–4/31	21° Gemini	6/37–4/38
Oct	5°–8° Sagittarius	2/15–12/15	19°–20° Sagittarius	9/29–5/31	21° Gemini	6/37–4/38
Nov	8°–12° Sagittarius	12/15–10/16	20°–22° Sagittarius	6/30–6/31	21°–19° Gemini	9/36–4/38
Dec	12°–15° Sagittarius	1/16–11/16	22°–24° Sagittarius	8/30–5/32	19°–17° Gemini	7/36–6/37

1987	Saturn	Return	Uranus	Opposition	Chiron	Return
Jan	15°–18° Sagittarius	2/16–12/16	24°–25° Sagittarius	6/31–5/32	17°–16° Gemini	7/36–5/37
Feb	18°–20° Sagittarius	12/16	25°–26° Sagittarius	7/31–6/32	16° Gemini	7/36–5/37
Mar	20°–21° Sagittarius	12/16–9/17	26°–27° Sagittarius	7/31–4/33	16°–17° Gemini	7/36–5/37
April	21°–20° Sagittarius	12/16–9/17	27°–26° Sagittarius	7/31–4/33	17°–19° Gemini	7/36–6/37
May	20°–19° Sagittarius	12/16	26°–25° Sagittarius	7/31–6/32	19°–21° Gemini	9/36–4/38
June	18°–16° Sagittarius	3/16–12/16	25°–24° Sagittarius	6/31–5/32	21°–24° Gemini	6/37–5/38
July	16°–15° Sagittarius	2/16–11/16	24°–23° Sagittarius	9/30–5/32	24°–26° Gemini	8/37–6/38
Aug	15° Sagittarius	2/16–11/16	23° Sagittarius	9/30–4/32	26°–28° Gemini	10/37–4/39
Sept	15°–16° Sagittarius	2/16–11/16	23° Sagittarius	9/30–4/32	28°–29° Gemini	6/38–4/39
Oct	16°–18° Sagittarius	2/16–12/16	23°–24° Sagittarius	9/30–5/32	29°–28° Gemini	6/38–4/39
Nov	18°–22° Sagittarius	12/16–10/17	24°–26° Sagittarius	7/31–6/32	28°–27° Gemini	6/38–4/39
Dec	22°–25° Sagittarius	1/17–11/17	26°–28° Sagittarius	7/31–5/33	27°–25° Gemini	8/37–3/39

KEY LIFE PASSAGES

1988	Saturn	Return	Uranus	Opposition	Chiron	Return
Jan	25°–29° Sagittarius	2/17–12/17	28°–29° Sagittarius	6/32–5/33	25°–24° Gemini	8/37–6/38
Feb	29° Sagittarius – 1° Capricorn	12/17–1/18	29° Sagittarius– 1° Capricorn	7/32–6/33	24°–23° Gemini	7/37–5/38
Mar	1°–2° Capricorn	12/17–9/18	1° Capricorn	8/32–6/33	23°–24° Gemini	7/37–5/38
April	2° Capricorn	1/18–9/18	1° Capricorn	8/32–6/33	24°–26° Gemini	8/37–6/38
May	2°–1° Capricorn	12/17–9/18	1°–0° Capricorn	7/32–6/33	26°–28° Gemini	10/37–4/39
June	0° Capricorn – 29° Sagittarius	12/17	29° Sagittarius	7/32–5/33	28° Gemini– 1° Cancer	6/38–5/39
July	28°–27° Sagittarius	3/17–12/17	29°–28° Sagittarius	6/32–5/33	1°–4° Cancer	8/38–6/39
Aug	27°–26° Sagittarius	2/17–12/17	28°–27° Sagittarius	8/31–5/33	4°–6° Cancer	10/38–3/40
Sept	26°–27° Sagittarius	2/17–12/17	27° Sagittarius	8/31–4/33	6°–7° Cancer	7/39–4/40
Oct	27°–29° Sagittarius	3/17–12/17	27°–28° Sagittarius	8/31–5/33	7° Cancer	7/39–4/40
Nov	29° Sagittarius – 2° Capricorn	12/17–9/18	28° Sagittarius– 0° Capricorn	6/32–6/33	7°–6° Cancer	7/39–4/40
Dec	2°–5° Capricorn	1/18–11/18	0°–2° Capricorn	7/32–4/34	6°–4° Cancer	10/38–3/40

1989	Saturn	Return	Uranus	Opposition	Chiron	Return
Jan	6°–9° Capricorn	2/18–12/18	2°–3° Capricorn	9/32–5/34	4°–2° Cancer	8/38–6/39
Feb	9°–12° Capricorn	3/18–1/19	3°–5° Capricorn	7/33–6/34	2°–1° Cancer	8/38–6/39
Mar	12°–13° Capricorn	1/19–9/19	5° Capricorn	8/33–6/34	1°–2° Cancer	8/38–6/39
April	13°–14° Capricorn	1/19–10/19	5° Capricorn	8/33–6/34	2°–3° Cancer	8/38–6/39
May	14°–13° Capricorn	1/19–10/19	5°–4° Capricorn	7/33–6/34	3°–6° Cancer	9/38–3/40
June	13°–11° Capricorn	12/18–9/19	4°–3° Capricorn	7/33–6/34	6°–9° Cancer	7/39–5/40
July	11°–9° Capricorn	3/18–1/19	3°–2° Capricorn	9/32–5/34	9°–12° Cancer	8/39–6/40
Aug	9°–7° Capricorn	2/18–12/18	2°–1° Capricorn	8/32–4/34	12°–14° Cancer	9/39–7/40
Sept	7°–8° Capricorn	2/18/–12/18	1°–2° Capricorn	8/32–4/34	14°–16° Cancer	6/40–4/41
Oct	8°–9° Capricorn	3/18–12/18	2° Capricorn	9/32–4/34	16°–17° Cancer	7/40–4/41
Nov	9°–12° Capricorn	4/18–1/19	2°–4° Capricorn	9/32–6/34	17°–16° Cancer	7/40–4/41
Dec	12°–15° Capricorn	1/19–11/19	4°–6° Capricorn	7/33–4/35	16°–14° Cancer	6/40–4/41

KEY LIFE PASSAGES

1990

	Saturn	Return	Uranus	Opposition	Chiron	Return
Jan	16°–19° Capricorn	2/19–12/19	6°–7° Capricorn	10/33–5/35	14°–12° Cancer	9/39–7/40
Feb	19°–22° Capricorn	3/19–1/20	7°–9° Capricorn	7/34–6/35	12°–11° Cancer	8/39–6/40
Mar	22°–24° Capricorn	1/20	9°–10° Capricorn	8/34–3/36	11° Cancer	8/39–6/40
April	24°–25° Capricorn	1/20–10/20	10°–9° Capricorn	8/34–3/36	11°–12° Cancer	8/39–6/40
May	25° Capricorn	1/20–10/20	9° Capricorn	7/34–6/35	12°–15° Cancer	9/39–7/40
June	25°–23° Capricorn	1/20–10/20	9°–8° Capricorn	7/34–6/35	15°–18° Cancer	7/40–5/41
July	23°–21° Capricorn	12/19–1/20	7°–6° Capricorn	10/33–5/35	18°–21° Cancer	8/40–6/41
Aug	21°–19° Capricorn	3/19–1/20	6° Capricorn	9/33–4/35	21°–24° Cancer	9/40–7/41
Sept	19° Capricorn	3/19–12/19	6° Capricorn	9/33–4/35	24°–26° Cancer	7/41–8/41
Oct	19°–20° Capricorn	3/19–12/19	6° Capricorn	9/33–4/35	26°–27° Cancer	7/41–8/41
Nov	20°–22° Capricorn	3/19–1/20	7°–8° Capricorn	7/34–6/35	27° Cancer	8/41
Dec	22°–26° Capricorn	1/20–11/20	8°–10° Capricorn	7/34–4/36	27°–25° Cancer	7/41–8/41

1991

	Saturn	Return	Uranus	Opposition	Chiron	Return
Jan	26°–29° Capricorn	2/20–12/20	10°–11° Capricorn	8/34–5/36	25°–23° Cancer	6/41–7/41
Feb	29° Capricorn – 2° Aquarius	3/20–1/21	12°–13° Capricorn	7/35–6/36	23°–22° Cancer	9/40–7/41
Mar	2°–5° Aquarius	4/20–2/21	13°–14° Capricorn	8/35–7/36	22°–21° Cancer	9/40–6/41
April	5°–7° Aquarius	1/21–11/21	14° Capricorn	9/35–7/36	21°–22° Cancer	9/40–6/41
May	7° Aquarius	2/21–11/21	14°–13° Capricorn	8/35–7/36	22°–25° Cancer	9/40–7/41
June	7°–5° Aquarius	1/21–11/21	13°–12° Capricorn	7/35–6/36	25°–28° Cancer	7/41–4/42
July	5°–3° Aquarius	1/21–2/21	12°–11° Capricorn	7/35–5/36	28° Cancer– 1° Leo	8/41–6/42
Aug	3°–1° Aquarius	4/20–1/21	11°–10° Capricorn	9/34–5/36	1°–5° Leo	9/41–7/42
Sept	1°–0° Aquarius	3/20–1/21	10° Capricorn	8/34–4/36	5°–7° Leo	7/42–8/42
Oct	0°–1° Aquarius	3/20–1/21	10°–11° Capricorn	8/34–5/36	7°–9° Leo	7/42–8/42
Nov	1°–3° Aquarius	4/20–1/21	10°–12° Capricorn	7/35–5/36	9°–10° Leo	8/42
Dec	3°–6° Aquarius	1/21–10/21	12°–14° Capricorn	7/35–7/36	10°–8° Leo	8/42

KEY LIFE PASSAGES

1992	Saturn	Return	Uranus	Opposition	Chiron	Return
Jan	6°–9° Aquarius	2/21–12/21	13°–15° Capricorn	8/35–4/37	8°–6° Leo	7/42–8/42
Feb	9°–13° Aquarius	3/21–2/22	15°–16° Capricorn	7/36–5/37	6°–4° Leo	10/41–8/42
Mar	13°–16° Aquarius	4/21–2/22	16°–17° Capricorn	7/36–6/37	4°–3° Leo	10/41–6/42
April	16°–18° Aquarius	2/22–11/22	17°–18° Capricorn	8/36–6/37	3° Leo	10/41–6/42
May	17°–18° Aquarius	2/22–11/22	17° Capricorn	8/36–6/37	3°–5° Leo	10/41–7/42
June	18°–17° Aquarius	2/22–11/22	17°–16° Capricorn	7/36–6/37	5°–9° Leo	7/42–8/42
July	17°–15° Aquarius	1/22–2/22	16°–15° Capricorn	7/36–5/37	9°–12° Leo	8/42–5/43
Aug	15°–13° Aquarius	4/21–2/22	15°–14° Capricorn	9/35–4/37	12°–16° Leo	10/42–7/43
Sept	13°–12° Aquarius	4/21–1/22	14° Capricorn	9/35–7/36	16°–19° Leo	10/42–7/43
Oct	12°–11° Aquarius	3/21–1/22	14° Capricorn	7/35–7/36	19°–22° Leo	7/43–8/43
Nov	12°–13° Aquarius	4/21–1/22	14°–15° Capricorn	9/35–4/37	22°–23° Leo	8/43
Dec	13°–16° Aquarius	4/21–2/22	15°–17° Capricorn	7/36–6/37	22°–33° Leo	8/43

1993	Saturn	Return	Uranus	Opposition	Chiron	Return
Jan	16°–19° Aquarius	2/22–12/22	17°–19° Capricorn	8/36–7/37	23°–21° Leo	8/43
Feb	19°–23° Aquarius	3/22–1/23	19°–20° Capricorn	9/36–5/38	21°18° Leo	7/43–8/43
Mar	23°–26° Aquarius	4/22–2/23	20°–21° Capricorn	7/37–6/38	18°–17° Leo	11/42–8/43
April	26°–29° Aquarius	2/23–3/23	21°–22° Capricorn	7/37–6/38	17° Leo	11/42–7/43
May	29° Aquarius– 0° Pisces	2/23–11/23	22°–21° Capricorn	7/37–6/38	17°–18° Leo	11/42–8/43
June	0° Pisces	3/23–11/23	21°–20° Capricorn	7/37–6/38	18°–21° Leo	7/43–8/43
July	29°–28° Aquarius	2/23–3/23	20°–19° Capricorn	9/36–5/38	21°–25° Leo	8/43–9/43
Aug	28°–26° Aquarius	2/23	19°–18° Capricorn	8/36–7/37	25°–29° Leo	9/43–7/44
Sept	26°–24° Aquarius	4/22–2/23	18° Capricorn	8/36–6/37	29° Leo– 3° Virgo	10/43–8/44
Oct	24°–23° Aquarius	4/22–1/23	18° Capricorn	8/36–6/37	3°–6° Virgo	8/44
Nov	23°–24° Aquarius	4/22–1/23	18°–19° Capricorn	8/36–7/37	6°–8° Virgo	8/44–9/44
Dec	24°–26° Aquarius	4/22–2/23	19°–21° Capricorn	9/36–6/38	8°–9° Virgo	9/44

KEY LIFE PASSAGES

1994	Saturn	Return	Uranus	Opposition	Chiron	Return
Jan	27° Aquarius–0° Pisces	2/23–11/23	21°–23° Capricorn	7/37–6/38	9°–7° Virgo	8/44–9/44
Feb	0°–3° Pisces	3/23–1/24	23°–24° Capricorn	9/37–7/38	7°–5° Virgo	8/44–9/44
Mar	3°–7° Pisces	12/23–2/24	24°–25° Capricorn	10/37–5/39	5°–3° Virgo	7/44–8/44
April	7°–10° Pisces	6/23–3/24	25°–26° Capricorn	7/38–6/39	3°–2° Virgo	11/43–7/44
May	10°–11° Pisces	3/24	26°–25° Capricorn	7/38–6/39	2°–3° Virgo	11/43–7/44
June	12° Pisces	3/24–12/24	25° Capricorn	7/38–5/39	3°–6° Virgo	7/44–8/44
July	12°–11° Pisces	3/24–12/24	25°–23° Capricorn	9/37–8/38	6°–9° Virgo	8/44–9/44
Aug	11°–9° Pisces	2/24–3/24	23°–22° Capricorn	8/37–6/38	9°–13° Virgo	9/44–6/45
Sept	9°–7° Pisces	6/23–3/24	22° Capricorn	8/37–6/38	13°–18° Virgo	10/44–8/45
Oct	6°–5° Pisces	4/23–2/24	22° Capricorn	8/37–6/38	18°–22° Virgo	10/44–9/45
Nov	5°–6° Pisces	4/23–2/24	22°–23° Capricorn	8/37–6/38	22°–24° Virgo	8/45–9/45
Dec	6°–7° Pisces	5/23–2/24	23°–25° Capricorn	9/37–8/38	24°–26° Virgo	9/45–10/45

1995	Saturn	Return	Uranus	Opposition	Chiron	Return
Jan	7°–10° Pisces	6/23–3/24	25°–27° Capricorn	7/38–7/39	26°–25° Virgo	9/45–10/45
Feb	10°–14° Pisces	3/24–1/25	27°–28° Capricorn	8/38–7/39	25°–24° Virgo	9/45
Mar	14°–18° Pisces	4/24–2/25	28°–29° Capricorn	9/38–4/40	24°–21° Virgo	8/45–9/45
April	18°–21° Pisces	6/24–3/25	29° Capricorn–0° Aquarius	7/39–6/40	21°–20° Virgo	8/45
May	21°–23° Pisces	3/25	0° Aquarius	8/39–6/40	20° Virgo	8/45
June	23°–24° Pisces	3/25–4/25	0° Aquarius–29° Capricorn	7/39–6/40	20°–21° Virgo	8/45
July	24° Pisces	3/25–4/25	29°–28° Capricorn	9/38–5/40	21°–24° Virgo	8/45–9/45
Aug	24°–22° Pisces	3/25	28°–27° Capricorn	8/38–7/39	24°–28° Virgo	9/45–10/45
Sept	22°–20° Pisces	2/25–3/25	27°–26° Capricorn	8/38–7/39	28° Virgo–3° Libra	10/45–8/46
Oct	20°–18° Pisces	6/24–3/25	26° Capricorn	8/38–6/39	3°–7° Libra	11/45–10/46
Nov	18°–17° Pisces	5/24–2/25	26°–27° Capricorn	8/38–7/39	7°–11° Libra	8/46–10/46
Dec	18°–19° Pisces	6/24–2/25	27°–29° Capricorn	8/38–5/40	11°–13° Libra	9/46–10/46

KEY LIFE PASSAGES

1996	**Saturn**	**Return**	**Uranus**	**Opposition**	**Chiron**	**Return**
Jan	19°–22° Pisces	6/24–3/25	29° Capricorn– 1° Aquarius	7/39–6/40	13°–14° Libra	10/46
Feb	22°–25° Pisces	3/25–12/25	1°–2° Aquarius	8/39–7/40	14°–13° Libra	10/46
Mar	25°–29° Pisces	4/25–2/26	2°–4° Aquarius	9/39–5/41	13°–11° Libra	9/46–10/46
April	29° Pisces– 2° Aries	6/25–3/26	4° Aquarius	7/40–5/41	11°–9° Libra	9/46–10/46
May	2°–5° Aries	6/25–4/26	4° Aquarius	7/40–5/41	8°–7° Libra	8/46–9/46
June	5°–7° Aries	3/26–12/26	4°–3° Aquarius	10/39–5/41	7°–8° Libra	8/46–9/46
July	7° Aries	4/26–12/26	3°–2° Aquarius	9/39–4/41	8°–10° Libra	9/46–10/46
Aug	7°–5° Aries	3/26–12/26	2°–1° Aquarius	8/39–7/40	10°–14° Libra	9/46–10/46
Sept	5°–3° Aries	3/26–4/26	1°–0° Aquarius	8/39–6/40	14°–18° Libra	10/46–7/47
Oct	3°–1° Aries	6/25–3/26	0° Aquarius	8/39–6/40	18°–22° Libra	11/46–8/47
Nov	1°–0° Aries	5/25–3/26	0°–1° Aquarius	8/39–6/40	22°–27° Libra	12/46– 10/47
Dec	0°–1° Aries	5/25–3/26	1°–3° Aquarius	8/39–4/41	27° Libra– 0° Scorpio	10/47

1997	**Saturn**	**Return**	**Uranus**	**Opposition**	**Chiron**	**Return**
Jan	1°–3° Aries	6/25–3/26	3°–5° Aquarius	10/39–6/41	0°–1° Scorpio	10/47–11/47
Feb	3°–6° Aries	3/26–4/26	5°–6° Aquarius	8/40–7/41	1°–2° Scorpio	10/47–11/47
Mar	6°–10° Aries	4/26–2/27	6°–7° Aquarius	9/40–7/41	2°–0° Scorpio	10/47–11/47
April	10°–13° Aries	5/26–3/27	7°–8° Aquarius	9/40–5/42	0° Scorpio– 27° Libra	10/47
May	14°–17° Aries	6/26–4/27	8° Aquarius	11/40–5/42	27°–26° Libra	9/47–10/47
June	17°–19° Aries	4/27	8°–7° Aquarius	9/40–5/42	26°–25° Libra	9/47–10/47
July	19°–20° Aries	4/27–5/27	7°–6° Aquarius	9/40–7/41	25°–26° Libra	9/47–10/47
Aug	20°–19° Aries	4/27–5/27	6°–5° Aquarius	8/40–7/41	26°–29° Libra	9/47–10/47
Sept	19°–17° Aries	4/27	5°–4° Aquarius	7/40–6/41	29° Libra– 3° Scorpio	10/47–11/47
Oct	17°–15° Aries	3/27–4/27	4° Aquarius	7/40–5/41	3°–7° Scorpio	11/47–8/48
Nov	15°–13° Aries	6/26–3/27	4°–5° Aquarius	7/40–6/41	7°–11° Scorpio	12/47–10/48
Dec	13° Aries	6/26–3/27	5°–7° Aquarius	8/40–7/41	11°–15° Scorpio	1/48–11/48

KEY LIFE PASSAGES

1998	Saturn	Return	Uranus	Opposition	Chiron	Return
Jan	13°–15° Aries	6/26–3/27	7°–8° Aquarius	9/40–5/42	15°–17° Scorpio	10/48–11/48
Feb	15°–18° Aries	3/27–4/27	8°–10° Aquarius	11/40–7/42	17°–18° Scorpio	11/48
Mar	18°–21° Aries	4/27–1/28	10°–11° Aquarius	8/41–7/42	18°–17° Scorpio	11/48
April	21°–25° Aries	5/27–3/28	11°–12° Aquarius	9/41–8/42	17°–15° Scorpio	10/48–11/48
May	25°–29° Aries	6/27–4/28	12° Aquarius	10/41–8/42	15°–13° Scorpio	10/48–11/48
June	29° Aries–0° Taurus	4/28	12° Aquarius	10/41–8/42	13°–12° Scorpio	10/48
July	1°–3° Taurus	4/28–5/28	11°–10° Aquarius	8/41–7/42	12° Scorpio	10/48
Aug	3° Taurus	5/28	10°–9° Aquarius	8/41–7/42	12°–14° Scorpio	10/48
Sept	3°–1° Taurus	4/28–5/28	9°–8° Aquarius	11/40–6/42	14°–17° Scorpio	10/48–11/48
Oct	1° Taurus–29° Aries	4/28	8° Aquarius	11/40–5/42	17°–21° Scorpio	11/48–8/49
Nov	29°–27° Aries	7/27–4/28	8°–9° Aquarius	11/40–6/42	21°–25° Scorpio	12/28–10/49
Dec	27°–26° Aries	6/27–3/28	9°–10° Aquarius	8/41–7/42	25°–29° Scorpio	1/49–11/49

1999	Saturn	Return	Uranus	Opposition	Chiron	Return
Jan	26°–27° Aries	6/27–3/28	10°–12° Aquarius	8/41–8/42	29° Scorpio–2° Sagittarius	11/49–12/49
Feb	27°–29° Aries	7/27–4/28	12°–14° Aquarius	10/41–5/43	2°–3° Sagittarius	11/49–12/49
Mar	29° Aries–3° Taurus	4/28–5/28	14°–15° Aquarius	8/42–7/43	3° Sagittarius	12/49
April	3°–7° Taurus	5/28–3/29	15°–16° Aquarius	9/42–7/43	3°–2° Sagittarius	11/49–12/49
May	7°–10° Taurus	6/28–4/29	16° Aquarius	9/42–7/43	2°–0° Sagittarius	11/49–12/29
June	11°–14° Taurus	8/28–5/29	16° Aquarius	9/42–7/43	0° Sagittarius–28° Scorpio	10/49–11/49
July	14°–16° Taurus	5/29	16°–15° Aquarius	9/42–7/43	28°–27° Scorpio	2/49–11/49
Aug	16°–17° Taurus	5/29–6/29	15°–13° Aquarius	8/42–7/43	27°–28° Scorpio	2/49–11/49
Sept	17°–16° Taurus	5/29–6/29	13° Aquarius	8/42–5/43	28° Scorpio–0° Sagittarius	10/49–11/49
Oct	16°–14° Taurus	5/29	13°–12° Aquarius	10/41–5/43	0°–4° Sagittarius	11/49–12/49
Nov	14°–11° Taurus	8/28–5/29	12°–13° Aquarius	10/41–5/43	4°–7° Sagittarius	12/49–10/50
Dec	11°–10° Taurus	7/28–4/29	13°–14° Aquarius	8/42–6/43	7°–11° Sagittarius	1/50–11/50

KEY LIFE PASSAGES

2000	Saturn	Return	Uranus	Opposition	Chiron	Return
Jan	10° Taurus	7/28–4/29	14°–16° Aquarius	8/42–7/43	11°–14° Sagittarius	2/50–1/51
Feb	10°–12° Taurus	7/28–4/29	16°–18° Aquarius	9/42–6/44	14°–16° Sagittarius	11/50–1/51
Mar	12°–15° Taurus	4/29–5/29	18°–19° Aquarius	8/43–7/44	16°–17° Sagittarius	12/50–1/51
April	15°–19° Taurus	5/29–3/30	19°–20° Aquarius	8/43–7/44	17°–16° Sagittarius	12/50–1/51
May	19°–23° Taurus	6/29–4/30	20° Aquarius	9/43–7/44	16°–14° Sagittarius	11/50–1/51
June	23°–26° Taurus	7/29–5/30	20° Aquarius	9/43–7/44	14°–12° Sagittarius	11/50–1/51
July	26°–29° Taurus	5/30–6/30	20°–19° Aquarius	8/43–7/44	12°–11° Sagittarius	2/50–11/50
Aug	29° Taurus– 0° Gemini	5/30–6/30	19°–18° Aquarius	8/43–7/44	11° Sagittarius	2/50–11/50
Sept	0° Gemini	6/30	18°–17° Aquarius	10/42–6/44	11°–12° Sagittarius	2/50–11/50
Oct	0° Gemini– 29° Taurus	5/30–6/30	17°–16° Aquarius	9/42–8/43	12°–15° Sagittarius	11/50–1/51
Nov	28°–26° Taurus	5/30–6/30	16°–17° Aquarius	9/42–8/43	15°–18° Sagittarius	12/50– 10/51
Dec	26°–24° Taurus	8/29–5/30	17°–18° Aquarius	10/42–6/44	18°–22° Sagittarius	12/50– 11/51

APPENDIX TWO

Key Chiron Passages Tables

THE "KEY CHIRON PASSAGES" TABLES show the sign and degree locations of the planet Chiron in the birth chart. Simply find the table that indicates your year of birth and then consult the horizontal line of information after your month of birth.

The first column indicates Chiron's location in your birth chart, the second column shows the time range of your first Chiron square, the third column indicates the time range of your Chiron opposition, and the fourth column shows the time range of your upper Chiron square. The time range of your Chiron Return is the last column in the Key Life Passages tables in appendix one. Or you can just add fifty years to your month and year of birth to get the time range of your Chiron Return. Numbers that are out of sequence exist because of "retrograde" motion of planets, which occurs at certain times of the year when planets appear to move backward in the sky from our viewing perspective on Earth.

In order to get an *exact* timing for these Chiron aspects, an astrologer must be consulted. However, the information given here is accurate enough to offer a very close time range. It is important to note that while the time ranges listed here cover the most intense phase of the Chiron aspects, the influence of the aspects on the individual tends to begin approximately a year before the dates listed and to continue for a year after these dates.

For individuals wishing to have a more exact location of planets in their birth charts and timing of these key life passages, an astrologer can be consulted or a computerized chart can be ordered free online from www.astrotheme .com/horoscope_chart_sign_ascendant.php. Also, many fine Apps are available for casting your chart, and you should try a few of them to see which ones work for you. If you need an ephemeris to cast your Saturn transits, there are many choices online. Have fun!

KEY CHIRON PASSAGES

1940	Birth Chart	1st Square	Opposition	Upper Square
Jan	17°–15° Cancer	11/45–8/46	1/53–11/53	5/72–2/74
Feb	15°–14° Cancer	11/45–7/46	1/53–10/53	4/72–3/73
Mar	14°–13° Cancer	10/45–6/46	12/52–1/53	6/71–3/73
April	14°–15° Cancer	11/45–7/46	1/53–10/53	4/72–3/73
May	15°–17° Cancer	11/45–8/46	1/53–11/53	5/72–2/74
June	17°–20° Cancer	11/45–9/46	2/53–12/53	6/72–2/75
July	20°–24° Cancer	12/45–10/46	3/53–11/54	6/73–2/76
Aug	24°–27° Cancer	9/46–10/46	2/54–1/55	6/74–2/77
Sept	27° Cancer–0° Leo	10/46–11/46	3/54–11/55	6/75–4/77
Oct	0°–1° Leo	11/46	1/55–12/55	5/76–2/78
Nov	1° Leo	11/46	2/55–12/55	6/76–2/78
Dec	1° Leo– 29° Cancer	11/46	1/55–12/55	5/76–2/78

1941	Birth Chart	1st Square	Opposition	Upper Square
Jan	29°–27° Cancer	10/46–11/46	3/54–1/55	6/75–3/77
Feb	27°–25° Cancer	10/46	2/54–1/55	5/75–2/77
Mar	25° Cancer	10/46	2/54–12/54	5/75–3/76
April	25°–26° Cancer	10/46	2/54–12/54	5/75–4/76
May	26°–28° Cancer	10/46–11/46	2/54–1/55	5/75–3/77
June	28° Cancer–1° Leo	10/46–11/46	4/54–12/55	7/75–2/78
July	1°–5° Leo	11/46–9/47	2/55–1/56	6/76–2/79
Aug	5°–8° Leo	12/46–10/47	4/55–12/56	6/77–4/79
Sept	8°–11° Leo	1/47–10/47	2/56–2/57	6/78–4/80
Oct	11°–13° Leo	10/47–11/47	4/56–12/57	5/79–2/81
Nov	13°–14° Leo	10/47–11/47	2/57–1/58	7/79–3/81
Dec	14°–13° Leo	10/47–11/47	2/57–1/58	7/79–3/81

KEY CHIRON PASSAGES

1942	Birth Chart	1st Square	Opposition	Upper Square
Jan	13°–11° Leo	10/47–11/47	4/56–12/57	5/79–2/81
Feb	11°–9° Leo	10/47	3/56–2/57	7/78–4/80
Mar	9°–8° Leo	1/47–10/47	2/56–1/57	6/78–3/80
April	8° Leo	1/47–10/47	2/56–12/56	6/78–4/79
May	8°–10° Leo	1/47–10/47	2/56–1/57	6/78–3/80
June	10°–13° Leo	10/47–11/47	3/56–12/57	5/79–2/81
July	13°–17° Leo	10/47–12/47	2/57–11/58	7/79–2/82
Aug	17°–21° Leo	11/47–9/48	4/57–2/59	6/80–5/82
Sept	21°–24° Leo	1/48–10/48	3/58–1/60	6/81–4/83
Oct	24°–27° Leo	2/48–11/48	3/59–12/60	6/82–2/84
Nov	27°–29° Leo	11/48	4/59–1/61	7/82–4/84
Dec	29° Leo	11/48	3/60–1/61	6/83–4/84

1943	Birth Chart	1st Square	Opposition	Upper Square
Jan	29°–27° Leo	11/48	4/59–1/61	7/82–4/84
Feb	27°–25° Leo	10/48–11/48	3/59–12/60	6/82–2/84
Mar	25°–23° Leo	1/48–10/48	2/59–1/60	5/82–4/83
April	23°–22° Leo	1/48–10/48	4/58–12/59	7/81–3/83
May	23°–24° Leo	1/48–10/48	2/59–1/60	5/82–4/83
June	24°–26° Leo	2/48–11/48	3/59–2/60	6/82–5/83
July	26° Leo–0° Virgo	10/48–12/48	4/59–2/61	7/82–4/84
Aug	0°–4° Virgo	11/48–9/49	3/60–2/62	6/83–4/85
Sept	4°–8° Virgo	12/48–11/49	3/61–2/63	6/84–6/85
Oct	8°–12° Virgo	2/49–12/49	3/62–2/64	8/84–5/86
Nov	12°–14° Virgo	11/49–12/49	3/63–1/65	7/85–6/86
Dec	14°–15° Virgo	12/49–9/50	5/63–1/65	8/85–3/87

KEY CHIRON PASSAGES

1944	Birth Chart	1st Square	Opposition	Upper Square
Jan	15°–14° Virgo	12/49–9/50	5/63–1/65	8/85–3/87
Feb	14°–12° Virgo	11/49–12/49	3/63–1/65	7/85–6/86
Mar	12°–10° Virgo	11/49–12/49	4/62–2/64	6/85–5/86
April	10°–9° Virgo	3/49–11/49	4/62–12/63	6/85–4/86
May	9° Virgo	3/49–11/49	4/62–2/63	6/85–3/86
June	9°–11° Virgo	3/49–11/49	4/62–1/64	6/85–4/86
July	11°–15° Virgo	11/49–9/50	3/63–1/65	6/85–3/87
Aug	15°–19° Virgo	12/49–11/50	3/64–2/66	6/86–5/87
Sept	19°–23° Virgo	1/50–12/50	3/65–2/67	7/86–4/88
Oct	23°–28° Virgo	12/50–10/51	3/66–12/68	6/87–6/88
Nov	28° Virgo–1° Libra	1/51–11/51	4/67–3/69	9/87–4/89
Dec	1°–3° Libra	2/51–12/51	4/68–2/70	7/88–5/89

1945	Birth Chart	1st Square	Opposition	Upper Square
Jan	3° Libra	12/51	6/68–2/70	7/88–5/89
Feb	3°–1° Libra	2/51–12/51	4/68–2/70	7/88–5/89
Mar	1° Libra–29° Virgo	1/51–11/51	5/67–3/69	6/88–4/89
April	29°–27° Virgo	1/51–11/51	4/67–1/69	8/87–6/88
May	27°–26° Virgo	12/50–10/51	6/66–2/68	7/87–5/88
June	26°–28° Virgo	12/50–10/51	6/66–12/68	7/87–6/88
July	28° Virgo–0° Libra	1/51–11/51	4/67–2/69	9/87–7/88
Aug	0°–4° Libra	2/51–12/51	4/68–3/70	6/88–5/89
Sept	4°–9° Libra	12/51–11/52	4/69–1/72	8/88–7/89
Oct	9°–13° Libra	2/52–1/53	5/70–2/73	7/89–5/90
Nov	13°–17° Libra	12/52–11/53	6/71–2/74	8/89–7/90
Dec	17°–20° Libra	2/53–12/53	6/72–2/75	6/90–8/90

KEY CHIRON PASSAGES

1946	Birth Chart	1st Square	Opposition	Upper Square
Jan	20°–21° Libra	3/53–1/54	6/73–3/75	7/90–4/91
Feb	21°–20° Libra	3/53–1/54	6/73–3/75	7/90–4/91
Mar	20°–18° Libra	2/53–12/53	4/73–2/75	7/90–8/90
April	18°–16° Libra	1/53–12/53	5/72–3/74	9/89–7/90
May	16°–15° Libra	1/53–11/53	5/72–2/74	9/89–6/90
June	15°–14° Libra	1/53–10/53	4/72–3/73	8/89–6/90
July	15°–17° Libra	1/53–11/53	5/72–2/74	9/89–7/90
Aug	17°–20° Libra	2/53–12/53	6/72–2/75	6/90–8/90
Sept	20°–24° Libra	3/53–11/54	6/73–2/76	7/90–6/91
Oct	24°–28° Libra	2/54–1/55	6/74–3/77	8/90–7/91
Nov	28° Libra–2° Scorpio	4/54–12/55	7/75–3/78	7/91–8/91
Dec	2°–6° Scorpio	2/55–11/56	4/77–3/79	8/91–6/92

1947	Birth Chart	1st Square	Opposition	Upper Square
Jan	6°–8° Scorpio	1/56–12/56	5/78–4/79	9/91–6/92
Feb	8° Scorpio	2/56–12/56	6/78–4/79	10/91–6/92
Mar	8°–7° Scorpio	2/56–12/56	5/78–4/79	9/91–6/92
April	7°–5° Scorpio	4/55–12/56	6/77–4/79	9/91–6/92
May	5°–3° Scorpio	3/55–1/56	5/77–2/79	8/91–6/92
June	3°–2° Scorpio	2/55–1/56	4/77–4/78	8/91–5/92
July	2°–3° Scorpio	2/55–1/56	4/77–4/78	8/91–5/92
Aug	3°–5° Scorpio	3/55–1/56	5/77–2/79	8/91–6/92
Sept	5°–8° Scorpio	4/55–12/56	6/77–4/79	9/91–6/92
Oct	8°–13° Scorpio	2/56–12/57	6/78–2/81	10/91–8/92
Nov	13°–17° Scorpio	2/57–11/58	7/79–2/82	8/92–5/93
Dec	17°–20° Scorpio	4/57–1/59	6/80–4/82	9/92–6/93

KEY CHIRON PASSAGES

1948	Birth Chart	1st Square	Opposition	Upper Square
Jan	20°–23° Scorpio	3/58–12/59	6/81–3/83	10/92–7/93
Feb	23°–24° Scorpio	2/59–1/60	5/82–4/83	11/92–7/93
Mar	24° Scorpio	3/59–1/60	6/82–4/83	7/93
April	24°–22° Scorpio	4/58–1/60	7/81–4/83	10/92–7/93
May	22°–20° Scorpio	3/58–11/59	6/81–2/83	10/92–7/93
June	20°–18° Scorpio	2/58–1/59	7/80–4/82	9/92–6/93
July	18° Scorpio	2/58–12/58	7/80–3/82	9/92–6/93
Aug	18°–20° Scorpio	2/58–1/59	7/80–4/82	9/92–6/93
Sept	20°–22° Scorpio	3/58–11/59	6/81–2/83	10/92–7/93
Oct	22°–26° Scorpio	4/58–2/60	7/81–5/83	10/92–8/93
Nov	26° Scorpio–0° Sagittarius	4/59–2/61	7/82–4/84	8/93–9/93
Dec	0°–4° Sagittarius	3/60–2/62	6/83–4/85	9/93–6/94

1949	Birth Chart	1st Square	Opposition	Upper Square
Jan	4°–7° Sagittarius	3/61–1/63	6/84–5/85	10/93–7/94
Feb	7°–8° Sagittarius	3/62–2/63	7/84–6/85	11/93–7/94
Mar	8°–9° Sagittarius	3/62–2/63	8/84–3/86	11/93–8/94
April	9°–7° Sagittarius	3/62–2/63	7/84–3/86	11/93–8/94
May	7°–5° Sagittarius	4/61–1/63	6/84–5/85	10/93–7/94
June	5°–3° Sagittarius	3/61–2/62	5/84–4/85	9/93–6/94
July	3°–2° Sagittarius	5/60–1/62	7/83–3/85	9/93–6/94
Aug	2°–3° Sagittarius	5/60–1/62	7/83–3/85	9/93–6/94
Sept	3°–5° Sagittarius	3/61–2/62	5/84–4/85	9/93–6/94
Oct	5°–8° Sagittarius	4/61–2/63	6/84–6/85	10/93–7/94
Nov	8°–12° Sagittarius	3/62–2/64	8/84–5/86	11/93–8/94
Dec	12°–15° Sagittarius	3/63–1/65	7/85–3/87	8/94–9/94

KEY CHIRON PASSAGES

1950	Birth Chart	Ist Square	Opposition	Upper Square
Jan	15°–18° Sagittarius	3/64–1/66	6/86–5/87	9/94–10/94
Feb	18°–20° Sagittarius	5/64–2/66	7/86–5/87	10/94–6/95
Mar	20°–21° Sagittarius	4/65–12/66	8/86–6/87	10/94–7/95
April	21° Sagittarius	4/65–12/66	9/86–6/87	10/94–7/95
May	21°–19° Sagittarius	3/65–12/66	7/86–6/87	10/94–7/95
June	19°–17° Sagittarius	4/64–2/66	6/86–5/87	9/94–10/94
July	17°–15° Sagittarius	3/64–11/65	6/86–4/87	9/94–10/94
Aug	15° Sagittarius	3/64–1/65	6/86–3/87	9/94
Sept	15°–17° Sagittarius	3/64–11/65	6/86–4/87	9/94–10/94
Oct	17°–19° Sagittarius	4/64–2/66	6/86–5/87	9/94–10/94
Nov	19°–22° Sagittarius	3/65–1/67	7/86–6/87	10/94–7/95
Dec	22°–26° Sagittarius	5/65–2/68	6/87–5/88	11/94–8/95

1951	Birth Chart	Ist Square	Opposition	Upper Square
Jan	26°–29° Sagittarius	6/66–1/69	7/87–6/88	12/94–9/95
Feb	29° Sagittarius– 1° Capricorn	5/67–3/69	6/88–4/89	9/95
Mar	1°–2° Capricorn	4/68–1/70	7/88–4/89	9/95
April	2° Capricorn	5/68–1/70	7/88–4/89	9/95
May	2°–1° Capricorn	4/68–1/70	7/88–4/89	9/95
June	1° Capricorn– 29° Sagittarius	5/67–3/69	6/88–4/89	9/95
July	29°–27° Sagittarius	4/67–1/69	8/87–6/88	8/95–9/95
Aug	27°–26° Sagittarius	6/66–2/68	7/87–5/88	12/94–8/95
Sept	26°–27° Sagittarius	6/66–2/68	7/87–5/88	12/94–8/95
Oct	27°–29° 2° Sagittarius	4/67–1/69	8/87–6/88	8/95–9/95
Nov	29° Sagittarius– 2° Capricorn	5/67–1/70	6/88–4/89	9/95
Dec	2°–5° Capricorn	5/68–1/71	7/88–6/89	9/95–10/95

KEY CHIRON PASSAGES

1952

	Birth Chart	1st Square	Opposition	Upper Square
Jan	5°–8° Capricorn	5/69–3/71	8/88–7/89	10/95–7/96
Feb	8°–10° Capricorn	4/70–2/72	6/89–4/90	11/95–8/96
Mar	10°–12° Capricorn	6/70–1/73	7/89–5/90	11/95–8/96
April	12° Capricorn	5/71–1/73	8/89–5/90	12/95–8/96
May	12°–11° Capricorn	4/71–1/73	7/89–5/90	11/95–8/96
June	11°–9° Capricorn	5/70–3/72	7/89–4/90	11/95–8/96
July	9°–7° Capricorn	4/70–1/72	9/88–7/89	10/95–7/96
Aug	7°–6° Capricorn	5/69–2/71	9/88–6/89	10/95–6/96
Sept	6° Capricorn	5/69–2/71	9/88–6/89	10/95
Oct	6°–8° Capricorn	5/69–3/71	9/88–7/89	10/95–7/96
Nov	8°–10° Capricorn	4/70–2/72	6/89–4/90	11/95–8/96
Dec	10°–13° Capricorn	6/70–2/73	7/89–5/90	11/95–8/96

1953

	Birth Chart	1st Square	Opposition	Upper Square
Jan	13°–16° Capricorn	6/71–2/74	8/89–6/90	12/95–9/96
Feb	16°–18° Capricorn	5/72–3/74	9/89–7/90	9/96–10/96
Mar	18°–20° Capricorn	4/73–2/75	7/90–8/90	9/96–10/96
April	20°–21° Capricorn	6/73–3/75	7/90–4/91	10/96
May	21°–20° Capricorn	6/73–3/75	7/90–4/91	10/96
June	20°–18° Capricorn	4/73–2/75	7/90–8/90	9/96–10/96
July	18°–16° Capricorn	5/72–3/74	9/89–7/90	9/96–10/96
Aug	16°–15° Capricorn	5/72–2/74	9/89–6/90	9/96
Sept	15° Capricorn	5/72–3/73	9/89–6/90	9/96
Oct	15°–16° Capricorn	5/72–2/74	9/89–6/90	9/96
Nov	16°–18° Capricorn	5/72–3/74	9/89–7/90	9/96–10/96
Dec	18°–20° Capricorn	4/73–2/75	7/90–8/90	9/96–10/96

KEY CHIRON PASSAGES

1954	Birth Chart	1st Square	Opposition	Upper Square
Jan	20°–23° Capricorn	6/73–2/76	7/90–5/91	10/96–11/96
Feb	23°–26° Capricorn	5/74–4/76	8/90–6/91	11/96–8/97
Mar	26°–27° Capricorn	5/75–2/77	9/90–7/91	11/96–8/97
April	27°–28° Capricorn	6/75–3/77	10/90–7/91	12/96–8/97
May	28° Capricorn	7/75–3/77	7/91	12/96–8/97
June	28°–26° Capricorn	5/75–3/77	9/90–7/91	11/96–8/97
July	26°–25° Capricorn	5/75–4/76	9/90–6/91	11/96–8/97
Aug	25°–23° Capricorn	5/74–3/76	8/90–6/91	11/96–7/97
Sept	23° Capricorn	5/74–2/76	8/90–5/91	11/96
Oct	23° Capricorn	5/74–2/76	8/90–5/91	11/96
Nov	23°–25° Capricorn	5/74–3/76	8/90–6/91	11/96–7/97
Dec	25°–27° Capricorn	5/75–2/77	9/90–7/91	11/96–8/97

1955	Birth Chart	1st Square	Opposition	Upper Square
Jan	27° Capricorn–0° Aquarius	6/75–4/77	10/90–7/91	12/96–9/97
Feb	0°–2° Aquarius	5/76–3/78	7/91–8/91	12/96–9/97
Mar	2°–4° Aquarius	4/77–4/78	8/91–5/92	2/97–10/97
April	4°–5° Aquarius	6/77–2/79	8/91–6/92	10/97
May	5° Aquarius	6/77–2/79	9/91–6/92	10/97
June	5°–4° Aquarius	6/77–2/79	8/91–6/92	10/97
July	4°–2° Aquarius	4/77–4/78	8/91–5/92	2/97–10/97
Aug	2°–0° Aquarius	5/76–3/78	7/91–8/91	12/96–9/97
Sept	0° Aquarius	5/76–4/77	7/91	12/96–9/97
Oct	0° Aquarius	5/76–4/77	7/91	12/96–9/97
Nov	0°–1° Aquarius	5/76–2/78	7/91–8/91	12/96–9/97
Dec	1°–3° Aquarius	6/76–4/78	7/91–5/92	1/97–10/97

KEY CHIRON PASSAGES

1956	Birth Chart	1st Square	Opposition	Upper Square
Jan	3°–6° Aquarius	5/77–3/79	8/91–6/92	9/97–10/97
Feb	6°–8° Aquarius	5/78–4/79	9/91–6/92	10/97–11/97
Mar	8°–10° Aquarius	6/78–3/80	10/91–7/92	11/97
April	10°–11° Aquarius	5/79–4/80	7/92	11/97–12/97
May	11° Aquarius	5/79–4/80	7/92	11/97–12/97
June	11°–10° Aquarius	5/79–4/80	7/92	11/97–12/97
July	10°–9° Aquarius	7/78–3/80	10/91–7/92	11/97
Aug	9°–7° Aquarius	5/78–3/80	9/91–7/92	10/97–11/97
Sept	7°–6° Aquarius	5/78–4/79	9/91–6/92	10/97–11/97
Oct	6° Aquarius	5/78–3/79	9/91–6/92	10/97
Nov	6°–7° Aquarius	5/78–4/79	9/91–6/92	10/97–11/97
Dec	7°–9° Aquarius	5/78–3/80	9/91–7/92	10/97–11/97

1957	Birth Chart	1st Square	Opposition	Upper Square
Jan	9°–11° Aquarius	7/78–4/80	10/91–7/92	11/97–12/97
Feb	11°–14° Aquarius	5/79–3/81	7/92–8/92	11/97–9/98
Mar	14°–16° Aquarius	5/80–4/81	8/92–9/92	12/97–9/98
April	16°–17° Aquarius	6/80–2/82	8/92–5/93	1/98–10/98
May	17° Aquarius	6/80–2/82	9/92–5/93	1/98–10/98
June	17°–16° Aquarius	6/80–2/82	8/92–5/93	1/98–10/98
July	16°–15° Aquarius	5/80–4/81	8/92–9/92	12/97–9/98
Aug	15°–13° Aquarius	7/79–4/81	8/92	12/97–9/98
Sept	13°–12° Aquarius	6/79–2/81	7/92–8/92	12/97–8/98
Oct	12° Aquarius	6/79–4/80	7/92–8/92	12/97–8/98
Nov	12°–13° Aquarius	6/79–2/81	7/92–8/92	12/97–8/98
Dec	13°–14° Aquarius	7/79–3/81	8/92	12/97–9/98

KEY CHIRON PASSAGES

1958	Birth Chart	1st Square	Opposition	Upper Square
Jan	14°–17° Aquarius	5/80–2/82	8/92–5/93	12/97–10/98
Feb	17°–19° Aquarius	6/80–4/82	9/92–6/93	1/98–10/98
Mar	19°–21° Aquarius	5/81–5/82	9/92–7/93	10/98–11/98
April	21°–22° Aquarius	6/81–2/83	10/92–7/93	10/98–11/98
May	22° Aquarius	7/81–2/83	10/92–7/93	11/98
June	22° Aquarius	7/81–2/83	10/92–7/93	11/98
July	22°–20° Aquarius	6/81–2/83	10/92–7/93	10/98–11/98
Aug	20°–19° Aquarius	5/81–4/82	9/92–6/93	10/98
Sept	19°–18° Aquarius	7/80–4/82	9/92–6/93	2/98–10/98
Oct	18°–17° Aquarius	6/80–3/82	9/92–6/93	1/98–10/98
Nov	17°–18° Aquarius	6/80–3/82	9/92–6/93	1/98–10/98
Dec	18°–19° Aquarius	7/80–4/82	9/92–6/93	2/98–10/98

1959	Birth Chart	1st Square	Opposition	Upper Square
Jan	19°–21° Aquarius	5/81–5/82	9/92–7/93	10/98–11/98
Feb	21°–23° Aquarius	6/81–3/83	10/92–7/93	10/98–11/98
Mar	23°–25° Aquarius	5/82–4/83	11/92–8/93	11/98–12/98
April	25°–27° Aquarius	6/82–2/84	7/93–8/93	11/98–8/99
May	27° Aquarius	7/82–2/84	8/93	12/98–8/99
June	27° Aquarius	7/82–2/84	8/93	12/98–8/99
July	27°–26° Aquarius	7/82–2/84	8/93	12/98–8/99
Aug	26°–24° Aquarius	6/82–5/83	7/93–8/93	11/98–12/98
Sept	24°–23° Aquarius	5/82–4/83	11/92–7/93	11/98
Oct	23°–22° Aquarius	7/81–3/83	10/92–7/93	11/98
Nov	22°–23° Aquarius	7/81–3/83	10/92–7/93	11/98
Dec	23°–24° Aquarius	5/82–4/83	11/92–7/93	11/98

KEY CHIRON PASSAGES

1960	Birth Chart	1st Square	Opposition	Upper Square
Jan	24°–26° Aquarius	6/82–5/83	7/93–8/93	11/98–12/98
Feb	26°–28° Aquarius	7/82–3/84	8/93	12/98–9/99
Mar	28° Aquarius–0° Pisces	5/83–4/84	8/93–9/93	12/98–10/99
April	0°–1° Pisces	6/83–5/84	9/93	1/99–10/99
May	1°–2° Pisces	7/83–5/84	9/93–5/94	1/99–10/99
June	2°–1° Pisces	7/83–5/84	9/93–5/94	1/99–10/99
July	1°–0° Pisces	6/83–5/84	9/93	1/99–10/99
Aug	0° Pisces–29° Aquarius	6/83–4/84	8/93–9/93	12/98–10/99
Sept	29°–28° Aquarius	5/83–4/84	8/93–9/93	12/98–9/99
Oct	28°–27° Aquarius	7/82–3/84	8/93	12/98–9/99
Nov	27° Aquarius	7/82–2/84	8/93	12/98–8/99
Dec	27°–28° Aquarius	7/82–3/84	8/93	12/98–9/99

1961	Birth Chart	1st Square	Opposition	Upper Square
Jan	28° Aquarius–0° Pisces	5/83–4/84	8/93–9/93	12/98–10/99
Feb	0°–2° Pisces	6/83–5/84	9/93–5/94	1/99–10/99
Mar	2°–4° Pisces	7/83–4/85	9/93–6/94	1/99–11/99
April	4°–5° Pisces	6/84–4/85	10/93–6/94	10/99–11/99
May	5°–6° Pisces	6/84–5/85	10/93–7/94	11/99
June	6° Pisces	7/84–5/85	10/93–7/94	11/99
July	6°–5° Pisces	6/84–5/85	10/93–7/94	11/99
Aug	5°–4° Pisces	6/84–4/85	10/93–6/94	10/99–11/99
Sept	4°–2° Pisces	7/83–4/85	9/93–6/94	1/99–11/99
Oct	2°–1 ° Pisces	7/83–5/84	9/93–5/94	1/99–10/99
Nov	1°–2° Pisces	7/83–5/84	9/93–5/94	1/99–10/99
Dec	2°–3° Pisces	7/83–3/85	9/93–6/94	1/99–10/99

KEY CHIRON PASSAGES

1962	Birth Chart	1st Square	Opposition	Upper Square
Jan	3°–4° Pisces	5/84–4/85	9/93–6/94	2/99–11/99
Feb	4°–6° Pisces	6/84–5/85	10/93–7/94	10/99–11/99
Mar	6°–8° Pisces	7/84–6/85	10/93–7/94	11/99–12/99
April	8°–9° Pisces	8/84–3/86	11/93–8/94	12/99
May	9°–10° Pisces	6/85–4/86	12/93–8/94	12/99
June	10° Pisces	6/85–4/86	8/94	12/99
July	10°–9° Pisces	6/85–4/86	12/93–8/94	12/99
Aug	9°–8° Pisces	8/84–3/86	11/93–8/94	12/99
Sept	8°–7° Pisces	7/84–6/85	11/93–7/94	11/99–12/99
Oct	7°–6° Pisces	7/84–5/85	10/93–7/94	11/99–12/99
Nov	6° Pisces	7/84–5/85	10/93–7/94	11/99
Dec	6°–7° Pisces	7/84–5/85	10/93–7/94	11/99–12/99

1963	Birth Chart	1st Square	Opposition	Upper Square
Jan	7°–8° Pisces	7/84–6/85	11/93–7/94	11/99–12/99
Feb	8°–10° Pisces	8/84–4/86	11/93–8/94	12/99
Mar	10°–12° Pisces	6/85–5/86	8/94	12/99–10/00
April	12°–13° Pisces	7/85–5/86	8/94–9/94	1/00–10/00
May	13°–14° Pisces	7/85–6/86	8/94–9/94	1/00–10/00
June	14° Pisces	8/85–6/86	9/94	1/00–10/00
July	14° Pisces	8/85–6/86	9/94	1/00–10/00
Aug	14°–12° Pisces	7/85–6/86	8/94–9/94	1/00–10/00
Sept	12°–11° Pisces	6/85–5/86	8/94	12/99–10/00
Oct	11°–10° Pisces	6/85–4/86	8/94	12/99–1/00
Nov	10° Pisces	6/85–4/86	8/94	12/99
Dec	10° Pisces	6/85–4/86	8/94	12/99

KEY CHIRON PASSAGES

1964	Birth Chart	1st Square	Opposition	Upper Square
Jan	10°–12° Pisces	6/85–5/86	8/94	12/99–10/00
Feb	12°–14° Pisces	7/85–6/86	8/94–9/94	1/00–10/00
Mar	14°–16° Pisces	8/85–4/87	9/94	1/00–11/00
April	16°–17° Pisces	6/86–4/87	9/94–10/94	2/00–11/00
May	17°–18° Pisces	6/86–5/87	9/94–10/94	3/00–12/00
June	18° Pisces	7/86–5/87	10/94	11/00–12/00
July	18° Pisces	7/86–5/87	10/94	11/00–12/00
Aug	18°–16° Pisces	6/86–5/87	9/94–10/94	2/00–12/00
Sept	16°–15° Pisces	6/86–4/87	9/94	2/00–11/00
Oct	15°–14° Pisces	8/85–3/87	9/94	1/00–11/00
Nov	14° Pisces	8/85–6/86	9/94	1/00–10/00
Dec	14° Pisces	8/85–6/86	9/94	1/00–10/00

1965	Birth Chart	1st Square	Opposition	Upper Square
Jan	14°–16° Pisces	8/85–4/87	9/94	1/00–11/00
Feb	16°–17° Pisces	6/86–4/87	9/94–10/94	2/00–11/00
Mar	17°–19° Pisces	6/86–5/87	9/94–10/94	3/00–12/00
April	19°–21° Pisces	7/86–6/87	10/94–7/95	12/00
May	21°–22° Pisces	9/86–6/87	10/94–7/95	12/00–9/01
June	22° Pisces	6/87	11/94–7/95	12/00–9/01
July	22°–21° Pisces	9/86–6/87	10/94–7/95	12/00–9/01
Aug	21°–20° Pisces	8/86–6/87	10/94–7/95	12/00
Sept	20°–19° Pisces	7/86–5/87	10/94–6/95	12/00
Oct	19°–18° Pisces	7/86–5/87	10/94	11/00–12/00
Nov	18°–17° Pisces	6/86–5/87	9/94–10/94	3/00–12/00
Dec	17°–18° Pisces	6/86–5/87	9/94–10/94	3/00–12/00

KEY CHIRON PASSAGES

1966	Birth Chart	1st Square	Opposition	Upper Square
Jan	18°–19° Pisces	7/86–5/87	10/94	11/00–12/00
Feb	19°–21° Pisces	7/86–6/87	10/94–7/95	12/00
Mar	21°–23° Pisces	9/86–4/88	10/94–7/95	12/00–10/01
April	23°–24° Pisces	6/87–4/88	11/94–8/95	1/01–10/01
May	24°–25° Pisces	7/87–5/88	11/94–8/95	1/01–11/01
June	25°–26° Pisces	7/87–5/88	12/94–8/95	1/01–11/01
July	26°–25° Pisces	7/87–5/88	12/94–8/95	1/01–11/01
Aug	25°–24° Pisces	7/87–5/88	11/94–8/95	1/01–11/01
Sept	24°–23° Pisces	6/87–4/88	11/94–8/95	1/01–10/01
Oct	23°–22° Pisces	6/87–4/88	11/94–7/95	12/00–10/01
Nov	22°–21° Pisces	9/86–6/87	10/94–7/95	12/00–9/01
Dec	21°–22° Pisces	9/86–6/87	10/94–7/95	12/00–9/01

1967	Birth Chart	1st Square	Opposition	Upper Square
Jan	22°–23° Pisces	6/87–4/88	11/94–7/95	12/00–10/01
Feb	23°–24° Pisces	6/87–4/88	11/94–8/95	1/01–10/01
Mar	24°–26° Pisces	7/87–5/88	11/94–8/95	1/01–11/01
April	26°–28° Pisces	7/87–6/88	12/94–9/95	2/01–12/01
May	28°–29° Pisces	9/87–6/88	8/95–9/95	3/01–12/01
June	29° Pisces	6/88	9/95	12/01
July	29° Pisces	6/88	9/95	12/01
Aug	29°–28° Pisces	9/87–6/88	8/95–9/95	3/01–12/01
Sept	28°–27° Pisces	8/87–6/88	8/95–9/95	2/01–12/01
Oct	27°–25° Pisces	7/87–5/88	12/94–8/95	1/01–11/01
Nov	25° Pisces	7/87–5/88	12/94–8/95	1/01–11/01
Dec	25° Pisces	7/87–5/88	12/94–8/95	1/01–11/01

KEY CHIRON PASSAGES

1968	Birth Chart	1st Square	Opposition	Upper Square
Jan	25°–26° Pisces	7/87–5/88	12/94/–8/95	1/01–11/01
Feb	26°–28° Pisces	7/87–6/88	12/94–9/95	2/01–12/01
Mar	28° Pisces–0° Aries	9/87–7/88	8/95–9/95	3/01–12/01
April	0°–1° Aries	6/88–4/89	9/95	12/01
May	1°–3° Aries	7/88–5/89	9/95–10/95	12/01–10/02
June	3° Aries	7/88–5/89	9/95–10/95	1/02–10/02
July	3° Aries	7/88–5/89	9/95–10/95	1/02–10/02
Aug	3°–2° Aries	7/88–5/89	9/95–10/95	12/01–10/02
Sept	2°–1° Pisces	7/88–4/89	9/95	12/01–1/02
Oct	1°Aries–29° Pisces	6/88–4/89	9/95	4/01–10/01
Nov	29° Pisces	6/88	9/95	4/01–10/01
Dec	29° Pisces	6/88	9/95	4/01–10/01

1969	Birth Chart	1st Square	Opposition	Upper Square
Jan	29° Pisces–0° Aries	6/88	9/95	4/01–10/01
Feb	0°–1° Aries	6/88–4/89	9/95	12/01–1/02
Mar	1°–3° Aries	7/88–5/89	9/95–10/95	12/01–10/02
April	3°–5° Aries	8/88–6/89	9/95–10/95	12/01–10/02
May	5°–6° Aries	8/88–6/89	10/95	1/02–11/02
June	6°–7° Aries	9/88–6/89	10/95–6/96	2/02–12/02
July	7° Aries	10/88–6/89	10/95–6/96	2/02–12/02
Aug	7°–6° Aries	9/88–6/89	10/95–6/96	2/02–12/02
Sept	6°–4° Aries	8/88–6/89	9/95–10/95	1/02–11/02
Oct	4°–3° Aries	7/88–6/89	9/95–10/95	12/01–10/02
Nov	3°–2° Aries	7/88–5/89	9/95–10/95	12/01–10/02
Dec	2° Aries	7/88–4/89	9/95	12/01–1/02

KEY CHIRON PASSAGES

1970	Birth Chart	1st Square	Opposition	Upper Square
Jan	2°–3° Aries	7/88–5/89	9/95–10/95	12/01–10/02
Feb	3°–5° Aries	8/88–6/89	9/95–10/95	12/01–10/02
Mar	5°–7° Aries	8/88–6/89	10/95–6/96	1/02–12/02
April	7°–8° Aries	10/88–7/89	10/95–7/96	2/02–12/02
May	8°–10° Aries	6/89–4/90	11/95–8/96	3/02–1/03
June	10° Aries	7/89–4/90	11/95–8/96	12/02–1/03
July	10° Aries	7/89–4/90	11/95–8/96	12/02–1/03
Aug	10°–9° Aries	7/89–4/90	11/95–8/96	4/02–12/02
Sept	9°–8° Aries	6/89–7/89	11/95–7/96	3/02–12/02
Oct	8°–7° Aries	10/88–7/89	10/95–7/96	2/02–12/02
Nov	7°–6° Aries	9/88–6/89	10/95–6/96	2/02–12/02
Dec	6° Aries	9/88–6/89	10/95	2/02–11/02

1971	Birth Chart	1st Square	Opposition	Upper Square
Jan	6°–7° Aries	9/88–6/89	10/95–6/96	2/02–12/02
Feb	7°–8° Aries	10/88–7/89	10/95–7/96	2/02–12/02
Mar	8°–10° Aries	6/89–4/90	11/95–8/96	3/02–1/03
April	10°–12° Aries	7/89–5/90	11/95–8/96	12/02–10/03
May	12°–13° Aries	8/89–5/90	12/95–8/96	1/03–11/03
June	13°–14° Aries	8/89–6/90	12/95–9/96	1/03–11/03
July	14° Aries	8/89–6/90	1/96–9/96	2/03–11/03
Aug	14°–13° Aries	8/89–6/90	12/95–9/96	1/03–11/03
Sept	13°–12° Aries	8/89–5/90	12/95–8/96	1/03–11/03
Oct	12°–10° Aries	7/89–5/90	11/95–8/96	12/02–10/03
Nov	10° Aries	7/89–4/90	11/95–8/96	12/02–1/03
Dec	10°–9° Aries	7/89–4/90	11/95–8/96	12/02–1/03

KEY CHIRON PASSAGES

1972	Birth Chart	1st Square	Opposition	Upper Square
Jan	9°–10° Aries	7/89–4/90	11/95–8/96	12/02–1/03
Feb	10°–11° Aries	7/89–4/90	11/95–8/96	12/02–9/03
Mar	11°–13° Aries	7/89–5/90	11/95–8/96	1/03–11/03
April	13°–15° Aries	8/89–6/90	12/95–9/96	1/03–12/03
May	15°–16° Aries	9/89–6/90	9/96	2/03–12/03
June	16°–17° Aries	9/89–7/90	9/96	2/03–12/03
July	17° Aries	6/90–7/90	9/96	3/03–12/03
Aug	17° Aries	6/90–7/90	9/96	3/03–12/03
Sept	17°–15° Aries	9/89–7/90	9/96	2/03–12/03
Oct	15°–14° Aries	8/89–6/90	1/96–9/96	2/03–12/03
Nov	14°–13° Aries	8/89–6/90	12/95–9/96	1/03–11/03
Dec	13° Aries	8/89–5/90	12/95–8/96	1/03–11/03

1973	Birth Chart	1st Square	Opposition	Upper Square
Jan	13°–14° Aries	8/89–6/90	12/95–9/96	1/03–11/03
Feb	14°–15° Aries	8/89–6/90	1/96–9/96	2/03–12/03
Mar	15°–16° Aries	9/89–6/90	9/96	2/03–12/03
April	16°–18° Aries	9/89–7/90	9/96–10/96	2/03–1/04
May	18°–20° Aries	7/90–8/90	9/96–10/96	4/03–10/04
June	20°–21° Aries	7/90–4/91	10/96	1/04–2/04
July	21° Aries	7/90–4/91	10/96	1/04–2/04
Aug	21°–20° Aries	7/90–4/91	10/96	1/04–2/04
Sept	20°–19° Aries	7/90–8/90	10/96	1/04
Oct	19°–18° Aries	7/90–8/90	9/96–10/96	4/03–1/04
Nov	18°–17° Aries	6/90–7/90	9/96–10/96	3/03–1/04
Dec	17°–16° Aries	9/89–7/90	9/96	2/03–12/03

KEY CHIRON PASSAGES

1974	**Birth Chart**	**1st Square**	**Opposition**	**Upper Square**
Jan	16°–17° Aries	9/89–7/90	9/96	2/03–12/03
Feb	17°–18° Aries	6/90–7/90	9/96–10/96	3/03–1/04
Mar	18°–20° Aries	7/90–8/90	9/96–10/96	4/03–10/04
April	20°–22° Aries	7/90–5/91	10/96	1/04–11/04
May	22°–23° Aries	8/90–4/91	10/96–11/96	2/04–12/04
June	23°–24° Aries	8/90–6/91	10/96–11/96	2/04–12/04
July	24° Aries	9/90–6/91	11/96	3/04–12/04
Aug	24° Aries	9/90–6/91	11/96	3/04–12/04
Sept	24°–23° Aries	8/90–6/91	10/96–11/96	2/04–12/04
Oct	23°–21° Aries	8/90–4/91	10/96–11/96	5/03–12/04
Nov	21°–20° Aries	7/90–4/91	10/96	1/04–2/04
Dec	20° Aries	7/90–8/90	10/96	1/04

1975	**Birth Chart**	**1st Square**	**Opposition**	**Upper Square**
Jan	20° Aries	7/90–8/90	10/96	1/04
Feb	20°–21° Aries	7/90–8/90	10/96	1/04–2/04
Mar	21°–23° Aries	8/90–4/91	10/96–11/96	1/04–12/04
April	23°–25° Aries	8/90–6/91	10/96–7/97	2/04–1/05
May	25°–27° Aries	9/90–7/91	11/96–8/97	3/04–10/05
June	27°–28° Aries	10/90–7/91	12/96–8/97	1/05–12/05
July	28° Aries	7/91	12/96–8/97	1/05–12/05
Aug	28° Aries	7/91	12/96–8/97	1/05–12/05
Sept	28°–27° Aries	10/90–7/91	12/96–8/97	1/05–12/05
Oct	27°–25° Aries	9/90–7/91	11/96–8/97	3/04–10/05
Nov	25°–24° Aries	9/90–6/91	11/96–7/97	3/04–1/05
Dec	24° Aries	9/90–6/91	11/96	3/04–12/04

KEY CHIRON PASSAGES

1976	Birth Chart	1st Square	Opposition	Upper Square
Jan	24° Aries	9/90–6/91	11/96	3/04–12/04
Feb	24°–25° Aries	9/90–6/91	11/96–7/97	3/04–1/05
Mar	25°–27° Aries	9/90–7/91	11/96–8/97	3/04–10/05
April	27°–28° Aries	10/90–7/91	12/96–8/97	1/05–12/05
May	28° Aries– 0° Taurus	7/91	12/96–9/97	1/05–12/05
June	0°–1° Taurus	7/91–8/91	12/96–9/97	2/05–1/06
July	1°–2° Taurus	7/91–8/91	1/97–9/97	3/05–1/06
Aug	2° Taurus	8/91	2/97–9/97	3/05–1/06
Sept	2°–1° Taurus	7/91–8/91	1/97–9/97	3/05–1/06
Oct	1° Taurus–29° Aries	7/91–8/91	12/96–9/97	2/05–1/06
Nov	29°–28° Aries	7/91	12/96	1/05–12/05
Dec	28°–27° Aries	10/90–7/91	12/96–8/97	1/05–12/05

1977	Birth Chart	1st Square	Opposition	Upper Square
Jan	27°–28° Aries	10/90–7/91	12/96–8/97	1/05–12/05
Feb	28°–29° Aries	7/91	12/96	1/05–12/05
Mar	29° Aries–0° Taurus	7/91	12/96–1/97	2/05–12/05
April	0°–2° Taurus	7/91–8/91	12/96–2/97	2/05–1/06
May	2°–4° Taurus	8/91–5/92	2/97–8/97	3/05–11/06
June	4°–5° Taurus	8/91–6/92	10/97	1/06–11/06
July	5°–6° Taurus	9/91–6/92	10/97	2/06–12/06
Aug	6° Taurus	9/91–6/92	10/97	2/06–12/06
Sept	6°–5° Taurus	9/91–6/92	10/97	2/06–12/06
Oct	5°–3° Taurus	8/91–6/92	10/97	4/05–11/06
Nov	3°–2° Taurus	7/91–5/92	2/97–10/97	3/05–1/06
Dec	2°–1° Taurus	7/91–8/91	1/97–9/97	3/05–1/06

KEY CHIRON PASSAGES

1978	Birth Chart	1st Square	Opposition	Upper Square
Jan	1° Taurus	7/91–8/91	1/97–9/97	3/05–1/06
Feb	1°–2° Taurus	7/91–8/91	1/97–9/97	3/05–1/06
Mar	2°–4° Taurus	8/91–5/92	2/97–10/97	3/05–11/06
April	4°–6° Taurus	8/91–6/92	10/97–11/97	1/06–12/06
May	6°–7° Taurus	9/91–6/92	10/97–11/97	2/06–1/07
June	7°–9° Taurus	9/91–7/92	10/97–11/97	3/06–1/07
July	9°–10° Taurus	10/91–7/92	11/97	4/06–11/07
Aug	10° Taurus	7/92	11/97	1/07–11/07
Sept	10°–9° Taurus	10/91–7/92	11/97	4/06–11/07
Oct	9°–7° Taurus	9/91–7/92	10/97–11/97	3/06–1/07
Nov	7°–6° Taurus	9/91–6/92	10/97–11/97	2/06–1/07
Dec	6°–5° Taurus	9/91–6/92	10/97	2/06–12/06

1979	Birth Chart	1st Square	Opposition	Upper Square
Jan	5° Taurus	9/91–6/92	10/97	2/06–12/06
Feb	5°–6° Taurus	9/91–6/92	10/97	2/06–12/06
Mar	6°–8° Taurus	9/91–6/92	10/97–11/97	2/06–1/07
April	8°–9° Taurus	10/91–7/92	11/97	3/06–1/07
May	9°–11° Taurus	10/91–7/92	11/97	4/06–11/07
June	11°–13° Taurus	7/92–8/92	11/97–8/98	2/07–1/08
July	13°–14° Taurus	8/92	12/97–9/98	3/07–1/08
Aug	14° Taurus	8/92	12/97–9/98	3/07–1/08
Sept	14°–13° Taurus	8/92	12/97–9/98	3/07–1/08
Oct	13°–12° Taurus	8/92	12/97–8/98	2/07–1/08
Nov	12°–10° Taurus	7/92–8/92	7/92–12/97	1/07–12/07
Dec	10°–9° Taurus	10/91–7/92	11/97	4/06–11/07

KEY CHIRON PASSAGES

1980	Birth Chart	1st Square	Opposition	Upper Square
Jan	9° Taurus	10/91–7/92	11/97	4/06–1/07
Feb	9°–10° Taurus	10/91–7/92	11/97	4/06–11/07
Mar	10°–11° Taurus	7/92	11/97	1/07–11/07
April	12°–13° Taurus	7/92–8/92	12/97–8/98	2/07–1/08
May	13°–15° Taurus	8/92	12/97–9/98	3/07–2/08
June	15°–17° Taurus	8/92–5/93	12/97–10/98	4/07–12/08
July	17°–18° Taurus	9/92–6/93	1/98–10/98	2/08–1/09
Aug	18° Taurus	9/92–6/93	2/98–10/98	3/08–1/09
Sept	18° Taurus	9/92–6/93	2/98–10/98	3/08–1/09
Oct	18°–16° Taurus	8/92–6/93	1/98–10/98	2/08–1/09
Nov	16°–15° Taurus	8/92–3/93	10/97–9/98	4/07–12/08
Dec	15°–14° Taurus	8/92	12/97–9/98	3/07–2/08

1981	Birth Chart	1st Square	Opposition	Upper Square
Jan	14°–13° Taurus	8/92	12/97–9/98	3/07–12/08
Feb	13°–14° Taurus	8/92	12/97–9/98	3/07–12/08
Mar	14°–16° Taurus	8/92–3/93	12/97–9/98	3/07–12/08
April	16°–17° Taurus	8/92–4/93	1/98–10/98	2/08–12/08
May	17°–20° Taurus	9/92–6/93	1/98–10/98	2/08–2/09
June	20°–21° Taurus	10/92–7/93	10/98–11/98	4/08–12/09
July	21°–23° Taurus	10/92–7/93	10/98–11/98	5/08–1/10
Aug	23° Taurus	11/92–7/93	11/98	3/09–1/10
Sept	23°–22° Taurus	10/92–7/93	10/98–11/98	2/09–1/10
Oct	22°–21° Taurus	10/92–7/93	10/98–11/98	5/08–12/09
Nov	21°–19° Taurus	9/92–7/93	10/98–11/98	3/08–12/09
Dec	19°–18° Taurus	9/92–6/93	2/98–10/98	3/08–1/09

KEY CHIRON PASSAGES

1982	Birth Chart	1st Square	Opposition	Upper Square
Jan	18° Taurus	9/92–6/93	2/98–10/98	3/08–1/09
Feb	18° Taurus	9/92–6/93	2/98–10/98	3/08–1/09
Mar	18°–20° Taurus	9/92–6/93	2/98–10/98	3/08–2/09
April	20°–22° Taurus	10/92–7/93	10/98–11/98	4/08–3/09
May	22°–24° Taurus	10/92–7/93	11/98	2/09–1/10
June	24°–26° Taurus	11/92–8/93	11/98–12/98	3/09–12/10
July	26°–27° Taurus	8/93	11/98–8/99	5/09–1/11
Aug	27°–28° Taurus	8/93	12/98–9/99	3/10–1/11
Sept	28°–27° Taurus	8/93	12/98–9/99	3/10–1/11
Oct	27°–26° Taurus	8/93	11/98–8/99	5/09–1/11
Nov	26°–24° Taurus	11/92–8/93	11/98–12/98	3/09–12/10
Dec	24°–23° Taurus	11/92–7/93	11/98	3/09–1/10

1983	Birth Chart	1st Square	Opposition	Upper Square
Jan	23° Taurus	11/92–7/93	11/98	3/09–1/10
Feb	23° Taurus	11/92–7/93	11/98	3/09–1/10
Mar	23°–24° Taurus	11/92–7/93	11/98	3/09–1/10
April	24°–26° Taurus	11/92–8/93	11/98–12/98	3/09–12/10
May	26°–29° Taurus	8/93–9/93	11/98–9/99	5/09–2/11
June	29° Taurus–0° Gemini	8/93–9/93	12/98–10/99	3/10–12/11
July	0°–2° Gemini	9/93–5/94	1/99–10/99	4/10–2/12
Aug	2°–3° Gemini	9/93–6/94	1/99–10/99	3/11–1/12
Sept	3° Gemini	9/93–6/94	2/99–10/99	3/11–2/12
Oct	3°–2° Gemini	9/93–6/94	2/99–10/99	3/11–1/12
Nov	2° Gemini–29° Taurus	8/93–5/94	12/98–10/99	4/10–1/12
Dec	29°–28° Taurus	8/93–9/93	12/98–9/99	3/10–2/11

KEY CHIRON PASSAGES

1984	Birth Chart	1st Square	Opposition	Upper Square
Jan	28° Taurus	8/93	12/98–9/99	3/10–1/11
Feb	28° Taurus	8/93	12/98–9/99	3/10–1/11
Mar	28°–29° Taurus	8/93–9/93	12/98–9/99	3/10–2/11
April	29°–1° Gemini	9/93	12/98–10/99	3/10–1/12
May	1°–4° Gemini	9/93–6/94	1/99–11/99	6/10–2/12
June	4°–6° Gemini	10/93–7/94	2/99–11/99	4/11–1/13
July	6°–8° Gemini	10/93–7/94	11/99–12/99	3/12–2/13
Aug	8 ° Gemini	11/93–7/94	12/99	4/12–2/13
Sept	8° Gemini	11/93–7/94	12/99	4/12–2/13
Oct	8°–7° Gemini	11/93–7/94	11/99–12/99	3/12–2/13
Nov	7°–6° Gemini	10/93–7/94	11/99–12/99	3/12–2/13
Dec	6°–4° Gemini	10/93–7/94	2/99–11/99	4/11–1/13

1985	Birth Chart	1st Square	Opposition	Upper Square
Jan	4°–3° Gemini	10/93–6/94	2/99–11/99	3/11–2/12
Feb	3° Gemini	10/93–6/94	2/99–10/99	3/11–2/12
Mar	3°–5° Gemini	10/93–6/94	2/99–11/99	3/11–12/12
April	5°–7° Gemini	10/93–7/94	11/99–12/99	5/11–2/13
May	7°–9° Gemini	11/93–8/94	11/99–12/99	3/12–1/14
June	9°–11° Gemini	12/93–8/94	12/99–9/00	5/12–2/14
July	11°–13° Gemini	8/94–9/94	12/99–10/00	3/13–1/15
Aug	13°–14° Gemini	8/94–9/94	1/00–10/00	5/13–1/15
Sept	14°–15° Gemini	9/94	1/00–11/00	3/14–2/15
Oct	15°–14° Gemini	9/94	1/00–11/00	3/14–2/15
Nov	14°–12° Gemini	8/94–9/94	1/00–10/00	4/13–1/15
Dec	12°–10° Gemini	8/94	12/99–10/00	6/12–2/14

KEY CHIRON PASSAGES

1986	Birth Chart	1st Square	Opposition	Upper Square
Jan	10°–9° Gemini	12/93–8/94	12/99–8/00	5/12–1/14
Feb	9° Gemini	12/93–8/94	12/99	5/12–1/14
Mar	9°–10° Gemini	12/93–8/94	12/99–8/00	5/12–1/14
April	10°–12° Gemini	8/94	12/99–10/00	6/12–2/14
May	12°–15° Gemini	8/94–9/94	1/00–11/00	4/13–2/15
June	15°–17° Gemini	9/94	2/00–11/00	3/14–1/16
July	17°–19° Gemini	9/94–10/94	3/00–12/00	5/14–2/16
Aug	19°–21° Gemini	10/94–7/95	12/00	4/15–1/17
Sept	21° Gemini	10/94–7/95	12/00	5/15–1/17
Oct	21° Gemini	10/94–7/95	12/00	5/15–1/17
Nov	21°–19° Gemini	10/94–7/95	12/00	4/15–1/17
Dec	19°–17° Gemini	9/94–10/94	3/00–12/00	5/14–2/16

1987	Birth Chart	1st Square	Opposition	Upper Square
Jan	17°–16° Gemini	9/94	2/00–11/00	4/14–1/16
Feb	16° Gemini	9/94	2/00–11/00	4/14–12/15
Mar	16°–17° Gemini	9/94	2/00–11/00	4/14–1/16
April	17°–19° Gemini	9/94–10/94	3/00–12/00	5/14–2/16
May	19°–21° Gemini	10/94–7/95	12/00	4/15–1/17
June	21°–24° Gemini	10/94–8/95	12/00–10/01	5/15–1/18
July	24°–26° Gemini	11/94–8/95	1/01–11/01	5/16–2/18
Aug	26°–28° Gemini	12/94–9/95	2/01–12/01	4/17–1/19
Sept	28°–29° Gemini	8/95–9/95	2/01–12/01	5/17–2/19
Oct	29°–28° Gemini	8/95–9/95	2/01–12/01	5/17–2/19
Nov	28°–27° Gemini	8/95–9/95	2/01–12/01	4/17–1/19
Dec	27°–25° Gemini	12/94–8/95	1/01–11/01	6/16–3/18

KEY CHIRON PASSAGES

1988	Birth Chart	Ist Square	Opposition	Upper Square
Jan	25°–24° Gemini	11/94–8/95	1/01–11/01	5/16–2/18
Feb	24°–23 Gemini	11/94–8/95	1/01–10/01	4/16–1/18
Mar	23°–24 Gemini	11/94–8/95	1/01–10/01	4/16–1/18
April	24°–26 Gemini	11/94–8/95	1/01–11/01	5/16–2/18
May	26°–28 Gemini	12/94–9/95	2/01–12/01	4/17–1/19
June	28° Gemini–1° Cancer	8/95–9/95	2/01–12/01	5/17–1/20
July	1°–4° Cancer	9/95–10/95	12/01–10/02	5/18–3/20
Aug	4°–6° Cancer	10/95	1/02–11/02	4/19–2/21
Sept	6°–7° Cancer	10/95–6/96	2/02–12/02	7/19–3/21
Oct	7° Cancer	10/95–6/96	2/02–12/02	4/20–3/21
Nov	7°–6° Cancer	10/95–6/96	2/02–12/02	7/19–3/21
Dec	6°–4° Cancer	10/95	1/02–11/02	4/19–2/21

1989	Birth Chart	Ist Square	Opposition	Upper Square
Jan	4°–2° Cancer	9/95–10/95	12/01–10/02	6/18–3/20
Feb	2°–1° Cancer	9/95	12/01–1/02	5/18–2/20
Mar	1°–2° Cancer	9/95	12/01–1/02	5/18–2/20
April	2°–3° Cancer	9/95–10/95	12/01–10/02	6/18–3/20
May	3°–6° Cancer	9/95–10/95	1/02–11/02	4/19–2/21
June	6°–9° Cancer	10/95–7/96	2/02–12/02	7/19–2/22
July	9°–12° Cancer	11/95–8/96	4/02–10/03	6/20–2/23
Aug	12°–14° Cancer	12/95 –9/96	1/03–11/03	5/21–3/23
Sept	14°–16° Cancer	1/96–9/96	2/03–12/03	5/22–2/24
Oct	16°–17° Cancer	9/96	2/03–12/03	6/22–3/24
Nov	17°–16° Cancer	9/96	2/03–12/03	6/22–3/24
Dec	16°–14° Cancer	1/96–9/96	2/03–12/03	5/22–2/24

KEY CHIRON PASSAGES

1990	Birth Chart	1st Square	Opposition	Upper Square
Jan	14°–12° Cancer	12/95–9/96	1/03–11/03	5/21–3/23
Feb	12° –11° Cancer	11/95–8/96	1/03–10/03	5/21–2/23
Mar	11° Cancer	11/95–8/96	1/03	5/21–1/23
April	11° –12° Cancer	11/95–8/96	1/03–10/03	5/21–2/23
May	12°–15° Cancer	12/95–9/96	1/03–12/03	5/21–1/24
June	15°–18° Cancer	9/96–10/96	2/03–1/04	5/22–12/24
July	18°–21° Cancer	9/96–10/96	4/03–11/04	5/23–3/25
Aug	21°–24° Cancer	10/96–11/96	1/04–12/04	5/24–3/26
Sept	24°–26° Cancer	11/96–7/97	2/04–1/05	4/25–2/27
Oct	26°–27° Cancer	11/96–8/97	4/04–10/05	6/25–3/27
Nov	27 ° Cancer	12/96–8/97	1/05–10/05	7/25–3/27
Dec	27°–25° Cancer	11/96–8/97	3/04–10/05	5/25–3/27

1991	Birth Chart	1st Square	Opposition	Upper Square
Jan	25°–23° Cancer	11/96–7/97	2/04–1/05	6/24–4/26
Feb	23°–22° Cancer	10/96 –11/96	2/04–12/04	5/24–2/26
Mar	22°–21° Cancer	10/96	1/04–11/04	5/24–1/26
April	21°–22° Cancer	10/96	1/04–11/04	5/24–4/26
May	22 °– 25° Cancer	10/96–7/97	2/04–1/05	5/24–4/26
June	25°–28° Cancer	11/96–8/97	3/04–11/05	5/25–3/27
July	28° Cancer–1° Leo	12/96–9/97	1/05–1/06	5/26–3/28
Aug	1°–5° Leo	1/97–10/97	3/05–12/06	8/26–3/29
Sept	5°–7° Leo	10/97 –11/97	2/06–1/07	5/28–4/29
Oct	7°–9° Leo	10/97 –11/97	3/06–11/07	6/28–6/29
Nov	9°–10° Leo	11/97	4/06–11/07	5/29–4/30
Dec	10°–8° Leo	11/97	3/06–11/07	7/28–4/30

KEY CHIRON PASSAGES

1992	Birth Chart	1st Square	Opposition	Upper Square
Jan	8°–6° Leo	10/97–11/97	2/06–1/07	5/28–3/30
Feb	6°–4° Leo	10/97	1/06–12/06	7/27–4/29
Mar	4°–3° Leo	9/97–10/97	4/05–11/06	6/27–3/29
April	3° Leo	9/97–10/97	4/05–1/06	6/27–4/28
May	3°–5° Leo	9/97–10/97	4/05–12/06	6/27–3/29
June	5°–9° Leo	10/97–11/97	2/06–1/07	5/28–3/30
July	9°–12° Leo	11/97–8/98	4/06–12/07	5/29–3/31
Aug	12°–16° Leo	12/97–9/98	2/07–12/08	7/29–2/32
Sept	16°–19° Leo	1/98–10/98	2/08–1/09	7/30–4/32
Oct	19°–22° Leo	10/98–11/98	3/08–12/09	6/31–3/33
Nov	22°–23° Leo	11/98	2/09–1/10	5/32–4/33
Dec	23° Leo	11/98	3/09–1/10	6/32–4/33

1993	Birth Chart	1st Square	Opposition	Upper Square
Jan	23°–21° Leo	10/98–11/98	5/08–1/10	5/32–4/33
Feb	21°–18° Leo	2/98–11/98	3/08–12/09	5/31–3/33
Mar	18°–17° Leo	1/98–10/98	2/08–1/09	5/31–4/32
April	17° Leo	1/98–10/98	2/08–12/08	5/31–3/32
May	17°–18° Leo	1/98–10/98	2/08–1/09	5/31–4/32
June	18°–21° Leo	2/98–11/98	3/08–12/09	5/31–3/33
July	21°–25° Leo	10/98–12/98	5/08–2/10	7/31–5/33
Aug	25°–29° Leo	11/98–9/99	4/09–2/11	7/32–5/34
Sept	29° Leo–3° Virgo	12/98–10/99	3/10–2/12	6/33–4/35
Oct	3°–6° Virgo	2/99–11/99	3/11–1/13	6/34–5/35
Nov	6°–8° Virgo	11/99–12/99	3/12–2/13	8/34–4/36
Dec	8°–9° Virgo	12/99	4/12–1/14	6/35–4/36

KEY CHIRON PASSAGES

1994

	Birth Chart	1st Square	Opposition	Upper Square
Jan	9°–7° Virgo	12/99	3/12–1/14	5/35–4/36
Feb	7°–5° Virgo	11/99–12/99	5/11–2/13	7/34–3/36
Mar	5°–3° Virgo	2/99–10/99	3/11–12/12	6/34–5/35
April	3°–2° Virgo	1/99–10/99	3/11–2/12	6/34–4/35
May	2°–3° Virgo	1/99–10/99	3/11–2/12	6/34–4/35
June	3°–6° Virgo	2/99–11/99	3/11–1/13	6/34–5/35
July	6°–9° Virgo	11/99–12/99	3/12–1/14	8/34–4/36
Aug	9°–13° Virgo	12/99–10/00	5/12–1/15	6/35–3/37
Sept	13°–18° Virgo	1/00–12/00	5/13–2/16	6/36–6/37
Oct	18°–21° Virgo	11/00	3/15–1/17	8/36–4/38
Nov	21°–24° Virgo	12/00–10/01	5/15–1/18	6/37–5/38
Dec	24°–26° Virgo	1/01–11/01	5/16–2/18	8/37–6/38

1995

	Birth Chart	1st Square	Opposition	Upper Square
Jan	26°–25° Virgo	1/01–11/01	6/16–2/18	8/37–6/38
Feb	25°–24° Virgo	1/01–11/01	5/16–2/18	8/37–6/38
Mar	24°–21° Virgo	12/00–10/01	5/15–1/18	6/37–5/38
April	21°–20° Virgo	12/00	4/15–1/17	6/37–4/38
May	20° Virgo	12/00	4/15–12/16	6/37–3/38
June	20°–21° Virgo	12/00	4/15–1/17	6/37–4/38
July	21°–24° Virgo	12/00–10/01	5/15–1/18	6/37–5/38
Aug	24°–28° Virgo	1/01–12/01	5/16–1/19	8/37–4/39
Sept	28° Virgo–3° Libra	3/01–10/02	5/17–3/20	6/38–6/39
Oct	3°–7° Libra	1/02–12/02	4/19–3/21	9/38–4/40
Nov	7°–11° Libra	2/02–1/03	4/20–1/23	7/39–6/40
Dec	11°–13° Libra	1/03–11/03	5/21–3/23	9/39–6/40

KEY CHIRON PASSAGES

1996	Birth Chart	1st Square	Opposition	Upper Square
Jan	13°–14° Libra	1/03–11/03	4/22–3/23	6/40–7/40
Feb	14°–13° Libra	1/03–11/03	4/22–3/23	6/40–7/40
Mar	13°–11° Libra	1/03–11/03	5/21–3/23	9/39–6/40
April	11°–8° Libra	3/02–1/03	5/20–1/23	7/39–6/40
May	8°–7° Libra	2/02–12/02	4/20–1/22	7/39–5/40
June	7°–8° Libra	2/02–12/02	4/20–1/22	7/39–5/40
July	8°–10° Libra	3/02–1/03	5/20–3/22	7/39–5/40
Aug	10°–14° Libra	12/02–11/03	4/21–3/23	8/39–7/40
Sept	14°–18° Libra	2/03–1/04	5/22–1/25	6/40–5/41
Oct	18°–22° Libra	4/03–11/04	5/23–2/26	8/40–6/41
Nov	22°–27° Libra	2/04–10/05	5/24–2/27	9/40–8/41
Dec	27° Libra–0° Scorpio	1/05–12/05	7/25–2/28	7/41–5/42

1997	Birth Chart	1st Square	Opposition	Upper Square
Jan	0°–1° Scorpio	2/05–1/06	6/26–3/28	8/41–6/42
Feb	1° Scorpio	3/05–1/06	8/26–3/28	9/41–6/42
Mar	1°–0° Scorpio	2/05–1/06	6/26–3/28	8/41–6/42
April	0° Scorpio–27° Libra	1/05–12/05	7/25–2/28	7/41–5/42
May	27°–26° Libra	4/04–10/05	6/25–2/27	7/41–8/41
June	26°–25° Libra	3/04–1/05	5/25–2/27	7/41
July	25°–26° Libra	3/04–1/05	5/25–2/27	7/41
Aug	26°–29° Libra	4/04–12/05	6/25–4/27	7/41–5/42
Sept	29° Libra–3° Scorpio	2/05–1/06	5/26–1/29	8/41–6/42
Oct	3°–7° Scorpio	4/05–1/07	6/27–4/29	10/41–8/42
Nov	7°–11° Scorpio	3/06–12/07	6/28–4/30	7/42–5/43
Dec	11°–15° Scorpio	2/07–2/08	6/29–4/31	8/42–6/43

KEY CHIRON PASSAGES

1998	Birth Chart	1st Square	Opposition	Upper Square
Jan	15°–17° Scorpio	4/07–12/08	6/30–3/32	10/42–7/43
Feb	17°–18° Scorpio	2/08–1/09	5/31–4/32	11/42–7/43
Mar	18°–17° Scorpio	2/08–1/09	5/31–4/32	11/42–7/43
April	17°–15° Scorpio	4/07–12/08	6/30–3/32	10/42–7/43
May	15°–13° Scorpio	3/07–2/08	5/30–4/31	9/42–6/43
June	13°–12° Scorpio	2/07–12/07	7/29–3/31	9/42–6/43
July	12° Scorpio	2/07–12/07	7/29–3/31	9/42–5/43
Aug	12°–14° Scorpio	2/07–1/08	7/29–4/31	9/42–6/43
Sept	14°–17° Scorpio	3/07–12/08	5/30–3/32	9/42–7/43
Oct	17°–21° Scorpio	2/08–12/09	5/31–3/33	11/42–8/43
Nov	21°–25° Scorpio	5/08–2/10	7/31–5/33	8/43–9/43
Dec	25°–29° Scorpio	4/09–2/11	7/32–5/34	9/43–7/44

1999	Birth Chart	1st Square	Opposition	Upper Square
Jan	29° Scorpio–2° Sagittarius	2/10–1/12	6/33–4/35	10/43–7/44
Feb	2°–3° Sagittarius	3/11–2/12	6/34–4/35	11/43–8/44
Mar	3° Sagittarius	3/11–2/12	6/34–4/35	7/44–8/44
April	3°–2° Sagittarius	3/11–2/12	6/34–4/35	11/43–8/44
May	2°–0° Sagittarius	3/11–2/12	7/33–4/35	1/44–7/44
June	0° Sagittarius–28° Scorpio	3/10–12/11	6/33–5/34	10/43–7/44
July	28°–27° Scorpio	2/10–1/11	5/33–4/34	9/43–6/44
Aug	27°–28° Scorpio	2/10–1/11	5/33–4/34	9/43–6/44
Sept	28° Scorpio–0° Sagittarius	3/10–12/11	6/33–5/34	10/43–7/44
Oct	0°–4° Sagittarius	4/10–2/12	7/35–5/35	10/43–8/44
Nov	4°–7° Sagittarius	4/11–2/13	7/34–3/36	8/44–9/44
Dec	7°–11° Sagittarius	3/12–2/14	5/35–5/36	8/44–10/44

KEY CHIRON PASSAGES

2000	Birth Chart	1st Square	Opposition	Upper Square
Jan	11°–14° Sagittarius	3/13–1/15	7/35–3/37	9/44–7/45
Feb	14°–16° Sagittarius	3/14–12/15	6/36–5/37	11/44–7/45
Mar	16°–17° Sagittarius	4/14–1/16	7/36–5/37	11/44–7/45
April	17°–16° Sagittarius	4/14–1/16	7/36–5/37	11/44–7/45
May	16°–14° Sagittarius	3/14–12/15	6/36–5/37	11/44–7/45
June	14°–12° Sagittarius	4/13–1/15	8/35–4/37	10/44–7/45
July	12°–11° Sagittarius	3/13–2/14	7/35–6/36	9/44–6/45
Aug	11° Sagittarius	3/13–2/14	7/35–5/36	9/44–10/44
Sept	11°–12° Sagittarius	3/13–2/14	7/35–6/36	9/44–6/45
Oct	12°–15° Sagittarius	4/13–1/15	8/35–4/37	10/44–7/45
Nov	15°–18° Sagittarius	3/14–2/16	6/36–6/37	10/44–8/45
Dec	18°–22° Sagittarius	3/15–2/17	8/36–5/38	11/44–9/45

Notes

ONE. I'M IN MIDLIFE CRISIS NOW!

1. Grof, *Spiritual Emergency*, 7.
2. Sannella, *Kundalini*.

TWO. THE FUNDAMENTALS OF ASTROLOGY

1. Sobel, "Dr. Zodiac."
2. Seymour, *Astrology*, 108.
3. Ibid., 127.

THREE. THE SATURN PRINCIPLE IN THE CYCLES OF LIFE

1. Graves, *The Greek Myths*, 31.

FOUR. THE URANUS PRINCIPLE IN THE CYCLES OF LIFE

1. Graves, *The Greek Myths*, 31.
2. Sannella, *Kundalini*, 4.
3. Scott, *Kundalini in the Physical World*, 188.
4. Chopra, *Quantum Healing*, 217.
5. Gerber, *Vibrational Medicine*, 154.
6. Chopra, *Quantum Healing*, 219.
7. Sannella, *Kundalini*, 12.
8. Ibid., 10.
9. Scott, *Kundalini in the Physical World*, 191.

10. Scott, *Kundalini in the Physical World*, 25.

11. Ibid., 7.

FIVE. URANUS AND PERSONAL EMPOWERMENT

1. Scott, *Kundalini in the Physical World*, 92.

2. Strieber, *Communion*, 242–43.

3. Swan, *Sacred Places*, 81.

4. Clow, *The Mind Chronicles*.

SIX. URANUS AND ENLIGHTENMENT

1. Chopra, *Quantum Healing*, 223.

SEVEN. THE CHIRON PRINCIPLE IN THE CYCLES OF LIFE

1. Clow, *Chiron*, xiii.

2. Lantero, *The Continuing Discovery of Chiron*, 31.

3. Ibid., 18.

4. Graves, *The Greek Myths*, 145.

5. Phillips, *Emergence of the Divine Child*, 29.

6. Gerber, *Vibrational Medicine*, 76.

7. Graves, *The Greek Myths*, 144.

TEN. TOWARD A GLOBAL SHAMANIC PARADIGM

1. White, *Kundalini, Evolution and Enlightenment*, 291–97.

2. Clow, *Alchemy of Nine Dimensions*, 138–65.

3. Argüelles, *The Mayan Factor*, 110–30.

4. Men, *Secrets of Mayan Science/Religion*, 120.

Bibliography

Arroyo, Stephen. *Astrology, Karma, & Transformation: The Inner Dimensions of the Birth Chart.* Davis, Calif.: CRSC Publications, 1978.

Arguelles, Jose. *The Mayan Factor: Path Beyond Technology.* Santa Fe, N. Mex.: Bear & Co., 1987.

Asher, Maxine. *Ancient Energy: Key to the Universe.* New York: Harper & Row, 1979.

Assagioli, Roberto. *The Act of Will.* Harmondsworth, England: Penguin, 1974.

Becker, Robert O. and Gary Selden. *The Body Electric: Electromagnetism and the Foundations of Life.* New York: William Morrow, 1985.

Bord, Janet and Colin. *Earth Rites: Fertility Practices in Pre-Industrial England.* Frogmore, England: Granada, 1983.

Chopra, Deepak. *Quantum Healing: Exploring the Frontiers of Mind/ Body Medicine.* New York: Bantam New Age, 1989.

Clow, Barbara Hand. *Chiron: Rainbow Bridge Between the Inner and Outer Planets.* St. Paul, Minn.: Llewellyn Publications, 1987.

———. *The Mayan Code: Time Acceleration and Awakening the World Mind.* Rochester, Vt.: Bear & Co., 2007.

———. *The Mind Chronicles: A Visionary Guide into Past Lives.* Rochester, Vt.: Bear & Co., 2007.

Clow, Barbara Hand with Gerry Clow. *Alchemy of Nine Dimensions: The 2011/2012 Prophecies and Nine Dimensions of Consciousness.* Charlottesville, Va.: Hampton Roads, 2010.

Colton, Ann Ree. *Kundalini West.* Glendale, Calif.: ARC, 1978.

Epstein, Alan. *Psychodynamics of Inconjunctions.* York Beach, Maine: Samuel Weiser, 1984.

Fox, Matthew. *Original Blessing.* Santa Fe, N. Mex.: Bear & Co., 1983.

Gerber, Richard. *Vibrational Medicine: New Choices for Healing Ourselves.* Santa Fe, N. Mex.: Bear & Co., 1988.

Gimbutas, Marija. *The Language of the Goddess*. San Francisco: Harper & Row, 1989.

Graves, Robert. *The Greek Myths*. Vol. 1. Harmondsworth, England: Penguin, 1955.

Griscom, Chris. *Ecstasy Is a New Frequency*. Santa Fe, N. Mex.: Bear & Co., 1987.

Grof, Stanislav and Christina. *Spiritual Emergency: When Personal Transformation Becomes a Crisis*. Los Angeles: Jeremy P. Tarcher, 1989.

Heinberg, Richard. *Memories and Visions of Paradise*. Los Angeles, Calif.: Jeremy P. Tarcher, 1989.

Hitching, Francis. *Earth Magic*. New York: Willam Morrow, 1977.

Kennedy, Jan. *Sex, Pleasure & Power: How to Emerge Spiritually Without Going Nuts*. San Diego, Calif.: Cosmoenergetics Publications, 1988.

Kowal, Charles. *Asteroids: Their Nature and Utilization*. Chichester, England: Ellis Horwood Limited, 1988.

Kuhn, Thomas. *The Structure of Scientific Revolutions*. Chicago: University of Chicago, 1970.

Lantero, Erminie. *The Continuing Discovery of Chiron*. York Beach, Maine: Samuel Weiser, 1983.

Lowen, Alexander. *Bioenergetics*. Harmondsworth, England: Penguin, 1976.

Maslow, Abraham. *The Farther Reaches of Human Nature*. Harmondsworth, England: Penguin, 1976.

McKenna, Terence and Dennis. *Imaginary Landscape: Mind, Hallucinogens and the I Ching*. New York: Seabury Press, 1975.

Men, Hunbatz. *Secrets of Mayan Science/Religion*. Santa Fe, N. Mex.: Bear & Co., 1990.

Michell, John. *The New View over Atlantis*. San Francisco: Harper & Row, 1969.

Motoyama, Hiroshi. *Theories of the Chakras: Bridges to Higher Consciousness*. Wheaton, Ill.: Quest, 1981.

Nolle, Richard. *Chiron: The New Planet in Your Horoscope, The Key to Your Quest*. Tempe, Ariz.: AFA, 1983.

Phillips, Rick. *Emergence of the Divine Child*. Santa Fe, N. Mex.: Bear & Co., 1990.

Reinhart, Melanie. *Chiron and the Healing Journey: An Astrological and Psychological Perspective*. London, England: Penguin, 1989.

Sannella, Lee. *Kundalini: Psychosis or Transcendence?* San Francisco: H.S. Dakin, 1976.

Scott, Mary. *Kundalini in the Physical World*. London: Routledge & Kegan Paul, 1983.

Sedgwick, Philip. *The Astrology of Transcendence: Leaps and Bounds in Geocosmic Study*. Birmingham, Mich.: Seek-It, 1980.

Settegast, Mary. *Plato Prehistorian: 10,000 to 5,000 b.c. Myth, Religion, Archaeology*. Hudson, N.Y.: Lindisfarne Press, 1990.

Seymour, Percy. *Astrology: The Evidence of Science*. Luton, England: Lennard, 1988.

Sheldrake, Rupert. *A New Science of Life: The Hypothesis of Formative Causation*. London: Blond and Briggs, 1981.

————. *The Presence of the Past: Morphic Resonance and the Habits of Nature*. New York: Times Books, 1988.

Shearer, Tony. *Lord of the Dawn, Quetzalcoatl*. Happy Camp, Calif.: Naturegraph, 1971.

Sobel, Dava. "Dr. Zodiac." *Omni* (Dec. 1990): 60–72.

Spence, Lewis. *The History and Origins of Druidism*. New York: Rider, 1925.

Strieber, Whitley. *Communion*. New York: Beach Tree Books, 1987.

————. *Transformation: The Breakthrough*. New York: Beach Tree Books, 1988.

Swan, James. *Sacred Places: How the Living Earth Seeks our Friendship*. Santa Fe, N. Mex.: Bear & Co., 1990.

Talbot, Michael. *Beyond the Quantum: God, Reality, Consciousness in the New Scientific Revolution*. New York: Macmillan, 1986.

————. *Mysticism and the New Physics*. New York: Bantam New Age, 1981.

Thompson, William Irwin. *At the Edge of History: Speculations on the Transformation of Culture*. New York: Harper and Row, 1971.

————. *Imaginary Landscape: Making Worlds of Myth and Science*. New York: St. Martin's Press, 1989.

————. *The Time Falling Bodies Take to Light*. New York: St. Martin's Press, 1982.

Von Franz, Marie Louise. *Alchemy: An Introduction to the Symbolism and the Psychology*. Toronto, Canada: Inner City Books, 1980.

Waters, Frank. *Mexico Mystique: The Coming Sixth World of Consciousness*. Chicago, Ill.: Swallow Press, 1975.

White, John. *Kundalini, Evolution and Enlightenment*. New York: Anchor Books, 1979.

About the Author

BARBARA HAND CLOW is an internationally acclaimed author, astrologer, spiritual teacher, and publisher. She is the author of *Chiron: Rainbow Bridge Between the Inner and Outer Planets* (1987). Her trilogy exploring past-life regression under hypnosis was published as *Eye of the Centaur: A Visionary Guide into Past Lives* in 1986; *Heart of the Christos: Starseeding from the Pleiades* in 1989; and *Signet of Atlantis: War in Heaven Bypass* in 1992. The trilogy was revised and released as one book, *The Mind Chronicles,* in 2007. *The Mayan Code: Time Acceleration and Awakening the World Mind* was also published in 2007. *Catastrophobia: The Truth Behind Earth Changes* was published in 2001, and then it was revised and released as *Awakening the Planetary Mind: Beyond the Trauma of the Past to a New Era of Creativity* in 2011. *The Pleiadian Agenda: A New Cosmology for the Age of Light,* which became an instant bestseller, was published in 1995. Her scientific analysis of *The Pleiadian Agenda* was published in 2004 and again in 2010 as *Alchemy of Nine Dimensions: The 2011/2012 Prophecies and Nine Dimensions of Consciousness.*

    The Mind Chronicles trilogy remains a significant contribution to the field of past-life regression, while *Chiron* explores the emerging archetype of healing by means of the newly discovered Chiron, ruler of the "wounded healer complex." Based upon these explorations of the subconscious and twenty-five years of counseling as a natal astrologer, she wrote *Liquid Light of Sex* in 1991. It is her astrological examination of the maturational passages in the lives of all humans. The newly revised 2013 version with updated tables is titled *Astrology and the*

Rising of Kundalini: The Transformative Power of Saturn, Chiron, and Uranus.

Barbara was the copublisher with Gerry Clow of Bear & Company in Santa Fe, New Mexico, from 1983 to 1998. She holds a master's degree in theology, has trained in many healing modalities, and is a practitioner of Ecstatic Body Postures developed by Dr. Felicitas Goodman of the Cuyamungue Institute in New Mexico. Because of her commitments to teaching, research, and writing, she is no longer available for astrological counseling. She is currently working on a novel to be called *The Ruby Crystal,* the first book in a trilogy exploring how evil enters the world. Barbara and Gerry are the parents of four children and live in Vancouver, British Columbia, Canada.

Index

Page numbers in *italic* indicate illustrations.

296